D1789250

EXMOOR

By the same author

THE NORTH DEVON COAST
THE SOUTH DEVON COAST
THE COASTS OF CORNWALL
GREAT MEN OF DEVON
THE WEST COUNTRY
DEVON VILLAGES

In preparation

THE WEST COUNTRY – An Anthology

irc 9

S68212

Lewisham Leisure

Library Service

Library materials must be returned on or before the
last date stamped or fines will be charged at the
current rate. Items can be renewed by telephone,
letter or personal call unless required by another
borrower. For hours of opening and charges see
notices displayed in libraries.

RESERVE STOCK

R156

A 8029 00 159049

James Boevey—who bought the Forest in 1651 and built the first house within its borders (see Chapter One).

EXMOOR

by

S. H. BURTON

LONDON

ROBERT HALE & COMPANY

Copyright © 1969 and 1974 by S. H. Burton

First published 1969
Second impression 1970
Second Edition (first publication under the Robert Hale imprint) 1974

ISBN 0 7091 4561 6

Some material used in this book has been taken from the
author's previous book published under the same title in 1952

Robert Hale & Company
63 Old Brompton Road
London S.W.7

LEWISHAM LIBRARY SERVICE

	BRANCH	COPY
LBN.		
SBN 0 7091 4561 6	09	01
CLASS NUMBER 914.238	CATEGORY	
BOOK-SELLER BRI	INVOICE DATE 23.8.74	
ACC. NUMBER S68212		

Printed and bound
in Great Britain by
REDWOOD BURN LIMITED
Trowbridge & Esher

CONTENTS

ILLUSTRATIONS

MAPS

Acknowledgement is due to The Exmoor Society, for permission to quote from its annual publication *The Exmoor Review*.

The block for the frontispiece was supplied by the Editor of *The Exmoor Review* who kindly gave permission for its use in this book.

The line drawing of a stag's head on page 50 was made by Phyl Burton; the maps on pages 23, 77, 79 and 85 were drawn by Geoffrey Sinclair; the moorland plants in Appendix II were drawn and described by Audrey Bonham-Carter; invaluable help with the first edition was received from Victor Bonham-Carter; all the photographs in the book were taken by the author.

Introduction

Not in the whole of Britain is there more varied beauty in so small a space as can be found inside the boundaries of the Exmoor National Park. It is so short a distance from north to south, from east to west; yet the contrast between, say, the wooded valleys near Cloutsham and the brooding moor at Rowbarrows is so complete that they might be hundreds of miles apart instead of barely a mile.

Perhaps this endless variety is the secret of Exmoor's fascination; it is certainly the reason why everyone has his own special Exmoor, and why— unless he knows the moor well—he tends to be quite ignorant of other people's Exmoor.

For some, Exmoor is the sea and the distant views of Wales. Others believe that Exmoor is its eastern borders—spectacular tree-filled valleys and Dunkery's purple heather. Others think that Tarr Steps and Winsford Hill are Exmoor. They are all quite right, of course, for Exmoor is all these things—and a thousand others, too.

Exmoor is a summer day at Three Combes' Foot—the shade of beech trees and the noise of water. Exmoor is a gale out by Chapman Barrows, so fierce that it is hard to stand upright by the graves of the ancient people. Exmoor is Dunster in August: crowded pavements, souvenirs—and St. George's Church with its miraculous screen. Exmoor is 'Doone Land'— but it is southern Badgworthy, too, where desolate combes join in the heart of the moor to create that beautiful valley. Exmoor is a stag belling in October mists; it is peat-bog at Exe Head; it is barley in Porlock Vale; it is foot-slogging over the squelching Chains; blackcock lekking at Hawkcombe; wild ponies galloping over the moor; deserted iron mines on the Barle; the Knight family tombs at Simonsbath; curlews calling over Wood Barrow; the weird Longstone; cream teas; coach tours; utter loneliness; wild grandeur; postcard prettiness; controversy; heart's ease.

This book is about all these things, because it is about Exmoor. If it succeeds in helping its readers to know and love more Exmoors than they knew and loved before, I shall be well content; for I shall then have repaid a debt—a debt I owe to Exmoor, and to those who have walked there with me.

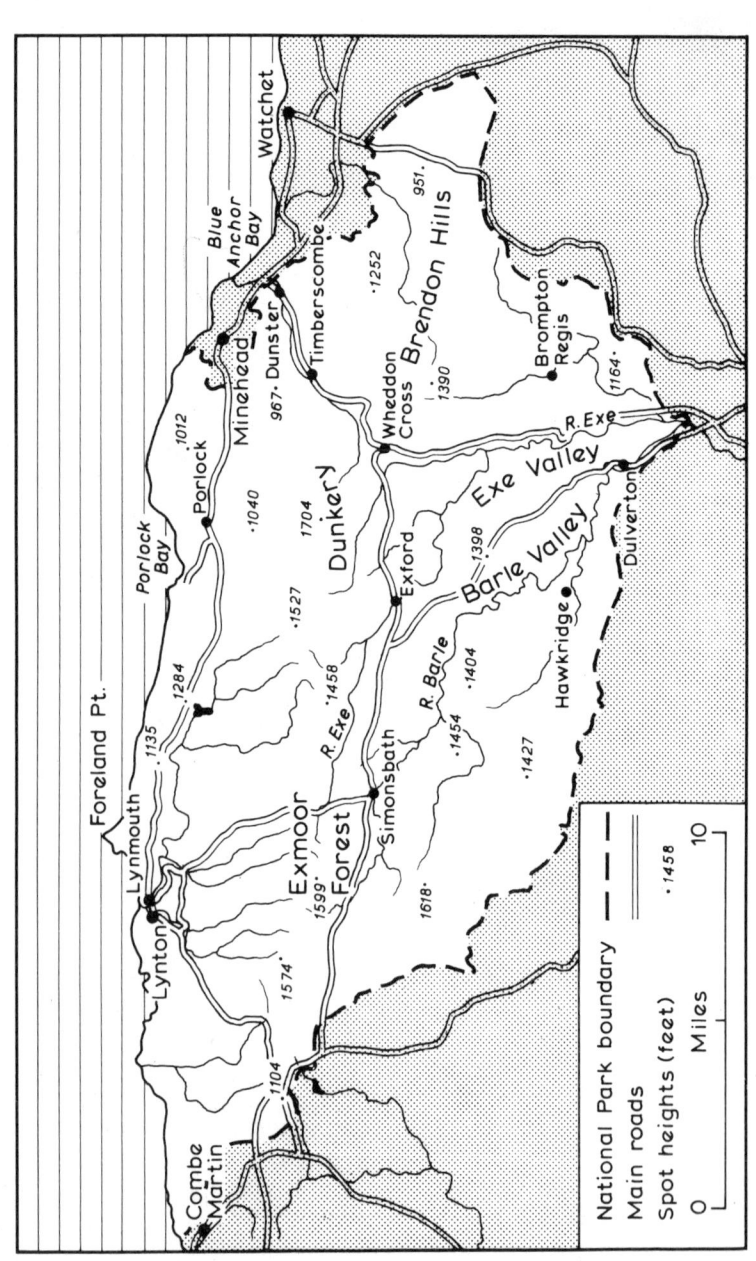

Foreland Pt.

Combe Martin
·1104
Lynton
Lynmouth
·1574
·1599
·1618
·1135
·1284
Exmoor Forest
·1458
R. Exe
Simonsbath
·1527
·1454
R. Barle
·1404
·1427
Porlock Bay
·1012
Porlock
·1040
Minehead
·967·Dunster
·1704
Dunkery
Exford
·1458
·1398
Hawkridge
Blue Anchor Bay
Watchet
Timberscombe
·1252
Wheddon Cross
·1390
Brendon Hills
·951
Brompton Regis
·1164·
R. Exe
Exe Valley
Barle Valley
Dulverton

National Park boundary — —
Main roads
Spot heights (feet)   ·1458

0   Miles   10

CHAPTER ONE

The History of Exmoor

THERE are not many references to Exmoor in the learned journals and text-books of archaeology for, compared with Dartmoor and most of the other National Parks, it has few of the more dramatic prehistoric remains such as stone avenues, standing stones and hut circles. That the megalithic monuments on Exmoor are neither as large nor as numerous as those elsewhere, however, argues nothing as to respective densities of population in prehistoric times. Outcropping of rock is the rule on Dartmoor, for example, and the exception on Exmoor where there are few accumulations of loose stone. Here, the materials for stockyards, monuments and dwellings had to be quarried, and even then the stone was unsuitable. Where free stone was available (Dunkery and Trentishoe, for instance) it was used for cairn-building, and the hut walls were probably of turf which has long since disappeared. The presence of *any* circles and avenues on Exmoor says much for the determination and ingenuity of its former inhabitants, and enough exist—together with the round barrows and the hill forts—to testify to the importance of the moor in the Bronze and Iron Ages.

It was not until post-Roman times that the richest agricultural lands of Britain were extensively farmed. Previously, inadequate tools or lack of organisation, or both, made the dense forests of the heavier soils an impenetrable barrier. In the last century before the Roman invasion the Belgic people with their efficient iron tools and developed political organisation were able to make progress in clearing the forests in the south-east; but for many hundreds of years before this it was to the downlands of the South Country, the Wiltshire Plain, and the uplands of Exmoor, Dartmoor and Bodmin that men turned for their living. (We know, too, that from about 1600 to 750 B.C. the Exmoor climate was drier and kinder then it has been at any time since.) Some cultivation was possible in the lower valleys and on the drier hillsides of Exmoor but in general they lived the life of hunters and pastoralists. The combes gave them shelter from the wind, wood for their fires and hut posts, water in abundance; on the open moorland there was wild life to provide food and clothing—bear, wild ox, ponies, and the red deer.

* I am indebted to the writings of Jacquetta Hawkes, Stuart Piggott, E.T. MacDermot and Charles Whybrow for some of the material included in this Chapter.

It is not possible to uncover more than fragments of Exmoor's history until the Norman Conquest, but the archaeological remains, and inferences drawn from the sweep of events discernible in more closely studied areas, enable the fragments to be pieced together. Like the other western uplands, Exmoor was a stronghold for the native inhabitants in time of trouble as wave after wave of invaders entered England in pre-Roman times. Neolithic settlers from the Mediterranean pushed up the South-West Peninsula bringing with them a knowledge of farming and pottery and a degree of skill and organising ability that enabled them to work their flint mines. They do not appear to have penetrated deeply into Exmoor, inhabited then—if at all—by Mesolithic hunters, for their most distinctive cultural mark, the long barrow, with its communal burials and death-fecundity symbolism, is not to be found anywhere on the moor. Yet recently discovered evidence argues that Neolithic man was a dweller on Exmoor and not merely a passing hunter.* On Parracombe Common, near Woolhanger, stands a small earth bank backed by a ditch, enclosing a flat area of moor. It is thought to be a *henge*—a sacred site—dating from the late Neolithic Period, about 2,000 B.C. (The small circular enclosure about a mile away—near Longstone Barrow—which was also thought to be a *henge* is, in fact, a denuded barrow.) The only other known traces of Neolithic times are the knapping floors (or flint 'factories') at Woody Bay Cross and Hawkcombe Head.

Bronze Age relics abound. The round-headed Indo-Europeans, whose invasions of Britain occupy 1,150 years of prehistory (from 1900 to 750 B.C.), pushed up the combes and along the ridgeways, leaving their impress for ever on the windy heights where they built their round barrows. Accounts of the Beaker Folk and of Wessex Culture, of the Food-Vessel and the Urn People, can be found in the writings of Jacquetta Hawkes, Stuart Piggott, L.V. Grinsell, and other archaeologists, and it would be beyond the purpose of this book to summarise their work. But even the casual traveller on Exmoor cannot fail to notice evidence of the settlement of the moor during this long period. The Bronze Age people were pastoralists and therefore found the moorland more attractive than did their Neolithic predecessors. The many round barrows—over 300 are now known and more are discovered every year—and the occasional stone avenues and circles prove the presence of a large and organised population.

The chief archaeological sites are described in the topographical surveys of later chapters, but it is useful to mention here the Bronze Age relics that are outstanding. First, the barrow-groups: eleven barrows at Chapman Barrows, eight of which are on the boundary between Challacombe and Parracombe parishes, a superb moorland site; eight at Five Barrows, another magnificent view; and smaller groups on Winsford Hill (the

* Charles Whybrow: "Antiquary's Exmoor—1", *The Exmoor Review*, No. 8.

Wambarrows), Dunkery, and Anstey Common, together with the cairn-barrows on Cosgate Hill and Trentishoe Down.

Many of the high points are crowned by single barrows: Leather Barrow, Cutcombe Barrow and Wiveliscombe Barrow on the Brendons; Chains Barrow in the Forest and Longstone Barrow just outside it. Several of the most prominent barrows are Forest boundary markers: Alderman's Barrow, Black Barrow, Wood Barrow and Setta Barrow. Few of the barrows, however, are named and most of them are not even marked on the maps.

It was not only his burial mounds that Bronze Age man left behind: his stone monuments on Exmoor are almost as numerous as the barrows, though, as has been said, they are small in comparison with Dartmoor's show pieces. We do not know much about the purposes for which—with great labour—these single stones, avenues (double and single), circles, triangles and quadrilaterals were erected. But as the churches and cathedrals of Christendom at once hallow and memorialise the dead and the living within shrines built to glorify God and provide for his worship, so we may suppose did the megalithic sanctuaries and memorials. What gods were worshipped we cannot know for sure, but may guess (from fragmentary evidence in the monuments themselves and by reasonable inference from anthropological findings elsewhere) that the sun, fire and sex were deified. It is probable, too that the more complicated patterns were of some astronomical significance.

The most striking of the standing stones is the Longstone (see Chapter Nine) and this remarkable and enigmatic memorial is neighboured by two other fine megaliths on Lyn Down. The best of the stone circles is on Withypool Hill; and there are two more* just to the west of the Exford-Porlock road, near Colley Water. There are stone rows (or alignments) near the headwaters of Badgworthy and to the south-west of Wood Barrow, having affinities with those found in South Wales rather than with the Dartmoor type. (This is not surprising: the sea journey between South Wales and Exmoor would have been easier than the land journey between Exmoor and Dartmoor.) In Ember Combe (on Wilmersham Common), W.J. Corney† discovered, in 1966, an alignment described in the following terms by the Archaeological Division of the Ordnance Survey Office: "The stone row is at SS 85654205, orientated S.W./N.E. on a west facing slope. It is unique for Exmoor and most closely resembles the Dartmoor rows . . ." This row has been singled out for special treatment here because it illustrates two important features of Bronze Age relics on Exmoor: fresh discoveries are always being made; and each new find may well upset

---

* Charles Whybrow queries the more southern of these two, preferring to classify it not as a circle but as one of the many miscellaneous 'rude stone monuments'.

† See article in *The Exmoor Review*, No. 8, pp. 48 and 49.

previous generalisations based on scanty knowledge. Corney's stone row destroys the notion that all Exmoor rows are of the South Wales and not the Dartmoor type. His other discoveries—not yet studied in detail—may well permit the evolution of sounder theories. As much remains to be discovered as is now known. The hut circles, with which both the map and the ground are dotted, deserve prolonged and expert attention, for map markings do not always correspond to field observation, and some that are marked are not authentic. Sometimes a supposed hut circle is a natural rock formation; often it is what is left of a cairn that was destroyed for road-making material, or of a barrow that has been demolished.

The numerous Bronze Age antiquities tell us of a peopled moor in the long-dead past; they also, when mutilated, tell a sad story of pillage. A great stone circle that once existed in the Valley of the Rocks was totally destroyed soon after 1850; and, despite the brave efforts made in this century to map and record and preserve, neglect and destruction still outpace preservation and study.

The Iron Age relics on Exmoor unfold an interesting story. We cannot know at what particular date iron tools were first used on the moor, nor whether when the first waves of iron-armed invaders reached the fringes of the upland they found inhabitants equipped with similar weapons. In the south and south-east of England it is clear that a gradual evolution from bronze to iron took place, hastened periodically by invasions from the Continent where iron had been used for generations. We may suppose on Exmoor a very slow development into the Early Iron Age over two or three hundred years from about 500 B.C., accompanied by an accelerating depopulation of the higher moor as the climate deteriorated. The increasing use of the confined lower valleys led to internal conflicts to complicate further a tense situation in which those already settled on and around Exmoor were under frequent threat from intruders. The main monuments of this troubled time and warlike people are the earthworks, built usually on a hill-top and improving on nature's defences by means of ramparts and ditches, varying in complexity from a simple circle to a comparatively intricate defensive system in which the gate was guarded by multiple trenches and wooden towers (long since gone) which exposed the attackers to cross-fire from slingers. Time, the elements, and the hoofs of sheep and cattle have worn down the walls which—surmounted as they once were by wooden palisades—must have been formidable.

Some of Exmoor's 'camps' were made in the early Iron Age to protect the men who built the round barrows from the onslaught of invaders approaching from the south-east. Others were thrown up, often on old and improved sites, by these same invaders when, having seized an area for their own use, they were in their turn menaced by the last of the 'Iron' conquerors who spread slowly across England in the last century B.C. The farmers appear to have lived in lonely and undefended settlements, retreating with their families and cattle to the shelter of the hill-forts (built by their chiefs) in troubled times. In a paper published in the *Proceedings* of the Devonshire Archaeological Society (1967), Charles Whybrow points out that a study of Exmoor hill-forts (few of which are multivallate) emphasises the contrast between these and the great *oppida* of Wessex (e.g. Maiden Castle) and of other and more fertile regions of the West Country (e.g. Hembury Fort). His conclusion is that Iron Age Exmoor supported a population "decidedly poverty-stricken by comparison with the peoples of Wessex or of other parts of Dumnonia".

It was chiefly on the heights commanding the valleys of the south and east that the Iron Age men of Exmoor built their forts. The Barle Valley is particularly well defended: Mounsey Castle and Brewer's Castle (both names are derived from Norman overlords), stone ramparted and much overgrown, keep watch over an ancient ford between Hawkridge and Dulverton. Higher upstream, lofty Cow Castle protects what was evidently a strategic site, the junction of the White Water and the Barle. Road Castle guards the middle Exe, while the lower Avill is commanded by the earthworks in Dunster Park. Coastal defences include an impressive linear rampart and ditch on Countisbury Hill, where the cliffs and the East Lyn gorge have been ingeniously incorporated in the plan of the fortress; and Bury Castle (near Selworthy), lying on a spur, its basically simple plan strengthened by additional outworks, probably added after the original construction. High up on western Exmoor, at the termination of the southern ridge, lies Shoulsbarrow (or Shoulsbury) Castle; an earthwork presenting unique features of site and construction, discussion of which is reserved for fuller treatment in Chapter Six.

Those energetic people, the Belgae, were still pushing deeper and deeper into the west at the time of the Roman invasion. While Rome was imposing law and order on eastern and southern Britain, Exmoor was still the scene of the bloody intertribal struggles that marked Belgic history. Thirty-three years before the Claudian conquest began, Cunobelin had established his capital at Camulodunum (Colchester) but outside the territory of this powerful king there were constant affrays. Cunobelin's policies were repeated by the Belgic invaders of the south coast who waged ceaseless war against the earlier settlers and drove westward with remorseless vigour, 'pacifying' with stern measures and strong hands. These western territories presented a problem to the Roman conquerors, and the Exmoor scene in Roman times must be related to the larger canvas. The work of Lady Aileen Fox and Dr. Ravenhill (both of Exeter University) enables a coherent account to be given.

There are within the boundaries of the National Park two undoubted Roman sites: Old Barrow, or Burrow (above Glenthorne), and Martinhoe. Both are forts and signalling stations and both have been excavated by the Exeter archaeologists just mentioned.* Additionally, in a paper delivered to the International Geographical Congress in 1964, Dr. Ravenhill linked Roman Exmoor with the political geography of Britain in the mid-first century A.D. What now follows derives from his fascinating reconstruction of events.

The two Roman earthworks (Old Barrow and Martinhoe Beacon) overlooking the Bristol Channel are very similar in site, construction and purpose. The structure of the hog's-back cliffs on which they were sited gave to them both extensive views of the South Wales coast from the Gower peninsula to Barry Island. Old Barrow stands 1,090 feet above sea level; Martinhoe Beacon 800 feet. Their position pre-supposes some kind of marine function: they are obviously not staging-posts on the route west, for easier ways lie to the south. The excavations by Lady Fox and Dr. Ravenhill revealed that Old Barrow was a Roman military outpost, occupied from approximately A.D. 48 to 54. Within the inner enclosure was a tented camp, and at the entrance six substantial timber posts were used to carry both the gates and an elevated signalling and look-out platform. The most remarkable difference between Old Barrow and Martinhoe Beacon is that the latter was equipped with wooden barracks—as compared with Old Barrow's tents—and finds on the site, such as a furnace, ovens, pottery and coins,† suggest a much longer occupation than at Old Barrow. It is thought that about sixty Roman soldiers manned Martinhoe Beacon between about A.D. 50 and 75.

It seems, then, that Old Barrow was built first and occupied until Martinhoe was ready. After a four-year overlap Old Barrow was abandoned and a permanent garrison was stationed at Martinhoe. The explanation of this sequence of events lies in the story of what was happening elsewhere in Britain.

In the summer of A.D. 43 a Roman army commanded by Aulus Plautius crossed the English Channel and defeated the Belgic tribal army on the Medway. Vespasian and the 2nd Augusta Legion were then given the task of conquering the whole of southern Britain, in pursuit of which assignment they overcame two powerful tribes and reduced over twenty fortresses. One of these tribes was the Durotriges, occupants of Dorset, south Wiltshire, south Somerset and east Devon. The Dumnonii, who lived in the rest of Devon and on Exmoor, were the inveterate enemies of the Durotriges whose might they feared. The Roman victory, therefore, caused them rejoicing, and we have every reason to suppose that they

* See *The Exmoor Review*, Nos. 3, 4 and 5.
† Now in the North Devon Athenaeum at Barnstaple.

Ruckham Combe seen from Furzehill—a typical Exmoor blend of scenery.

Wood Barrow Gate—a lonely, lovely place where the Bronze Age people lived.

Ponies out by Hoaroak Water—Exmoors and crossbreds.

The Ridge Road—climbing up to Anstey Barrows.

looked favourably on Rome and co-operated with the new conquerors (see Chapter Six). By about A.D. 50 the Romans had a firm grip on southern Britain as far as the line of the Fosse Way. With friendly tribes to the west of the Fosse they would probably have been content to pause for a while. The Silures of Wales and the Marches, however, were actively hostile and —inspired by Caratacus, who had escaped from the Medway battle—they thrust fiercely across the Fosse and (more damaging because less easily countered) they invaded the territory of tribes friendly to Rome, at once causing dissatisfaction with and contempt for Roman 'protection', and stirring tribal feeling against the Imperial power.

Plautius had meanwhile been succeeded as Governor by Ostorius Scapula, who quickly realised that fortifications must be built beyond the Fosse, and it seems likely that Old Barrow was constructed as part of this new policy. It would be a grim life up there for the garrison. Tacitus, in a vivid account* of the hardships of the campaign along and beyond the frontier, makes clear how formidable the Silures were and how effectively they employed guerilla tactics. The Old Barrow finds show that the Roman soldiers lived rough; communications were precarious and only essential military supplies and equipment were sent from the other side of the Fosse.

The 'military presence' (of between fifty and sixty men at Old Barrow) was clearly considered sufficiently useful to justify the efforts needed to build and maintain first Old Barrow and then Martinhoe. The Dumnonii were probably glad of the garrison as a safeguard against attack by their beaten but still dangerous neighbours, the Durotriges, whose territory ran to within a few miles of the Exmoor coast. But the Romans' chief purpose was to keep watch on Silurian ships approaching from South Wales. It is unlikely that they expected a full-scale invasion for there is no evidence that the Silures were capable of large sea-borne operations. Yet so power- fully had Caratacus inspired the western tribes with the spirit of revolt, and so bitter was the war in South Wales and the Borders, that they feared the spreading of the fire. Even the Dumnonii might not be proof against incitement by the Silures, while the Durotriges would almost certainly rise again if agitators from Wales landed on the coast of Exmoor and crossed into Durotrigian territory. A signalling station was the answer. From Old Barrow the look-outs could warn the Roman fleet in time for fast-sailing scout ships to intercept Silurian intruders before they could land.

The last years of Old Barrow were difficult for Rome. The revolt of the Brigantia diverted troops from the war in Wales, and though Caratacus was captured the Silures were as active as ever, pushing deep into Roman territory. Ostorius died in A.D. 52 and his successor, Aulus Didius,

* *The Annals*, Book xii.

concentrated on driving back the Silures, being well satisfied after that to hold them off until his recall to Rome in A.D. 58.

It is almost certain that Martinhoe Beacon was built and Old Barrow abandoned during this period of consolidation. A watch on the coast was as necessary as ever, and Martinhoe had certain advantages over Old Barrow. Standing on a lower site—but with as extensive a view of the South Wales coast—it is less exposed to the elements and less frequently mist-covered. Closer to the cliff edge than Old Barrow, it offered much better sightings of in-shore ships—a great asset in bad weather.

Between A.D. 58 and 61, life at Martinhoe was tense. The new Governor, Paulinus Suetonius, was campaigning in North Wales and the Silures might at any time seize their chance to break out. When the eastern tribes under Boudicca revolted the whole of the 2nd Legion remained on guard over those troublesome people, though Suetonius needed all the troops he could muster to subjugate East Anglia.

Between A.D. 61 and 71, Rome concentrated on pacifying the territory she held. In these ten years of Romanisation Martinhoe kept watch, for the Silures were untamed; but life became easier. The excavations traced a steady improvement in the garrison's amenities—an improvement best described in Dr. Ravenhill's own words:

> No longer was it necessary to use native pottery; there were mortaria and the much more sophisticated Gaulish Samian dishes; there was time between watches to game and dice, and even wine and oil to supplement the diet and no doubt improve morale.

In A.D. 69 Vespasian became Emperor and ordered his army in Britain to move forward again. Under Petilius Cerealis the Brigantes were subdued; and in A.D. 74 Julius Frontinus attacked the Silures and conquered this most energetic and warlike of tribes.

Soon afterwards, as the excavations revealed, the troops were withdrawn from Martinhoe. The lonely garrison on the Exmoor coast had no further part to play in the history of Roman Britain.

And, indeed, the history of Roman Exmoor ends there. There is no other trace of Roman occupation or settlement. Rumours of 'Roman' iron workings may be discounted, and the Roman coins that have been found at various places within the National Park boundaries, prove nothing.* Bleak Exmoor offered little to the Romans, and the tribesmen of the fringes could be adequately policed and supervised with little effort.

From the withdrawal of the Romans from Britain in A.D. 410 to the coming of the Saxons we know nothing of Exmoor's story. The Caratacus

---

* "... any passing traveller might lose a coin, or even a purseful." "Antiquary's Exmoor—II", *The Exmoor Review*, No. 9.

Stone on Winsford Hill (see Chapter Seven) and another inscribed stone above Lynton prove that the tribes living on the edges of the central moor had absorbed a measure of Romanisation. We know, too, that some of the farmers (on Lyn Down and near Parracombe, for example) found it expedient to fortify their settlements: a fact from which something may be guessed about life on Exmoor when the Romans had gone. But 'The Dark Ages' are darker on Exmoor than anywhere else.

Evidence of Anglo-Saxon conquest and occupation is found chiefly in names. It is clear from these that the new invaders pushed along the valleys and the coast, finally ringing the upland with their settlements. Within the Forest itself there are only two place-names (Elsworthy and Pinkworthy) to argue Saxon habitation; but this is not surprising, for the newcomers were farmers—interested only in seizing good land. This fact explains why the Anglo-Saxon conquest of South Devon* took place several years before the Celtic farmers of the Exmoor fringes were dispossessed.

The drive to the west left Exmoor undisturbed until sometime after A.D. 690, at which date the Wessex King Ine established a fortress at Taunton. This useful base provided the support and protection needed by the expeditions, and it seems likely that the Saxons had got what they wanted of Exmoor by about 710. We can only speculate about the resistance that they may have encountered for, as far as is known, no important battles took place. If the Iron Age forts were again used in a hopeless attempt to stem the Anglo-Saxon advance, archaeologists have yet to find evidence of this. It is likely that the Celtic farmers were overwhelmed one by one and settlement by settlement. Some undoubtedly fled before death could reach them and established new communities where, at any rate for some time, they and their descendants lived unmolested. The evidence derives from a cluster of wholly or partly Celtic place names in the south-western fringes: Charles, High Bray and Molland are well-known examples, but they are all just outside the National Park boundary. The Anglo-Saxons were too numerous, too well-armed and organised, for the scattered Exmoor Celts to hold out long. They moved up the valleys with considerable speed; and—though they had no appetite for settling there—they cut across the middle of the moor, following the Harepath (a Saxon word, meaning 'army road'). The Harepath is the great central trackway running from the Quantocks to Barnstaple; hundreds of years old when the Saxons took it over for their own use, renamed it in their own tongue, and moved men and supplies along it to overwhelm those whose distant forefathers had trodden out the way.†

Apart from their place-names—*Are* (Oare), *Stocke* (Stoke Pero),

---

* See W.G. Hoskins: "The Westward Expansion of Wessex", Occasional Paper No. 13, Leicester University Press, 1960.
† The Harepath is traced in some detail in Chapter Six.

Hernola (Horner), *Winesford* (Winsford), these are just a few examples—the Anglo-Saxons left few traces of their 350 years of undisturbed possession. The Domesday Book of 1086 tells us something of the life they lived. It listed the manors ('home-farms' to which were appended smaller farms and holdings and which varied greatly in size, from single farms with a few serfs' hovels attached, to considerable estates); using the alien tongue, it classed the inhabitants as villeins, bordars and serfs. The villeins and bordars were peasant-farmers, owing duties to the manor but farming a separate holding; the serfs were little better than slaves. The land was classified as pasture, meadow, ploughland and wood; and all round the cultivated and inhabited areas lay the Exmoor 'waste'. Domesday also listed the stock: oxen, goats, sheep and horses, making special mention of *equas indomitas* and *equas silvestres*—the wild ponies of the moor, herds of which were kept on some of the manors.*

Though battles were fought against Danish pirates at Watchet and Porlock in 919 and 989, and though the then-outlawed Harold made a descent on Porlock Bay in 1052, the more stirring and troublesome events of history left the area described in this book virtually untouched between the establishment of Anglo-Saxon dominance and the arrival of the Normans. Apart from the raids just mentioned, and one serious attempt at invasion (see Chapter Twelve), the Danes kept away, and the main interest in these years for the student of Exmoor lies in the early stages of its evolution as a Royal Forest. In early Saxon times unclaimed land could be shared out by the king—with the Witan's consent—among his favoured followers. The climate and soil of the moor, however, were of such a character that there was little competition for it among a people as conscious as the Saxons of the value of the heavier soils and as capable of working them. As the king's power grew, the unclaimed lands of England —and Exmoor with them—came to be regarded as royal property, the older idea of 'trusteeship' dying out. This process was completed by the Norman Conquest, after which event any lingering notions of national ownership ceased abruptly, and the land became the royal demesne.

Concurrently, however, the inhabitants of the Saxon settlements in the skirts of the moor were claiming, by usage, rights of 'commons'. Cattle were turned out for summer grazing and peat was dug. By the time of the Conquest such rights were sufficiently recognised for moorland commons to be attached by the Normans to the manors established on the more fertile borders.

The redistribution of the manors and the establishment of the Forest were the most noteworthy acts of the Normans. Castle-building—to hold down the Saxons and to guard their new-won estates against their nearest

* See Hope L. Bourne: "The Ancient Farms of Exmoor", *The Exmoor Review*, No. 5.

Norman rivals—was little called for on Exmoor, for much of it was un-inhabited. No Norman work is left at Dunster, though it once existed. Bury Castle (near Dulverton) is undoubtedly a motte-and-bailey—perhaps erected on the site of an Iron Age fort—but little is known of its history.* The other Norman fortification of note is Holwell Castle in Parracombe, described by Charles Whybrow as "almost a textbook model of the earth-work of a Norman private fortress".† Study of its construction and of its site illuminates the history of a period that has left few tangible records within the National Park. The moats, the gateway, the bailey ramparts and the motte are all remarkably well preserved, testifying to the original strength of the fortress, which dominates old Parracombe and commands the ford and the medieval cross-roads.

This Norman Age, however difficult to trace 'on the ground', pro-foundly affected the history of Exmoor in creating the Forest. Altitude and climate would in any case have delayed occupation and development of the central upland, but the work of the Normans ensured that until quite recent times (see Chapter Two) the heart of Exmoor remained a waste land, sombre, barren and remote.

Manwood's *Treatise of the Forest Lawes*, written in the reign of Elizabeth I, is authoritative in its account of the development of the Royal Forests as game preserves for beasts of the chase. In Saxon times the increase of population and habitations and the clearing of the woodlands for agri-culture destroyed many of the wild creatures:

> . . . and wolves and such like ravenous beasts being thus destroyed, the residue being beasts of pleasure as well as delicate meat, the kings of this land began to be careful for the preservation of them, and in order thereto to privilege certain woods and places so that no man may hurt or destroy them there; and thus the said places became Forests.

The term 'forest' as applied to Exmoor does not imply the former existence of extensive woodland. G.T. Turner‡ defined a medieval forest as

> a definite tract of land within which a particular body of law was enforced, having for its object the preservation of certain animals *ferae naturae*.

Though it was not until the reign of Henry II that Forest Law was fully codified, Turner's definition holds good from the Conquest onwards, the will of the king and his desire to reserve the beasts of the chase to his own

---

* A good deal is known about Bampton Castle—besieged by King Stephen when the rebel Robert de Bampton owned it—but this great mound is outside the National Park.

† *The Exmoor Review*, No. 4, p. 39.

‡ *Select Pleas of the Forest*, Selden Society, 1901.

use proving effective long before the formalised 'particular body of law' of later times. Though Forest Law contained several new provisions, in the main it made explicit conditions and penalties that had become established in early Norman days.

Before describing Forest Law on Exmoor it will be helpful to say something about the officials whose duty it was to administer it. A full account of the Forest Officers can be found in Turner's book; here, the complicated system will be outlined only as it affected the moor, and the detailed and legalistic explanations of Turner and MacDermot will be simplified.

First in the national Forest Hierarchy came the Justice of the Forest, an executive rather than a judicial officer. It seems that in earlier times he presided over the Forest Court, but by the thirteenth century this had ceased to be the case. At first there was one Justice for the whole of England, but in 1238 two were appointed: one for the Forests North of the Trent, and one for the Forests South of the Trent. The Justice supervised the whole of the Forest administration in his area, holding regular enquiries into the state of the Forests, examining proposed royal grants of liberties and enquiring into breaches of Forest Law. The office became a sinecure, and on the death in 1846 of Mr. Thomas Greville—the last Justice of the Forests South of the Trent—was abolished. The salary for the office in the thirteenth century was £100; in 1800 it was £2,000.

By far the most important figure in Exmoor's affairs was the Warden of the Forest.* From 1204, and probably from the Conquest, this was an hereditary post until it became merged in the Crown in the person of Edward IV. From 1461 to 1508 the Wardenship was granted to each holder of office for his lifetime, reverting to the Crown on his death; but after 1508 the Wardens leased the Forest itself as well as its custody from the monarch, but only for as many years and on what terms their influence and bargaining power enabled them to secure. The perquisites of the Warden of Exmoor included the profits arising from the Forest Court and a quaintly named item: "the attachment of pigs in the fence month". The fence month was the thirty-one days beginning fifteen days before and ending fifteen days after Midsummer Day. During this period, when the hinds were supposed to be calving (see Chapter Three), no pigs were allowed within the Forest and any found there were forfeit. Cattle and sheep were also forbidden in the fence month, and rights of common were suspended, forfeiture again being the penalty for fence month offences. These were valuable assets of office, and it seems that the early Wardens sometimes contrived to retain for their own use at least part of the tolls levied on moorland grazing; money which should have been sent to the king. After 1508, of course, when the Wardens became lessees of the

---

* Confusing changes of this title were made from time to time. It seems best to use only the one, and that the most usual, name.

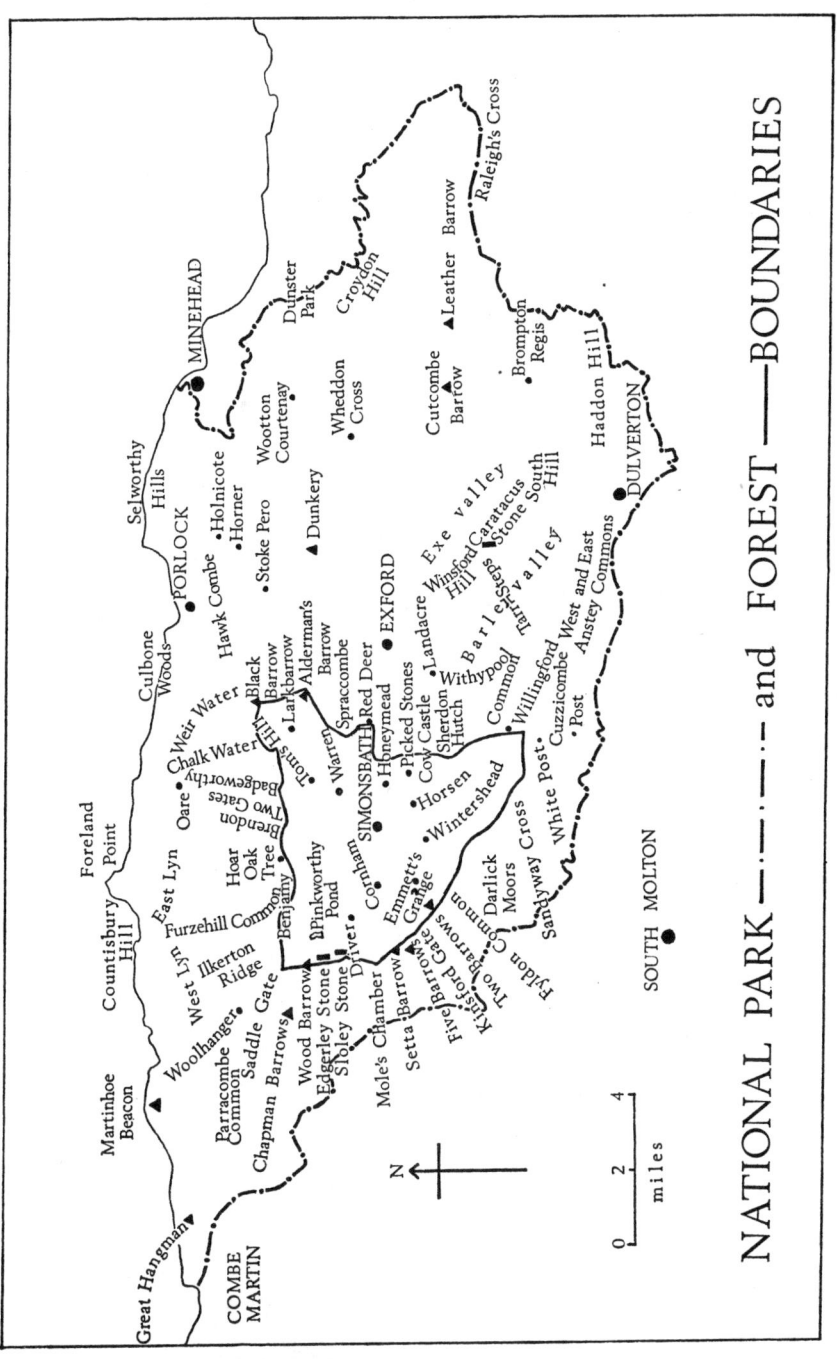

NATIONAL PARK — · — · — and FOREST ——— BOUNDARIES

Forest itself as well as of its custody, the profits of the herbage as well as all other rights of the Crown became legally theirs for the duration of their lease.

The Foresters were appointed by the Warden and carried out game-keeper's duties, also assisting at cattle driving at the beginning and end of the summer grazing. The Crown paid them nothing and, as is shown by the thirteenth-century petitions of the men of Somerset, the Wardens often failed to do so, expecting them to live off the country. It was a common practice for the Wardens to charge fees for making Foresters, who then recouped themselves at the expense of Forest dwellers (in the centuries when the Forest boundary stretched miles beyond the empty plateau round which in later years it shrank), wrongfully impounding their cattle and sheep, making false charges of offences against Forest Law, and thus thriving upon a well-organised system of blackmail and extortion. The statutory establishment of Foresters was three, one on horseback and two on foot; but to judge by the 'Grievances' presented by the men of Somerset in 1279, the Wardens were in the habit of exceeding this number and thus increasing their own revenue.

Turner divided the history of Forest Law into three periods: the first lasted until 1217 when the Charter of the Forest was issued; the second period lasted until 1301 when Edward I disafforested many areas; the third lasted until the sale of the Forest in 1818. During the first period the King's will and usage built up a body of Forest customs and laws harshly conceived and administered. From the issue of the Charter (1217) until 1301, Forest Law was rigidly enforced and frequent 'eyres' (assizes) were held to administer it, but the more brutal features of the Law were softened later in this period. After 1301 Forest Law decayed and eyres were rarely held.

The Assize of the Forest issued in 1184, in the reign of Henry II, is the earliest-known pronouncement of Forest Law. Its first article reads thus:

> First he (the King) forbids that anyone offend him concerning his venison or his forests in anything: and he wills not that they confide in this that he will have mercy on them for their chattels (as) hitherto (on those) who have offended him as to his venison or his forests. For now if anyone shall offend him and be convicted thereof, he will have full justice on him as was done in the time of King Henry his grandfather.

'Full justice' could mean the loss of life, or blinding, or other mutilation, but since the twelfth article of the Assize makes provision for second and third offences we may assume that 'full justice' often stopped short of the heaviest penalty that could be exacted. In the reigns of Henry II, Richard and John, fines appear to have been the commonest form of punishment, backed by physical penalties for those who could not pay.

The kings just mentioned all made large afforestations, but though the Charter of 1217 confirmed Forest Law in all established Forest areas it disafforested their newly-added tracts, to the great relief of the inhabitants. In another respect too, the Charter afforded relief. Its tenth article did something to humanise Forest Law:

> Henceforth let no man lose life or members for venison, but if anyone be taken and convicted of the taking of venison, let him be heavily ransomed, let him lie in our prison for a year and a day; and if after a year and a day he can find pledges, let him go forth from prison, but if not, let him abjure the realm of England.

The Wardens of Exmoor ruled over the Forest under the provisions of this Charter until, in the reign of Edward I, great changes were made. The boundaries of the king's land were contracted by the Perambulation of 1300; but the Ordinance of the Forest in 1306 was a more important development, for it made trial by jury essential to conviction for Forest offences and in several other ways upheld the rights of the subject against the Warden and his Foresters. The preamble shows how heavily Forest Law had pressed on Exmoor in the years between the Conquest and the issue of the Ordinance:

> We have indeed learned from the information of our faithful and the frequent cries of the oppressed, whereby we are disturbed with excessive commotion of mind, that the people of the same realm are by the officers of our forests miserably oppressed, impoverished and troubled with divers wrongs, being everywhere molested. For sometimes the accusations of the Forest . . . are not made by inquests of good and lawful men . . . but on the word of one or perhaps two of the foresters . . . who out of hatred or otherwise maliciously that they may extort money from someone, accuse or indict whom they will; and thereupon follow grievous attachments, and an innocent man is punished, who hath incurred no fault or offence at all. Moreover the people is oppressed by the multitude of foresters and other officers, who not having the wherewithal to get their living by other means, must needs live on the country near the forest, and what is worse, they do justify this their way of living in right of their office . . .

Such frank admissions must have been occasioned by a formidable—and piteous—body of evidence.

From the time of this Ordinance until (in 1508) Exmoor was leased to its Wardens by the Crown, Forest Law steadily decayed; and though in 1661 and 1718—and in the so-called 'Black Act' of 1722, which made deer-stealing a felony without Benefit of Clergy and thus liable to the death penalty—severe punishments were sporadically revived in an attempt to stamp out poaching, there was never a return to the reign of terror so graphically described in the Ordinance. An Act of 1776 repealed all previous Acts and specified heavy fines for the first offence against the deer and seven years transportation for the second; its provisions were reinforced by an Act of 1802 which increased the fines. Such were the Forest Laws until Exmoor ceased to be Crown Land.

Some account must now be given of the Free Suitors and the Suitors at Large, two categories of Exmoor borderers who, collectively and individually, have played a considerable part in the history of the moor.*

The Free Suitors were the owners (or their tenants) of fifty-two ancient holdings in the parishes of Hawkridge and Withypool. The principal duties which they had to perform at the command of the Warden of Exmoor Forest were: first, to drive the Forest nine times a year for ponies, cattle and sheep. Only two excuses were accepted for the non-performance of this duty: ". . . if the suitor's Wife be in travill with Child or that they have laid theire dow to Leaven to Bee baked that daye, and such persons are excusable for that tyme onely." Second, to perambulate the Forest with the Warden or his deputy once every seven years. Third, to serve on the jury of the coroner's inquest on any corpse found within the Forest. In return, the Free Suitors received valuable rights of grazing and fuel-gathering, being permitted to keep a stated number of beasts on the Forest and to cut turf, heath and fern without charge. They were also entitled to fishing rights in the Barle.

MacDermot explained the origin of the Free Suitor's privileges and duties in an unpublished letter to H.C.N. Bond (13 June 1934). He pointed out that they were originally undertenants of the |Odburvilles, who were Wardens of the Forest from the Conquest until they were succeeded by William de Wrotham in King John's reign. The Odburvilles owned Withypool and Hawkridge and recruited Forest helpers from their tenants in those parishes. By the time William de Wrotham became Warden, the rights and duties of the Free Suitors were firmly established, and throughout the subsequent history of the Forest they were sturdily defended. At the final disafforestation the Free Suitors were awarded an average allotment of 31 acres as the equivalent of their former rights on the Forest.

The Suitors at Large were of two kinds: the representatives of the ancient 'townships' or tithings bordering the moor, and the individual landowners whose property abutted the Forest. Each had rights of commons which they had to justify by appearing at the Forest Courts. The representatives of the tithings brought with them the parish branding-iron with which all beasts pastured on the Forest had to be marked. Unmarked

* See "Withypool Common: A Study in Depth" by Victor Bonham-Carter, Geoffrey Sinclair and F.C.J. Milton, *The Exmoor Review*, No. 9, for additional information.

beasts, except those belonging to the Free Suitors, were charged for by the Warden at full rate, or impounded as strays. The landowners were allowed representation by their bailiffs at the court on payment of a 'Lord's Fine' which came in time to be regarded as a quit rent payable to the Warden. After the Commonwealth, the borderers' rights were standardised by a provision which entitled them to pasture at half the rates paid by 'strangers', and this arrangement lasted until disafforestation when, like the Free Suitors, they received allotments of land in lieu of their rights of common. As C.S. Orwin pointed out, however, "the right to graze a cow upon a common found no equivalent, in utility, in the allotment of an acre or two of land, always unfenced and often remote, and it is no wonder that purchase and absorption by larger neighbours was the rule."* Beyond doing suit to the courts and paying the dues, the Suitors at Large had no other duties save that of maintaining Forest boundary marks where these bordered their own land. The end of the Forest was no blessing to them.

The Forest Courts referred to above were the Swainmote Courts, held yearly at Hawkridge and Landacre. These courts had jurisdiction over the Forest and the commons on its borders. The Hawkridge Court was always adjourned to Withypool in the afternoon, meeting at the inn or the pound. During the seventeenth century both courts moved to Simonsbath where the last was held in 1818. In earlier times the Swainmotes decided all disputes about Forest rights and pasture dues, as well as civil actions of trespass and debt; but by the eighteenth century their legal functions had dwindled and they existed solely to collect Suitors' dues and, as the records vividly reveal, to sample the Warden's hospitality. (As will be shown later in this Chapter only one Warden of the Forest deliberately incurred the hostility of the Suitors.) The affairs of the Free Suitors in so far as those lay on Withypool Common—outside the Forest Boundary—were regulated by the Manor Court functioning through the Court Leet or Court Baron. This met every three years or so right down to 1921, long after the Forest had been extinguished, fining unauthorised grazers, non-attenders at the Court, and collecting chief and rack rents.

Despite changes in Forest Law and the decay of the Swainmote, though Wardens came and went and Free Suitors fought for their rights, while France was won and lost and the Armada repulsed, through Civil War and Commonwealth, through '15 and '45, Seven Years' War and Napoleonic struggle, the life of the Royal Forest continued unchanged. Early each spring the Warden's men 'cried the moor', announcing at the neighbouring market towns the rates at which he would pasture cattle, sheep and horses on the Forest during the summer grazing season. Before 1570

* *The Reclamation of Exmoor Forest.*

the charge was 1s. 8d. a score for sheep and 2d. a head for cattle and horses. In 1642 it was 3s. 4d. a score and 6d. a head. In 1654 charges rocketed to 6d. a head for sheep, 3s. for cattle and 5s. for horses, but the next year the dues dropped to 4d., 2s., 4s.* And the rates charged in 1655 remained unchanged until 1818, when the Forest was sold.

The sheep went into the Forest between March and May, each owner's tally being entered in the 'Forest Book', and remained until shearing time. The Warden's tellers checked the sheep going off the moor, any not already entered in the Forest Book being charged at double the current rate. Thus wisely did the Warden put a premium on honesty. Most of the sheep came from the farms to the south of the Southern Ridge, and throughout June tellers were stationed at Span Head. It is likely that there was another 'telling-house' at Mole's Chamber. On 28 June, the Warden (or his deputy) and the Free Suitors made the annual round-up ('drift' or 'prey') for sheep. They searched the Forest, driving all unshorn sheep into the Withypool pound. The Free Suitors then sheared all but their own sheep, the fleeces going to the Warden even though the offending sheep had been properly entered in the Forest Book. (This discouraged owners from illegally extending the sheep-grazing period.) Then the Free Suitors' sheep were removed from the pound, while those that had been properly booked were turned into the Forest again, to be claimed in due course—minus their fleeces—by their owners. All others remained in the pound, either to be claimed and redeemed or to become the Warden's property. The sheep that had been taken off the Forest for shearing, and checked through the telling-houses, were driven back onto the moor after 28 June, being counted in by the tellers and remaining there until October, when the season ended. Pasturing dues for the whole season were payable at Withypool on St. James's Day (25 July).

Drifts for cattle and horses were not made on fixed days, but there were usually two for cattle before St. James's Day. 'Rother beast' (cattle) drifts were begun very early in the morning so as to catch any 'nightleared' beasts of the borderers who had daytime grazing rights only. The drifters were not always scrupulous about Forest boundaries, and evidence deposed in 1662 suggests that many a rother beast was wrongfully impounded at Withypool. Edward III had forbidden this practice as long ago as 1334, but Forest life and customs changed little in a mere 300 years.

'Widge beasts' (ponies and horses) were liable to be driven five times a year, but fortunately for the Free Suitors fewer preys were usually considered sufficient. 'Unbooked' cattle and widge beasts had to be impounded for a year and a day and produced at the Swainmote before they became the Warden's property. The 'Little Pound' at Withypool was in use until the

---

* These sudden fluctuations are explained later in this Chapter in the account of James Boevey's Wardenship.

end of the Forest, but the new pound built at Simonsbath in the seventeenth century became the main one.

Turf cutting was let by the Wardens and some quarrying was permitted. These two sources of income were worth £14 in 1736. Rights of hawking, hunting, fowling and fishing, and of seizure of the goods and chattels of outlaws, felons and fugitives provided a useful addition to the Warden's revenue. It was, however, the ample income from the grazing that made the Wardenship of Exmoor so lucrative an office—and so eagerly sought after at the fixed rent of £46 13s. 4d. a year.

Legally, the Warden had very wide powers. He was entitled to appoint his own coroner, and, after 1661, to prevent sheriffs, justices of the peace, bailiffs, and other officers from entering the Forest. From 1508 to 1814—when the last Crown lease fell in—the Forest of Exmoor was a little kingdom and the Warden was its near-absolute ruler.

Of the long line of Wardens, one or two call for special mention in this brief survey of Exmoor's history. William de Wrotham, who received the Wardenship from John in 1204, was an energetic and powerful man. He was one of the King's justices, warden of the Stannaries of Devon and Cornwall, warden of the seaports, and sheriff of Devon in 1198. John's charter granting him the office is our first certain proof that the Wardenship of the Forest had become hereditary: ". . . to hold to him and to his heirs of us and our heirs for ever, freely, quietly, wholly, honourably, fully, in all things and all places. . . ." It was to this charter that subsequent hereditary Wardens referred if their tenure was challenged. De Wrotham's success in procuring so satisfactory a condition is an early indication of the value attached to the Wardenship.

The reign on Exmoor of Sabina Pecche (1295–1308) is of interest in that she was the first woman to hold the office. Not for another 400 years did she have a successor, when Mrs. Margaret Boevey became the second, and last, woman Warden. Richard de Plessy died in 1289, leaving as his heirs his three sisters. The Wardenship went to Sabina, the eldest, though her husband Nicholas acted in right of his wife until his death in 1295. Her son (also Nicholas) succeeded Sabina, and it was during his Wardenship that Edward II sent his huntsmen to Exmoor to kill twenty stags. This is the only known instance of a royal command for the king's deer on Exmoor, for the remoteness of the Forest from the royal palaces prevented the monarchs from troubling the royal beasts. Edward II, however, was a lavish entertainer and as, under strong political pressure, he had dis-afforested large areas of other Forests he may well have been reminded of his far-distant Exmoor by a pressing need for venison. The frontispiece of E. J. Rawle's *Annals of Exmoor Forest* appears to provide another example of a royal requisition of Exmoor deer. It is a reproduction of a warrant of Charles I addressed "To the ranger of our Forrest of Exmore" and commanding that he deliver to the bearer of the warrant "one fatt stagg of this season". But there are odd features about this, and the document must have been signed by the king under a misapprehension, since —from 1508 onwards—though the Forest remained royal property it was leased, and with it all the king's rights over the deer. Nor had the king a 'ranger' of Exmoor. If an officer with that title did exist, he was the Warden's servant and not the king's. It is more than likely that Charles I was confusing Exmoor with his other Forests, forgetting the very special provisions that applied to the former.

The most remarkable of the Wardens was James Boevey.* In 1649, 'The Commons of England assembled in Parliament' (as the Rump called itself) passed "An Act for the sale of the Honours Manors and lands heretofore belonging to the late King, Queen and Prince". The other Royal Forests were excluded but, because it had for so long been leased to private individuals, Exmoor was treated as a Chase and not as a Forest, being therefore included in the Act. In accordance with the terms of this Act, the moor was surveyed and perambulated in 1651 (see Chapter Five), and soon afterwards James Boevey bought the freehold. Thus, for the first time, the Forest passed out of the Crown's possession.

Boevey was a wealthy merchant of Dutch ancestry, a well-known man, meriting a long description in John Aubrey's *Brief Lives*:

> Left off trade at 32, and retired to a country life, by reason of his indisposition, the ayre of the citie not agreeing with him. Then in these retirements he wrote *Active Philosophy* (a thing not done before) wherein he enumerated the Arts and Tricks practised in Negotiation, and how they were to be ballanced by prudentiall rules ... He speakes the Lowe Dutch, High Dutch, French, Italian, Spanish and Lingua Franco, and Latin besides his owne ... As to his person he is about 5 foot high, slender body, straight hair exceeding black and curling at the end, a dark hazell eie, of a midling size, but the most sprightly I have beheld. Browes and beard of the same colour as his haire. A person of great temperance, and deepe thoughts, and a working head never idle. From 14 he had a candle burning by him all night, with pen, inke, and paper, to write downe thoughts as they came into his head; that so he might not lose a thought. Was ever a great lover of Naturall Philosophie. His whole life has been perplexed in law-suites, which have made him expert in humane affairs, in which he alwaies over-came. He had many law-suites with powerfull adversaries; one lasted 18 years ... For his health he never had it very well, but indifferently, alwaies a weake stomach, which proceeded from the agitation of the braine ...

Aubrey completed his description with a list of Boevey's 'thirty two works mostly philosophical', which included *The Art of Building a Man: or*

* Pronounced *Boovy*.

Education, The Art of Governing the Tongue, The Art of Gaining Wealth, The Government of Amor Conjugalis and, 'in Two Tomes', *Of Amor Concupiscentiae.*

"No person inhabited within the Forest"*—according to evidence given before the Parliamentary Commissioners—when Boevey arrived in his kingdom, but several rough tracks met at Simonsbath and it was here that he built his house, now known as Simonsbath Lodge. And to this new house he brought his new wife, Isabel de Visscher—the first Mrs. Boevey (Susanna der Weyer) having died in 1649. Whether they wintered there we do not know. It would have been a lonely life; but Mr. Boevey would have had long, quiet evenings in which to write his learned and curious books.

The house still stands. Built by Boevey in the style of the prosperous yeoman's house of fifty years earlier, it has been added to at various times since, assuming eventually the shape of a capital E. In Boevey's time a detached wool-chamber was erected to the west of the main house and this, in due course, was joined to the first building whose date of completion is announced by the '1654' carved on the beam above the old kitchen fireplace.

In addition to building "the first house in the Forest", Boevey made the first farm in the Forest, enclosing 108 acres between Ashcombe and Lime Combe, bounded to the south by the Barle. He also made Simonsbath the administrative centre of his realm, building (and using!) the pound and causing the Swainmote Courts to be held in the 'Great Hall' of his house. These things lay in his power, for the freehold of the Forest was his.

It was his ambition to extend his domination beyond the Forest boundaries and to extinguish the rights of those who, as he put it, ". . . have and doe make divers claymes and pretences to receive privileges in the said Chase". From the first day of his ownership he was determined to make an assault on the commoners. He opened his campaign in 1654 when he filed a bill attacking all the rights of the Free Suitors, dropping the action, however, when preliminary enquiries revealed the strength of their position. But this was merely a tactical withdrawal, for it was at this same time that he began to formulate his claim that his Exmoor property included all the adjoining commons. He was thus preparing to take on the Suitors at Large as well as the Free Suitors.

His next step was to raise the agistment (grazing) rates very steeply. There was an immediate outcry, but many farmers took a more effective reprisal than protesting: they boycotted the pasturing, and Boevey was forced to drop the rates the next year, though not back to the old levels. At the same time he obtained a judgement from the Courts that the

---

* A measure of the contraction of the Forest boundaries (see p. 24).

Warden had the right to fix the rates at whatever level he pleased.

At the Restoration in 1660 all former Crown lands were resumed by the king, and Boevey's enemies not unnaturally assumed that they had seen the last of their tormentor. He had, however, made his plans and though he lost the freehold he still retained the Forest on lease, becoming a tenant of the Crown at the old rent of £46 13s. 4d. This secured for him all the advantages that Wardens had enjoyed since 1508; and his new pasturing rates and cunning plans put him in a fair way to making more money out of the Wardenship than had ever been done before. The intricacies of his smart deal with the Crown, however, resulted in a lease that was for the lifetime of Lady Thurles (a daughter of the Sir John Poyntz to whom, and to whose daughter, Queen Elizabeth I had leased the Forest for their lives). The life of an old lady of seventy-three was not the best of securities, and Boevey persuaded her son, the Marquis of Ormond, to apply to the Crown for the Forest lease after his mother's death. In July 1660 and in January 1661 letters patent were issued to Ormond giving him the lease for four lives and thirty-one years, the lives being aged seventy-three, fifty, twenty-six and twenty-one. Mr. James Boevey—to whom the lease was immediately transferred by Ormond—could now feel that he had all the time he needed to exploit his Wardenship to the full.

It is ironical that Boevey's business should have been so rapidly and successfully concluded whereas many loyal dispossessed Cavaliers, or their orphans, waited fruitlessly for recognition of their just claims to recompense. Boevey's planting of a new Hoar Oak Tree (see Chapter Five) not only restored an important Forest boundary mark but afforded him the opportunity of an ostentatious demonstration of loyalty.* The rapacious little Warden had cause to feel loyal!

In the autumn of 1660 Boevey brought another lawsuit about pasturing dues against seventeen farmers but was then, fortunately for the Exmoor borderers, involved in litigation concerning his first wife's property in Holland. The case lasted for a long time and left him with no leisure to go to law over Exmoor. Between 1672 and 1674, indeed, he was in prison at the Hague. (He had such powerful friends at Court that the Lords of the Treasury represented to the king that he should insist on reparation being made by the Dutch to James Boevey who had been unjustly imprisoned and had in consequence suffered damage estimated at £30,000. We do not know whether the compensation was paid.)

Upon his release he returned to Exmoor and at once opened the biggest fight of his career by seeking to prove that the Forest was not bounded by the perambulations of the Free Suitors but that it included all the commons on its borders, the tithes of which rightfully belonged to him as Warden.

---

* The oak, of course, being a nationally recognised symbol commemorating Charles II's escape after the Battle of Worcester in 1651.

The case lasted four years, Boevey employing all his skill in so congenial a cause. In the Michaelmas Term of 1679 judgement was given against him. He never had a leg to stand on.

He came to Simonsbath less frequently after this. In all his remaining lawsuits he was described as "of Cheam in the County of Surrey". There was a tradition that he took to coining in his old age and used a cellar in his house at Cheam for that purpose. If the rumour reached far-away Exmoor it undoubtedly secured universal credence.

The permanent effects of his long Wardenship—forty-three years, the longest of all—were Simonsbath Lodge, the only house in the Forest until the nineteenth century; the farm that he made; the creation of Simonsbath as the moorland's administrative 'capital'; the new pasturing rates, which remained in force until 1819; and the 'Boevey' Hoar Oak Tree.

When Isabel died he married Margaret Cresset as his third wife, and on his death in January 1696 she became the second woman to be Warden of the Forest; but she lacked his zest for Exmoor conquest and, after eight years, she sold the remainder of her lease to Robert Siderfin, whose name may still be read on the older Ordnance Maps, between Draydon Knap and South Hill on the northern slopes of Winsford Hill.

The last of the Wardens of Exmoor Forest were the three Sir Thomas Dyke Aclands whose successive reigns endured from 1767 to 1814, when the last Crown lease expired. Their Wardenships are chiefly memorable for the revival of stag-hunting and the consequent protection of the deer from poachers (see Chapter Three), and for their careful breeding of the Exmoor ponies and the strengthening of the stock (see Chapter Four).

The story of the end of the Forest and of the remarkable men who owned Exmoor in the nineteenth century forms the content of the next Chapter.

CHAPTER TWO

The Knights of Exmoor

IN May 1810 Sir Thomas Acland, then Warden and lessee of the Forest, made application to the Lords of the Treasury for a renewal of his lease which was due to expire in 1814. His application was referred to a new government department: the Commission of His Majesty's Woods, Forests, and Land Revenues. The Commissioners, sensitive to Parliament's insistence that Crown lands should be used wherever possible for growing timber for the navy, ordered a survey of Exmoor and directed that particular enquiries be made into the possibility of growing oak timber there. This survey was still in progress in 1812 when Sir Thomas made a second application for the renewal of his lease, adding on this occasion that, if the Government preferred, he would buy the freehold.

The surveyor's report and the Commissioners' suggestions for the disposal of the Forest were ready in June 1814. The surveyor, Mr. Richard Hawkins, after endorsing the description of the Forest given in the Surveyor-General's report of 1783—"a large Tract of heathy, uninclosed Ground . . . the profits whereof arise chiefly from depasturing Sheep, with some little addition from Horned Cattle and Colts"—then gave a fuller account of the farm that James Boevey had made and of the pasturing:

> The small farm . . . called Simon's Bath Farm is situated nearly in the centre of the Forest, and contains about 108 acres, . . . and the Farm-house is licensed and frequented as an Inn . . . the remainder of the Forest is uninclosed, and used for depasturing Sheep and Cattle . . . there is no Timber or other Trees on the Forest, except four Ash Trees, two of them of considerable size and length, three large Beech Trees, Twenty-three Sycamores, and seven Lime Pollards; in all Thirty-seven Trees and Pollards, which are growing about the said Farm-house.

(As will soon be shown, it is significant that Hawkins made no mention of the Hoar Oak Tree.) His reference to the Farm-house fills in a gap in the history of Mr. Boevey's house. It had declined in status since its builder's death and had suffered a good deal from indifferent and indigent tenants. One of these, Dennicombe, burned some of the doors, the window frames and the wainscotting for firing. He was eventually gaoled at Ilchester as a debtor. It fared better as an inn, for the tracks that met at Simonsbath brought what moorland travellers there were to the massive front door that had resisted even Dennicombe's attacks. It was from the Simonsbath inn that poor Tucker and his grand-daughter set out to meet their deaths in a blizzard on their way home to Badgworthy (see Chapter Ten).

Hawkins's report gave some interesting figures for Forest pasturing. He estimated 32,000 sheep (including those of the Free Suitors and the Suitors at Large) and 640 horses. The nett profits of the Warden were quoted as £403 8s. 3¾d. Not a bad return on the Crown rent.

But the most important part of the survey followed: Hawkins stated that large areas of the Forest could be planted with oak, ash, beech, birch, larch and fir, and he argued that it would be to the Crown's advantage to inclose and divide the Forest rather than to renew the lease, selling some parts and retaining those suitable for timber. Had he visited the Hoar Oak Tree before committing himself to this opinion he would not have been so sanguine about raising oaks on Exmoor. His duties took him there during the final Perambulation of 1815 (preparatory to the award of allotments to the Crown and to those who, by former Wardenship or Borderers' rights, were considered to have a claim upon the land) but the improbable scheme of turning the Forest into a nursery for navy timber lurked at the back of the Commissioners' minds until, in June 1818, they finally decided to sell.

Much legal and surveying work was necessary, however, before that, and Hawkins's views were reinforced by a Mr. Wasbrough, a local surveyor, who wrote independently to the Commissioners urging inclosure and allotment rather than the renewal of the lease. The Commissioners accordingly recommended to the Treasury that an inclosure should be made, with due regard for the former Warden's claims (especially to tithes) and to the rights of the Borderers. They added that the King's allotment could either be used for timber-growing or sold, and the money so gained could be spent on timber land elsewhere.

An Act for Inclosure was passed in 1815, and in the next year the Inclosure Commissioners were busy surveying, making out proposed allotments, and designating areas suitable for the provision of road-building and repairing materials and watering places for cattle. They also reserved twelve acres of land at Simonsbath for the erection of a church and the provision of a burying-ground and a parsonage,

(in anticipation of the time when) it may happen that some part of the said Forest may hereafter become inhabited (in which case the Church) shall be named and called *The Parish Church of Exmoor*; and the said Forest shall for ever thereafter form and be a distinct Parish of itself, and shall be called by the Name of *The Parish of Exmoor*.

In two awards (in 1817 and 1819) the Inclosure Commissioners allotted 10,262 acres to the Crown, 3,201 acres to Sir Thomas Acland, 1,880 acres to Sir Charles W. Bamfylde, and parcels of land to the Free Suitors and the Suitors at Large in lieu of their ancient rights. The small allotments were as near a just award as such awards can ever be; but the poor men who received little soon sold their allotments to the rich men who received much. The parcels of land were not adequate compensation for the loss of their Forest grazing.

With the second and final award in May 1819 the Royal Forest of Exmoor ceased to exist. A thousand years of history ended in accordance with the provisions of the Inclosure Act:

> And be it further enacted that after the final Award . . . all and every the Lands and Grounds lying and being within the Boundaries of the said Forest . . . shall be and the same are hereby disafforested, and shall be and continue exonerated and discharged for ever thereafter from all Forestal Rights, Jurisdictions and Authorities whatsoever . . . and from all Forestal Rents, Customs, and Services which his Majesty, His Heirs and Successors . . . could otherwise claim therein.

Before the details of the lesser allotments were settled by the final award, the Commissioners of Woods and Forests decided not to retain the King's allotment:

> Upon a full consideration of all the circumstances connected with this property, and particularly its great distance from any other Estate of the Crown; the difference of opinion which prevailed as to any considerable portion of it being adapted for the Cultivation of Naval Timber, and the necessity of an entire new local Establishment, if it had been retained for that purpose, it appeared to us, that it would be most beneficial to the interests of the Crown, to dispose of the whole . . .

Accordingly, they advertised it as for sale by tender: seven were received, the highest being that put in by John Knight. *The Taunton Courier* reported the sale in August 1818:

> Mr. Knight of Worcestershire has purchased the allotment . . . given in right of the Crown on Exmoor Forest, for £50,000. The property is near Simond's-Bath; and the greater part is to be inclosed by a wall, in the centre of which a handsome residence is to be built. The spot affords great facilities for this purpose, and will, under the judicious plans in contemplation, become an enviable possession.

The purchase of the Bamfylde and Acland allotments and the conveyance of the Simonsbath Farm followed rapidly, leaving John Knight in sole possession of what had been the Forest.

In the second half of the eighteenth century and the first half of the nineteenth, English agriculture was transformed. A rapidly growing industrial population made heavy demands upon the country's food supply. The stimulus brought the response, and new methods of cultivation, the four-course rotation, the science of agricultural engineering, fertilisers, new crops, the drill and the mechanical hoe were all discovered. In addition large areas of uncultivated ground were brought under the plough and to improved pasture. The rural England that we see about us today is very largely a product of those years. Coke of Norfolk is known to all: what is not so widely known is that he was but one of many who spent their lives in trying to realise his ambition of making "two blades of grass grow where only one grew before—and two rabbits fighting for that".

John Knight came of an enterprising and courageous stock. His ancestor, Richard Knight, had made a fortune as an iron-master in Cromwell's time; and his descendants expanded the foundries, both the elder and the younger branches achieving great success at the original Shropshire forges and at the new ones at Wolverley. Despite this material prosperity there was little of the philistine in the family; the artistic bent of Richard Payne Knight (of the elder branch), who left a fine collection of classical bronzes, coins and gems to the British Museum, typified the imaginative impulse that marked them.

They had, too, a strong dynastic tendency. The sole condition that Richard Payne Knight attached to his bequest was that the Museum should appoint a perpetual 'Knight Family Trustee'. As early as 1818, before his Exmoor reign had properly begun, John Knight planned a great house at Simonsbath, in the middle of the wilderness; and his son, Sir Frederic Winn Knight, fought bravely through all his problems until the death of *his* son, at the age of twenty-eight, destroyed his hopes of founding a line.

We are nearer now to an understanding of John Knight's motives in buying Exmoor. In the first place, the need to increase agricultural efficiency was appreciated by all thinking men of his day. Here was another desert which must be made to bloom. Secondly, it would be an adventure, and the Knights had always been great men for a struggle. The risks were high, but so were the possible rewards; and the smoking chimneys of the Wolverley foundry would provide adequate resources for buying, breaking, and cropping Exmoor. Then too, there was something of a social *cachet* to be derived from the possession of a former Royal Forest. Wealth might come from iron, but the landowners still led England and a status that really counted could be rooted only in the soil. Two or three generations of Knights on the Forest, on land that had been for a thousand years part of the demesne of the Kings of England, would be a full satisfaction of the dynastic ambitions so strongly implanted in the family.

There was the artistic impulse too. John Knight was neither poet nor painter, but he loved the moor he bought. Living at Simonsbath, he came to know the Forest in all its moods and at all seasons. He rode over every mile of his moorland kingdom; neither the solitude nor the storms, the mud nor the snow deterred him. He brought his family from Wolverley to live in the quiet house in the Forest, to the darkness of the long winters, to the beauty of nearby Long Combe and the flying shadows on the windy hills.

Romance and practicality sometimes warred within him: courage and tenacity never failed to sustain his initial acceptance of risk when the stakes seemed worthwhile. He had a vision of corn waving on Tom's Hill and to achieve that impossible dream he pitted himself and his all against the moor.

It must not be thought that he came green to his task. He was already farming in Worcestershire and had done some land reclamation there. He had made a special study of Coke's great work at Holkham and he was technically equipped for the agricultural engineering that lay ahead. As a newtomer to the Forest what he necessarily lacked was a knowledge of the ways of the moor.

For many years the work of the Knights was slighted. Not until 1929, when C.S. Orwin published *The Reclamation of Exmoor Forest*, did it receive its full due. The wilder schemes of John and the mining projects of Frederic were remembered; the wise and patient work that discovered how to farm Exmoor was ignored. Even the sensible and well-informed Page* showed no real comprehension of these pioneers but, as Orwin pointed out, those best qualified to judge at the time knew the value of the best of the Knights' work. When T.D. Acland (the future eleventh baronet) heard the news of John Knight's death in 1850 he said:

> He will long be remembered as the first person who had the spirit to commence a great agricultural work which Mr. Billingsley foretold fifty years ago . . . The present proprietor [Frederic Knight] wants neither the energy nor the will to do his duty . . . and to bring the Forest into a condition which an English gentleman may look upon with well-grounded satisfaction.

The final result may not have assumed the precise shape envisaged by John Knight, but if he could have seen the outcome of his and his son's work his satisfaction would have been well-grounded indeed.

Frederic Winn Knight, who assumed control of Exmoor policy and administration in 1841, spent much of his youth at Simonsbath. Unlike his father, he had grown up on the moor and this helps to explain his success in evolving a sounder agricultural system. He was a determined and

---

* John Lloyd Warden Page: *An Exploration of Exmoor and the Hill Country of West Somerset.*

energetic man, fitted for the heavy responsibilities that he was born to. Nor was Exmoor his sole activity: he was Member of Parliament for West Worcestershire for forty-four years, and Parliamentary Secretary to the Poor Law Board in 1852 and again in 1858–59. Directorships of the Bank of London and of the National Provincial Insurance Association made considerable demands on his time. He was active in the Volunteer movement, his K.C.B. (1886) being a recognition of his work for that body. But these other commitments were always additional to his Exmoor work and plans which were the chief activity of his life and foremost in his hopes. He and his wife identified themselves with the moor and its concerns—the farms that were created, the community that was established, the staghounds—in a way that was not possible for John Knight. Exmoor for them was home: the centre of their lives, the scene of all their strivings, their resting place at the end.

The first phase of the Knight family's epic struggle lasted from the purchase of the Forest until 1841, when John Knight relinquished personal direction of the Exmoor projects.

Early in 1819 the moor was 'cried' and an advertisement in *The Taunton Courier* announced that the rates for sheep pasturing were raised from 5d. to 1s. There is no evidence of a boycott similar to that which followed Boevey's first big increase and forced him to moderate his demands. Nor can a parallel be drawn between the actions of John Knight and Boevey: the old rates had been in force since 1655 and had long ceased to represent the value of the grazing. Knight's new charges were not excessive in the circumstances.

The first constructional work undertaken was the building of the Forest wall to enclose the whole of Knight's estate. By 1824 most of it was finished —twenty-nine miles in all—and, as described in Chapter Five, considerable stretches survive to remind the walker of the energy and money expended so long ago. The story is told that the men of Brendon used to demolish after dark what Knight's men had built during the day; but as their raids were confined to that section running along the old Badgworthy enclosures the work was not much delayed. There may be truth in the story, for there was opposition to Knight in this area, caused partly by legitimate dissatisfaction with the moorland allotments made to the Suitors at Large, and partly by an unfounded fear that he planned to enlarge his territory at the expense of Brendon Common. A pound that he built in this part of the Forest suffered considerable damage, but the trouble eventually died away.

Higher up the moor he made Brendon Two Gates, a name that survives and deserves explanation. Where roads cut the Forest Wall, ingenious double gates were erected to prevent cattle and sheep from straying. These gates were hung on opposite sides of the same hanging-post and closed, without fastenings of any kind, against the same clapping-post. Thus they were easy to open and shut, but a wind that blew one gate open was, at the same time, blowing the other shut. There was another of these contrivances between Red Deer and Honeymead.

John Knight also undertook in his first phase the improvement and making of roads, realising that he could not get supplies to his estate, produce away from it, or colonists to settle on it until transport was adequate. The land set aside in the Inclosure Awards for the making of public roads had followed the routes of existing trackways, and Knight metalled the tracks from Exford and Sandyway to Simonsbath. He also constructed a good highway from Simonsbath to link with the lowland road to South Molton, and drove an excellent carriage road north across the moor to Brendon and Lynmouth. Twenty years later, Frederic Knight made a good road across Challacombe Common to enable him to transport lime cheaply from Combe Martin. In all, the Knights constructed twenty-two miles of public roads and in so doing made the settlement of the moor possible.

After living for a time at Lynton, John Knight and his family moved to James Boevey's old house at Simonsbath, behind which was to be built the mansion referred to in the press announcement of the sale of the king's allotment. A family tradition tells that he intended to bring furniture, fittings and woodwork from Wolverley House, which was to be dismantled; but the Great House at Simonsbath was never completed and the shell remained a gaunt mockery until it was pulled down in 1899.

It was from Simonsbath Lodge that John Knight supervised the construction of what has become an enigma of the moor—Pinkworthy Pond.* The Barle rises on the desolate Chains and, to the south of this plain, across the headwaters of the infant river, a dam was built by gangs of Irish labourers. The lake so formed is about seven acres in extent and 30 feet deep at its southern end.† What purpose it was intended to serve is not certainly known, for the family papers do not explain it. The Exmoor opinion that it was built to supply water for a canal is vague about the canal's function. A so-called canal runs from the Pond in the direction of Simonsbath, but this dry ditch is not linked to Pinkworthy, nor would the volume of water have been adequate to do more than float toy boats down to the moorland 'capital'; and John Knight was sufficiently conversant with engineering to know this. Another suggestion is that Pinkworthy was intended to supply water power for mining machinery. There are strong objections to this theory: although John Knight acquired the mineral rights of his Exmoor property it was not until Frederic's day that mining was

---

* Pronounced *Pinkery*; see, too, Badgworthy, pronounced *Badgery*.
† For a detailed description see Chapter Seven.

Middle Exmoor—looking east down Chetsford Water.

Pinkworthy Pond—desolate birthplace of the River Barle.

Looking up the Barle—a view from Sandyway-Withypool road.

Near Cornham Ford on the Barle.

Tarr Steps—medieval or prehistoric? But certainly the finest bridge of its type in England.

St. Luke's, Simonsbath—the Church that the Knights built on Exmoor.

attempted, and there is no evidence that his father seriously contemplated mining on the moor. Even if he had done so, the mineral area known at the time that Pinkworthy was constructed was situated lower down the Barle, where water power was readily available if needed. Orwin suggested that the 'canal' was to be an irrigation channel and supports his theory with a family tradition that it was never linked up with Pinkworthy because a mistake was made in the surveying and the channel would have tapped the Pond at too high a level. The likeliest of all explanations is that John Knight wanted to adorn his property with a large lake. Such a sheet of water would offer both aesthetic and sporting advantages: it was part of the 'improvements'—in the eighteenth-century sense of the term.

During the Pinkworthy period, too, big draining operations were begun. The iron pan (described in Chapter Five) accounts for the peaty water-logged condition of much of the Forest, and John Knight was at once aware of the need for adequate drainage. Many miles of channels were cut, notably on Trout Hill, down the Pinfords, and across the Chains, but they were relatively ineffective, since the pan was not cracked. To this day they provide nasty pitfalls for the unwary walker in these wild areas.

Throughout this first period of Forest management a far-reaching agricultural experiment was conducted. Knight continued to let the grazing as had been done for hundreds of years, but his true intention was to revolutionise the life of Exmoor by bringing it under cultivation. Since Boevey's day there had been enclosed fields round Simonsbath, and both here and in new stretches of the Barle valley he began to plough. The laborious process was performed with energy and skill. The rough grass was burnt and—at great expense, since there were no moorland sources of lime—the soil was heavily limed to neutralise its acid sourness. Then bullock teams, six beasts to each plough, cut through the soil. On 'dry' land they ploughed down to the clay subsoil; on 'wet' land the pan had to be broken by subsoil ploughing, a lengthy and, therefore, expensive operation. It must be stressed that John Knight's methods were perfectly sound. If Exmoor was to be reclaimed, this was the way to do it, and the land he broke has never reverted. Where he went wrong was in trying to grow on his broken land the crops that he was used to growing on his Midland farm. He never realised that the four-course rotation was an impossibility on his bleak upland. He should have built windbreaks, but it was not until Frederic's day that the need for these was fully realised; he should not have tried to grow wheat and barley; it was Frederic who learnt the lesson. In the father's time good chance occasionally provided a fair cereal crop in sheltered fields on the broken land. Such illusory successes confirmed his faith in his hopeless quest, and to the end he was trying to farm his 2,500 acres of ploughland in an 'orthodox' manner. The secret of success on Exmoor remained to be discovered by his son.

Considering the difficulties involved it says much for John Knight's energy and determination that so large an acreage should have been ploughed, but the cost was great and there was no prospect of a return while he persisted with a four-course system. His stock-rearing experiments on the other hand were successful, and to these he gave much time and thought. In one month alone he travelled 1,000 miles by coach and bought 100 head of cattle—West Highland bullocks and Herefords. The former did well in the summer but could not winter on the Forest without hay or corn. They also had the disadvantage of being very wild: a letter of Frederic Knight's describes how a drift of these beasts to market developed into a running fight, the bulls attacking passers-by and several of the animals having to be shot. Eventually, Devons and Shorthorns replaced the 'foreigners'.

Sheep, too, were brought onto the moor in great herds, and it was John Knight who introduced the Cheviots now so common on Exmoor. He had much trouble both with them and with the native 'Horns' at first. Summer agistment was one thing, and well understood by the local shepherds he employed, but sheep ranching on the scale he planned was quite another. The district had always been lawless—an extra-parochial and county-border paradise for deer-poachers and sheep-stealers. So bad did things get that he employed Irishmen as guards, but found that their habit of fighting among themselves was as troublesome as the thefts they were supposed to prevent. It was difficult to find reliable men who would endure the solitude of the Forest, and by the end of John Knight's regime, little colonisation had taken place.

Another interesting experiment of the first phase was the crossing of native Exmoor mares with Dongola Arab stallions to increase the size and 'quality' of the ponies. But the 'improved' foals could not winter on the moor, and after this lesson was learnt Knight concentrated on increasing the native herds, understanding more clearly the true value of the home-bred animal.

By 1840 John Knight's splendid energy began to fail, and in the following year he handed over to his son the management of Exmoor. Despite many failures he had achieved much: in particular he had shown that the land could be improved; and his large-scale experiments with sheep and cattle had provided experience which enabled Frederic to discover the true way to farm the moor. The greatest weakness was his failure to colonise. Exmoor could not be tamed by one man alone, however great his energy, however bold his plans.

In 1842 he retired to Rome, dying there in 1850. To the end he was vitally concerned with the Forest and was kept fully informed of all developments in the grand design that he had conceived with such ardour and prosecuted with such courage.

The second phase of the reclamation lasted from 1841 until 1850 and initiated a change of policy. Frederic Knight abandoned his father's policy of large-scale centralised experiment in favour of a landlord-tenant system, in which the tenants were given considerable financial inducements to make a success of the new farming policies worked out by Knight and his very able agents.

There were several reasons for this change, one being financial. The cost of John Knight's work had been great, and in 1840 the fortune of the elder branch of the family, which John and Frederic had every reason to suppose would be theirs in due course, was held by the Courts to be settled in the female and not the male line. This was a severe blow, and even had Frederic been in favour of a continuation of his father's policy he would have been hard pressed to find the capital. But he had in any case been convinced for some time that colonisation was essential for success, so he now pressed on with the creation of tenant farms. Already there were farm buildings at Honeymead and Cornham; by 1842 houses were built and tenants found. This was the period of Robert Smith's agency; he and Knight planned and made Emmett's Grange, Driver, Duredown, Warren, Horsen, Wintershead, Pinkworthy, Tom's Hill and Larkbarrow. The agreements on which they were let were largely the work of Smith: very low rents for the first four years, rising each four years thereafter until the twenty-year leases expired. The leases also provided for compensation to tenants for durable improvements made at their own expense. Thus it was hoped to aid the tenant in the early years when he was having his hardest struggle with the moor, the landlord taking a higher return as the farm prospered. It was Smith, too, who first planted beech hedges on a large scale as windbreaks, buying huge quantities of beech nuts for sowing in the Simonsbath plantations.

Frederic Knight had long realised that the four-course system and Exmoor were incompatible. Now that he was in charge he worked out with Smith a policy of root and grass growing. Here lay the true path for the Exmoor farmer: for centuries the high moor had carried summer flocks; the task now was to improve the more sheltered lands by ploughing and liming—as in John Knight's day—but to use them as in-fields for the newly-made farms, growing sheep fodder so that the ewes could be winter-folded on roots and grasses ready for the spring lambing.

By 1850, then, a revolutionary change had occurred: the true farming method was being evolved and colonisation was at last under way.

Yet the struggle was by no means over. Just though Smith's agreements were, the first tenants of the new farms failed almost to a man. There were two reasons for this. Many of the tenants were unsuited to the grim battle that faced them; attracted by the very low rents of the early years of the tenancies, they had left 'soft' farming country and had no knowledge of what their new life demanded. Again, though the later and higher rents represented only a fair return to the landlord on the capital value of land and buildings, to say nothing of general estate costs—roads, plantations, boundary fences, initial improvements—they were higher than moor farms could yet be made to yield.

Between 1850 and 1860 Frederic Knight might well have expected to see some return for all his hard work and heavy and continuing expenditure. Instead, he had deep disappointments as tenants failed* and land was not taken up. His courage and resourcefulness did not desert him, however: to these years belong the mining ventures (about which more is said later in this Chapter) and, on the home farm, he experimented with what he called 'continuous cropping'—a grass and root rotation which made possible in later years the big scale sheep-ranching that he perfected as the true Exmoor system.

This troubled decade saw one major triumph. The population had grown sufficiently for the erection of the church and parsonage and the creation of the parish envisaged in the Inclosure Act. Frederic Knight had already built a school at Simonsbath, and in 1856 the little church of St. Luke and its parsonage were built and blessed. When John Knight bought the Forest it contained one house in which lived a family of five. In 1852 there were 281 people on Frederic Knight's estate and thirty children attending the Simonsbath school. It was time for the extra-parochial wasteland to become a civil and ecclesiastical parish.

In 1866 Robert Smith retired, to be succeeded as agent by Frederick Loveband Smyth. Knight was once again fortunate in his chief subordinate. Developing his predecessor's work at Emmett's Grange and Knight's 'continuous cropping', Smyth introduced the practice of reclaiming rough land by raising successive rape crops. After preliminary burning and top-soil ploughing an annual rape crop could be produced—if sufficient lime was used—for three or four years in succession. Four years of successive liming, burning, and sheep-treading decomposed the peaty soil right down to the pan, which was then broken by subsoil ploughing and the land sown with a mixture of rape and grass seed to form permanent pasture. Each rape crop in the first four years was eaten off by sheep, and Smyth's records showed that they improved on average 2s. a head per week during this preparatory period.

With this method as its basis the boldest and most successful of the Exmoor experiments was launched. Five thousand Blackface and Cheviot ewes were brought to Exmoor from the Scottish Highlands and the Border, their shepherds coming with them to settle on the moor. Most of the sheep were brought by sea to Lynmouth, but one flock came by rail to

---

* 'Ruined on Exmoor' is a phrase found in several contemporary memoirs—e.g. Sir Thomas Acland's description of a servant girl's father, *Sir Thomas Acland : Memoir and Letters.*

Bristol and was then driven the eighty miles to Simonsbath by its shepherd, the redoubtable John Gourdie: his name, a hundred years later, is still legendary on the moor. The sheep ranching succeeded so well that a quicker method of subsoil ploughing was needed to replace the bullock teams. A ten-horse-power stationary steam engine, winches, hawsers, and a Sutherland plough provided the ingenious and efficient answer. By 1879 Frederic Knight knew that he had won. This vast—and last—pioneering venture was the successful climax to the sixty years of constant and hitherto unremunerative toil which he and his father had given to their Forest land.

In the same period (1866 to 1879) the tenant farms began to improve. The unsuccessful tenants were gradually replaced by local men who were prepared for the hard life and ready to apply the Knight methods. Tenants who had begun their working life in the service of the Knight estate now took over Warren, Honeymead, Picked Stones and Duredown. Not all the farms succeeded, and not all were let; but by 1880 there were some thriving tenants to prove that the right man using the right methods could do well on a Knight farm.

When things were at their worst—in the 1850 to 1860 period—Frederic Knight involved himself in the iron mining project which is sometimes remembered when his true and enduring work is forgotten. Here and there in the Forest, and particularly in the southern area, round Cornham and Blue Gate, are surface workings, often called 'Roman' though with little justification. Yet some of the workings are undoubtedly old and the existence of iron ore on the moor has been known for hundreds of years. John Knight made no attempt to investigate the mineral wealth of his estate, but round about 1850 a variety of circumstances impelled Frederic to look into the possibilities of mining the moor. Money was scarce; the new system of tenant farming seemed to be failing; and from a purely material point of view the Exmoor experiment looked like a costly failure. On the adjacent Brendon Hills iron was being mined very profitably, and there seemed no reason why Exmoor should not prove equally productive. Obtaining the services of a first-rate mining engineer, Frederic Knight went into the question thoroughly. The expert's report was so encouraging that he was able to interest the Dowlais Iron Company in the possibility of working the deposits and, after an investigation by its own surveyors and engineers, the Company came to terms with Knight in 1855, agreeing on a rent of £1,000 a year plus a royalty of 1s. a ton on every ton of ore above 20,000. Every precaution had been taken, the best opinion in the country obtained, and when the first operations began at Cornham Ford there was no reason to anticipate anything but success.

It would be unprofitable to recount in detail the events of the next few years. The story is one of constantly recurring hope and disappointment. New shafts were dug; new adits driven; iron was found everywhere, but nowhere in sufficient quantities to justify continued working. The ore was high grade, but the veins were always too thin. By 1858 the Dowlais Company had spent £6,000 in mining £950-worth of ore.

In the meantime Knight had been pressing on with the construction of a light railway to take the ore to the coast.* In 1856–7 he surveyed the whole route and prepared two-thirds of the bed. The railway was to run from Simonsbath to Porlock Weir, following the winding 1,400 foot contour over its high moorland route. At the Simonsbath end it was to climb out of the Barle valley by a long curving incline; at Porlock Weir the precipitous drop of nearly 1,400 feet was to be negotiated by rope-worked inclines, the descending laden trucks pulling empties to the top by gravity—a method then being used on the Brendons. Apart from these two terminal stretches the route across the moor is level, nowhere exceeding a gradient of one in 250: traction could, therefore, have been supplied either by pony or locomotive.

No ground work was carried out at the proposed termini, but the beginnings of the level bed can be traced from near Whit Stones (the junction of the Porlock Hill and Exford roads) to Warren Farm, a distance of some six and a half miles. Gettins's accurate observations provide this description:

> For most of its length it consists of two parallel low banks about eighteen ins. high and twenty-seven feet apart at the top, with a flat 'road space' between. It is often obscured by heather and rushes, but clearly identifiable when seen lengthwise. The banks seem to be spoil heaps of surface peat and soil cleared from the road space. The bank on the uphill side is usually the larger and may have served to deflect surface water to culverts at intervals. It does not seem sufficiently wide or of suitable material to carry a railed track, which presumably was to have been laid on ballast deposited in the road space.

The Warren Farm to Prayway Head section of the route provided some interesting problems but the general direction was made plain in Knight's scheme. The track was to cross the Exe somewhere near Exe Head, circle back to Prayway and then proceed by 'sweeping curves' over Duredown and down to the Barle.

But not a line was ever laid. Having dug much of the bed, Knight applied to the Dowlais Company for the delivery of the rails which it had contracted to supply. The Company, convinced by now that the Exmoor deposits were not an economic proposition, refused to proceed with the railway; and though a Court judgement in November 1859 upheld

* See "The Exmoor Mineral Railway": G.L. Gettins, *The Exmoor Review*, No. 8.

Knight's claim, Dowlais opted to make a new agreement with him by which, on payment of £7,000, the Company was released from any further obligation in connection with the railway or the mines. Knight never wavered in his belief that more determination in prosecuting the mining project would have resulted in success. Although he received compensation the abandonment of the scheme was a heavy blow, coming as it did when the reclamation was proving both expensive and disappointing.

Nor was the eventual success of the great agricultural innovation an unclouded triumph. In 1879 Frederic Sebright Winn Knight, Sir Frederic's only son, died at the age of twenty-eight. His father, whose dearest wish it had been to hand on to his son a secure inheritance, did not fully recover from the shock and grief. From then until his own death in 1897 he retained his interest in and love for his Exmoor estate but consolidation, not conquest, was the aim in this final period. There were no new experiments. The steam ploughs completed the tasks they had begun and were then silent, leaving thousands of acres in their wild, unbroken state.

If there was no fresh conquest, however, there was no retreat. The sound farming policy evolved after so many years of costly experiment was steadily pursued. At Sir Frederic's death the Forest was flourishing as never before. The eighties and nineties were bad years for agriculture, but the new farms on Exmoor stood up to the depression as well as any. His had been no selfish goal or narrow achievement. With a courage and resourcefulness unsurpassed in the records of agricultural pioneers he established a thriving community. The farms of modern Exmoor, their herds and flocks, the village of Simonsbath, the parish church where he and Lady Knight are buried, are the direct outcome of this man's toil and vision—a toil prolonged and a vision cherished through years of disappointment.

Knight sold the reversion of his estate to Earl Fortescue whose own more fertile lands at Castle Hill provided good wintering and fattening for stock. There was thus a partial return to the policy of using the moor chiefly for summer grazing. The sheep-ranching continued, however, and a ewe flock of 5,000 was maintained on the unimproved lands. At the autumn round-up the surplus ewes were sold off and ewe lambs required for flock development were taken to the lower ground to winter. But the flock itself wintered on the moor, hay being fed to it only in the severest weather.

The tenant farms showed a steady capacity to survive bad times. Until after the second world war most of the farmers were local men and most of the labour was supplied by the family. The life was hard, but between the wars, radio and the motor car and the new industry of catering for summer visitors did much to lessen the loneliness.

It was still chiefly on sheep and Knight methods that the farming depended: roots and grasses grown on Knight fields were essential for wintering the breeders and finishing stock for market; and until recent years only Knight fields were available for this purpose. For two whole generations after Frederic's death the Exmoor farmer relied upon the work done and the money spent by John Knight and his son.

CHAPTER THREE

The Wild Red Deer

EXMOOR, and the wooded valleys south and west of the National Park, is, with the Scottish Highlands, the last of the secure haunts of the wild red deer in Britain. Poachers have drastically reduced their numbers in the Quantocks, where they used to flourish, but their Exmoor home is still safe. The shooting—authorised and otherwise—of the war years caused a serious decline, but the herds have increased since, and it is probable that there are something like 800–1,000 deer in the National Park now. They are the loveliest and largest of our wild mammals; a direct link with the prehistoric past, and a unique inheritance to be cherished by all who value the richness and variety of the wild life of Britain.

The most notable feature of the stag is his head, for which, together with his flesh and his fleetness, he is chiefly prized. The term 'head' should be explained: it is the name most properly used for the elaborate growth of antler which is the glory of this royal animal.* A massive horn (or 'beam') curves gracefully outwards and upwards from either side, having tines and points projecting from it. On Exmoor the three lateral projections on each beam are called 'rights'. The lowest is the brow; the next the bay; and the third the trey. Points or 'brockets' project upwards from the top of each beam.

There are two ways of describing the head. For example, a stag is described as having "all his rights (i.e. brow, bay and trey on each beam) and four and five (or three and four, etc.†) a'top". Or he may be described as 'a thirteen pointer'. The stag in the sketch answers this description, having brow, bay and trey on each beam (six points) plus three points on one beam and four on the other, making thirteen points in all. The record for a stag taken by the Devon and Somerset is twenty points.

Since Charles Palk Collyns wrote his *Notes on the Chase of the Wild Red Deer* in 1862 there has been one important modification of red deer lore. It is now known that the head is not necessarily an accurate indication of the stag's age. Differences in the feed obtained by calves and even full-grown stags, injuries sustained during 'velvet' periods, and naturally-occurring variations between individual specimens make it impossible to deduce age from rights and points with any certainty. The state of the

* See the outline sketch on page 50.
† That is, four and five (or three and four) points or brockets.

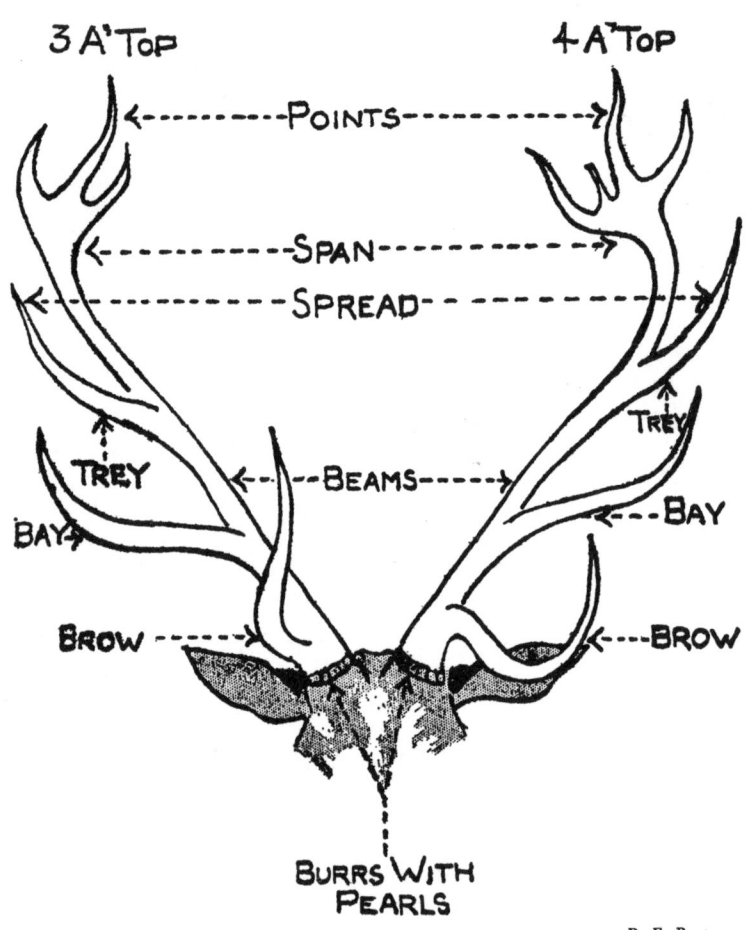

3 A'TOP   4 A'TOP

POINTS

SPAN

SPREAD

TREY

BEAMS

BAY

TREY

BAY

BROW

BROW

BURRS WITH PEARLS

P. E. Burton.

A FULL-GROWN STAG'S HEAD

teeth is often a better guide to age than is the head; the slots are the best guide of all—but only to an experienced eye.

No two heads are identical and a perfect head is rare. What follows, then, should be regarded as a general statement rather than a precise and universal description. The male calf has no horns until he is a year old. Between one and two he throws out a knob of bone about two inches high on each side of his brow, and 'spires' (slender upright horns) grow out of these. The young stag at this stage is called a 'pricket'—a name, like all other hunting terms, of great antiquity. In the third year the brow rights are added, and in the next the trey. The middle (or bay) rights come in the fifth year; in the six, points are added 'a'top'.* Between the sixth and eighth years more points grow a'top and the head increases in size, length and strength, the beams thickening and becoming deeply serrated. The round ball of horn from which the whole of this growth springs is called the burr, and the rough excrescences round the burr are called the pearls. A fine head weighs from five to ten pounds, depending on the number of points. The girth of the beams between brow and bay rights will be from four to six inches (the record is six and a half); and the span, measured from the inside curve of each beam, may be up to three feet or even a little over. As the stag ages the head often deteriorates in size and in shape until, in extreme cases, only an upright spire projects at each side. Such a stag is called a 'backer'.

The fact that the head is 'mewed' or cast every year is not always realised. The Exmoor stags drop their antlers between the middle and the end of April, but shedding may be retarded by a cold and late spring and often occurs in May. The older stags cast theirs earlier than the young ones. It is rare to see a full-grown stag with horns still on after middle May, but prickets sometimes carry theirs until the end of that month. Just before mewing time the stags retire to the deepest coverts, where the heads are cast; this accounts for the fact that so few of the precious trophies are found and that shedding is so very rarely seen. When the new growth begins to sprout they move into clearer territory, because the tissue of blood-vessels (the 'velvet') that covers the growing horn and feeds it is very sensitive; the lightest blow will cause pain and bleeding. Thus the dense undergrowth in which the stag lies during the casting period is a most unsuitable harbour for him when he is in velvet. This is a miserable time. Flies swarm round the growing antlers, irritating the poor beast, and the fear of knocking the velvet keeps him standing for hours on the same spot—his head bent low, ears twitching, feet stamping, as he tries to drive the flies away.

By late August or early September the head is fully renewed and the velvet dries up. When the now superfluous membrane begins

* Points count only if a crop can be hung from them.

to peel off the stag rubs his antlers against trees to assist the process.

> When his heade is growne out to the full bignesse, then he rubbeth of that pyll, and that is called "the fraying of his heade", and afterwards he burnisheth the same, and then his heade is said to be full sommed.*

Collyns says that in forty-six years he saw only two stags killed before 10 September whose heads were entirely free of velvet; whereas, over the same period, he saw only one killed after 10 September with any velvet on his horns. But in very exceptional cases velvet has been seen in late October.

The description just given of the mewing and renewing of antlers is valid only for Exmoor. Red deer in captivity shed and get their horns earlier; and the Highland deer's seasons, owing to the different climate, vary from what is generally the rule on the moor. As to the belief that hinds eat the cast antlers, there is no Exmoor evidence in support of an old, and unattractive, notion.

When it is remembered that only some sixteen or eighteen weeks elapse from the mewing of the head to its full renewal the remarkable nature of the occurrence will be more properly appreciated. Every year of its adult life the stag produces a great mass of horn in this comparatively brief time. Nor, of course, are the antlers merely ornamental. During the fights that sometimes take place in the rutting season, and when a stag is at bay, they can be used with deadly effect. The keen brow rights are the most dangerous of the stag's weapons, being up to twenty inches long.

The coat of the deer is ruddy-brown in colour, and so thick that even Exmoor storms cannot penetrate it. For a week or two in spring while the thicker, darker coat of winter is shed, the deer is yellowish and shabby, but the lighter red-brown summer coat soon grows. The underparts are paler, shading out to buff: the short, tufted tail (the 'single') is brown. The face is of the same colour as the coat but shades off to a light grey about the jaws. A dark brown stripe of wiry hair—sometimes called the mane—extends from between the ears to the shoulders. The stag's throat and neck are covered with coarse hair which thickens in the autumn and forms a ruff in winter. The ears of both stag and hind are large yet delicate; their hearing is acute, and their sense of smell remarkably sensitive. The nobility of the stag's eye and the full softness of the hind's complete the alert beauty of the face.

Hinds are ready to mate in their second year; they generally produce only one calf a year, but twins sometimes occur. The calves are born in June after a gestation period of eight months. They are lovely creatures, as leggy as colts, and dappled like the fallow deer for the first three or four months, after which their coats take the characteristic red deer colour. The young female calf is not so fully spotted as the male. The hind is skilled in

---

* John Turberville: *Art of Venerie*, 1575.

the defence of her calf. If on the run, she accommodates her pace to that of the calf, but if the danger is pressing she will butt the calf into adequate cover, returning when she has drawn and shaken off the pursuit. The calf lies up during the night while the hind is feeding; the mother's return is announced by a soft 'bark' and a gentle nuzzling. Danger is signalled to the calf by a sharp warning bark and the stamp of a forefoot. The later development of the deer depends greatly upon the length of time that it keeps its mother: the calf that is long suckled grows rapidly and strongly and, if a male, develops a better head. For the first month of its life the calf shows no fear of man, being vastly inquisitive. Protective timidity soon develops.

For much of the year deer are gregarious and move about in herds that usually vary in size from half a dozen to thirty. To see more than this number in one herd is exceptional, but herds of 100 have been counted. They often move in single file, the stags bringing up the rear, with the biggest stag last of all. He is the master of the herd and rounds up stragglers. In June the hinds move into coverts alone to calve, and the stags leave the herd during the mewing and velvet periods. They are often accompanied during the summer and early autumn, however, by a young stag—their 'esquire'—which they urge ruthlessly out of the covert if danger threatens, while they themselves, the warrantable stags, lie close and motionless in the undergrowth, bodies pressed to the ground, legs tucked under them and antlers low. Their protective colouring is very effective in the combes, where antlers are not conspicuous among stems and branches, and tawny coats harmonise with red soil and rustling bracken. Many visitors to the moor are disappointed that they do not see deer: the only way to be sure of doing so is to go into one of the noted coverts and wait silently and without moving. Success may not come without repeated visits and hours of patient watching on each occasion, but there is no point in wandering aimlessly about the open moor or in the wooded valleys 'looking for deer', especially in the summer. They may be seen by chance if they are on the move, and the prospects are hopeful on a hunting day; but people have visited Exmoor regularly for twenty years without seeing deer. Yet patience and a knowledge of their habits will certainly be rewarded.

The rutting season is in October,* lasting throughout the month. Towards the end of September the necks of the full-grown stags begin to swell, their bodies become tense and tucked up. No longer pacific, they adopt the fierce bearing and aggressive restlessness of the mating season. They tear up the ground with their antlers, paw at earth banks and shake bushes and small trees, 'belling' vigorously as they challenge their rivals and assert their mastery over the herd of hinds that each tries to collect. For eleven months of the year the stag occasionally 'barks'—in a variety of

---

* Again, there are exceptions. Late-born stags may rut as late as December or even February, but this is very rare.

tones; but at the rut he 'bells'. The noise is difficult to describe, unforgettable once heard. It is something between the bellowing of a bull and the roar of a lion, and trails off into a coughing grunt. A weird sound in a lonely combe, especially after dark. Collyns described how, in his early years at Dulverton, he first heard the bell when riding home at two in the morning:

> I have heard the sound often since, and now know it well; but to my dying day I shall not forget the dark, dreary night when I first heard the dismal, infernal noise, or the effect it produced on me.

During the rut the stag will advance boldly on a chance-encountered walker or rider. There is little danger provided there is room to manoeuvre. Goss said:

> My experience is that so long as wild deer are in the open they will, as soon as they realise they are up against a human being, run away.*

If the stag is met in a confined space—a steep combe or dense woodland— immobility is the way to safety. Some horses are frightened by the smell of rutting stags, and such a stag will sometimes chase a bolting horse. The viciousness of the rut can cause fights from which death results. Having obtained a harem for himself, the stag is vigilant against intruding rivals. Should one arrive and show fight they meet head on, antler locked with antler, bodies straining massively forward, heads twisting sideways and down to force the enemy to lower his guard. The effort is immense and the weaker must eventually try to break off the engagement. This is the moment of greatest danger: as the loser turns away the victor lunges viciously, piercing the soft flank with his keen brow tine.

Commonly, however, the stag in possession is not seriously threatened. Belling and stamping are often enough to send the newcomer on his way. Hornless stags—known on Exmoor as 'notts'—are utterly outcast during the rut. Not only are they incapable of challenging horned stags with hinds,† but horned stags which have not yet succeeded in collecting hinds drive them viciously from their presence. The sight of notts in company with horned stags is a sign that the rut is over.

The exertions of the rut, the constant vigilance and poor feeding, reduce the stag to a sorry state by the end of the month. His coat is bedraggled, and the coarse dark hair of his ruff accentuates—in ugly contrast with his thin, drawn-up body—the still-swollen neck. By mid-November he has recovered; his winter coat is thick and ruddy, his body has filled out, and

---

* *Memories of a Stag Harbourer.*
† Clearly, some notts succeed in the rut, for notts persist on the moor!

the aggression of his bearing has disappeared. The herds collect for the winter months and peace reigns once more.

The food of the deer is varied. In winter they eat ivy in the woods and pick what they can from hay and strawstacks—a diminished source now that baling is the rule and straw so scarce. If the weather is severe their raids on clamped root crops are desperate. They uncover the stored crops by scrabbling with their feet and, unless interrupted, eat voraciously through the night. Cabbage fields are raided too. Acorns and chestnuts, bramble leaves, hips, haws and rowan berries, as well as the tips of the 'worts', are all part of their winter diet. In spring and summer they live well: rape fields and young corn crops provide especial delicacies, but without raiding the farmlands they can find tender ash and beech shoots, young grass and mosses. They are given to cider-apples in the autumn and will travel miles from their coverts to raid the lowland orchards, swallowing the fruit whole and returning to the combes for cud-chewing.

As will be plain from that account of the feeding and breeding habits of the red deer, they live mainly outside the old Forest boundary. Evidence on this point given in a lawsuit in 1617 largely holds today:

> If any redd deere do come or strake within the said Forest they are very fewe and such as breed and harbour in the lands and woods of his Majesties subjects in Devon and Somerset bordering near the Forest, and never harbour and but seldom feed in the said Forest.

The Knights, by creating farms and fields, provided the deer with some food within the Forest and there are more harbouring there now than formerly; but the great coverts lie to the south, the east and the north— Culbone woods, the Horner valley, Cutcombe woods, the lower Barle and Exe valleys, the Molland coverts, the Bray valley. Deer often cross the open moor and can sometimes be found in upland combes, but the Forest is still pre-eminently the place where they are hunted.

Forest Law as it applied to the deer was outlined in Chapter One; its object was to preserve the deer for hunting. Though deer hunting itself is so ancient, however, the horse and hound method is comparatively modern. From pre-Conquest days until the eighteenth century, hounds were used to rouse and drive the deer, which were then shot with longbow or crossbow. In 1286 Maurice de la Barre held land "of the king in chief by serjeanty of three barbed arrows and a salmon on the king's coming into Exmoor to hunt"; and the warrant that sent royal huntsmen to Exmoor in Edward II's reign makes it clear that the method used was that of coursing and shooting. While Forest Law was strictly enforced the deer must have been little troubled except by very infrequent royal command. The only people allowed to kill deer (except by special warrant, rarely granted) were "archbishops, bishops, earls and barons passing through the Forest" who were allowed by the Charter of the Forest to take 'one or two beasts'. But such privileged travellers across Exmoor were not frequent in the middle ages.

After 1508, when the Forest itself as well as its custody was leased from the Crown, the Wardens had the right to hunt the deer "with hounds, greyhounds, bows and arrows and other appurtenances of the chase, and to take, kill, and carry away and dispose of them at their pleasure". Collyns's statement that Hugh Pollard (then Warden) kept a pack of stag-hounds at Simonsbath in 1598 has led to the false conclusion that he hunted in the modern manner. A Star Chamber case of the same period makes it clear that hounds did not hunt without assistance from marks-men. The offenders were stated by the Warden to have "hunted with houndes, weaponyd with crossbowes some of them, and other some with hunting staves, with intent to have killed sondrye red deare". The Warden further charged that one of them "did then and there in a peaceable manner . . . with a crossebowe kyll one redd deare". And if Pollard kept staghounds he certainly did not keep them at Simonsbath, for in 1598 there was nowhere at Simonsbath to keep them; nor anywhere for the Warden to live, either there or elsewhere in the Forest. The hound and shooting method of hunting lasted until the Civil War, when all regular hunting ceased, not to be revived on Exmoor for about 100 years.

In 1750 the second Earl of Orford became Warden. He was succeeded by his son, who held the lease until 1767 when he parted with it to the first Sir Thomas Acland. Wardens such as these were bound to revive the hunting and, of course, in the second half of the eighteenth century, to use the modern method of horse and hound. In one of his more excitable passages Collyns described the regime of the second Sir Thomas:

> Those, indeed, were palmy days. Then flourished such hospitality as, even in our hospitable west country has never been surpassed. The doors of Holnicote and Pixton . . . and Highercombe, the hunting and shooting lodge of the family, were open to all comers. Good cheer and a kindly welcome greeted alike nobleman and commoner. During the hunting season the rooms of the houses were filled by those who first presented themselves, unbidden, but welcome, guests; and when neither house nor stable would hold other guest or steed for the night, still the late-comer found hospitable welcome at the board, and sought his couch in the homely village inn, to dream over the merry evening passed, and anticipate the incidents of the approaching hunting morn.

Nimrod, writing in the *Sporting Magazine*, gave details of the gross custom of drinking the stag's health performed during this 'golden age', which lasted until 1825.

In more chivalrous times, or I should say in those times when the natural ebullition of feeling was less controlled by the forms and ceremonies of society than it is at the present day, the head of the deer, after a good run, was produced in the evening with a silver cup in its mouth out of which the favourite toast was drunk. The custom is still kept up by the huntsman, whippers-in, farmers, and others, and the operation is performed in the following manner. The cup is placed in the stag's mouth, secured with a cord to prevent its falling out. When it is filled to the brim, each person who is to drink it holds a horn in each hand, and brings it to his mouth, when he must finish it at one draught and then turn the head downwards, bringing the top of it in contact with his breast, to convince his companions that he has drunk it to the dregs, otherwise he is subject to a fine.

Such contemporary writing transmits the spirit of this remote and exuberant period of 'The Devon and Somerset's' long history.

The second Sir Thomas Acland and Colonel Basset were each Masters at various periods between 1775 and 1801. Sport was good in these years, and also during the Mastership of Squire Worth of Washfield, near Tiverton, who ran the hounds as a subscription pack. The first Earl Fortescue took over in 1812 and remained as Master until 1818, killing over 100 deer in those six years. Collyns called them 'glorious days':

When a good stag had been killed, the custom was for James Tout, the hunts-man, to enter the dining-room at Castle Hill after dinner in full costume, with his horn in his hand, and after he had sounded a mort, 'Success to Stag-hunting' was solemnly drunk by the assembled company in port wine.

In 1812 it was estimated that there were about 200 head of deer in the moorland coverts, "perhaps 100 short of what there was in old Sir Thomas Acland's time". Two famous stags were known by name: Brown George of the Dulverton coverts, and the Old Span Deer of Upper Bray.*

In 1818 the hounds again became a subscription pack, but things went badly and in 1825 they were taken to London and sold, being bought by a German baron who hunted with them in his native land for many years. These old staghounds—the only pack in the country—merit some attention, for their like has never been seen again in England. The exact origin of their breed is not certainly known but Collyns stated that the blood-hound and the old southern hounds were among their ancestors. They stood twenty-six inches high and were "hare pied, yellow, yellow and white, or badger pied". They had long ears, deep muzzles, large throats, and deep chests.

---

* These details are taken from Lord Graves's letter to Earl Fortescue in 1812. See *The Exmoor Review*, No. 7.

In tongue they were perfect, and when hunting in water, or on a half-scent, or baying a deer, they might be heard at an immense distance. Even when running at speed they always gave plenty of tongue, and their great size enabled them to cross long heather and the rough sedgy pasturage of the Forest without effort or difficulty.

Capable of great speed, they were like their quarry in appearing to run well within themselves, and "few horses could live with them in the open".

Apart from its speed, the deer has two characteristics that make it especially difficult to hunt. First, there is its habit of taking to the water. It is a powerful swimmer and will often travel in water for two or three miles, both to refresh itself and to throw its pursuers off the scent. It also 'soils' by plunging itself into a river or stream and may then remain quite still, its antlers flat on the surface, or immersed, only its nostrils breaking the water. So concealed, it is extremely hard to detect. Its second ruse is to rejoin the herd in covert or put up a young stag or hind, so 'staining' the scent and throwing hounds on a false trail. The old stag-hounds were as cunning as the deer:

> Their rarest quality, perhaps, was their sagacity in hunting in the water. Every pebble, every overhanging bush or twig which the deer might have touched, was quested as they passed up or down the stream, and the *crash* with which the scent, if detected, was acknowledged and announced, made the whole country echo again . . . They ran almost in a line, one after the other, not carrying a head, like foxhounds, but each hound apparently revelling in the scent, and doing his work for himself; not putting his faith in his neighbour, but trusting to his own nose, and to that alone.

Between 1825 and 1855 Exmoor hunting was in a poor way. It was only the energy and enthusiasm of Collyns that kept the sport alive. He organised subscription lists, convened meetings, wrote letters, and alternately pleaded with and bullied the hunting men of Devon and Somerset. In some years there was no hunting; in others, what little there was met with ill fortune. In 1837 Collyns conjured up yet another subscription pack—known for the first time as 'The Devon and Somerset Staghounds'—but sport was poor, and by 1841 subscriptions had dwindled so alarmingly that £531 was owing to Collyns as Treasurer. Hunting was kept alive by desperate expedients. In 1849, for example, a pack used to hunting carted deer in the Cheltenham country was brought to Exmoor for one season. Its Master was confident that his hounds would find the wild red deer an easy quarry after their experience with stall-fed beasts. In two months he took just three deer.

The turning point came in 1855 when Fenwick Bisset took over. His long reign as Master—he resigned in 1881—saw the Devon and Somerset securely established and a fine pack bred up. The deer population grew again after the onslaught of the poachers in the black days. Yet Bisset's early difficulties would have defeated most men. He was a complete novice, and the landowners, apart from a few enthusiasts, gave him half-hearted help; the poachers were still active, and the unschooled hounds killed more sheep than deer. In his first season the pack was out on twenty-five days and killed five deer; in his second, seven (two of them unwarrantable) were killed in thirty days.

Gradually, he won through, and for twenty years the hunt flourished under him. The end of his Mastership was marred by an outbreak of rabies in 1879 which necessitated the destruction of the pack he had so skilfully built up and trained. Nothing so clearly revealed his quality as his reaction to this disaster: he started afresh and in two years had got another pack together.

Since Bisset's day the Devon and Somerset has survived two world wars when little hunting was possible. During both, the deer population diminished, as it always does when hunting is in decline. Each post-war period brought economic problems; the rising costs of feeding hounds and horses, of wage-bills and equipment, of the Deer Damage Fund, placed a heavy strain on resources. The fact that the Hunt flourishes today requires explanation.

Stag-hunting on Exmoor is not the sport of a leisured few: it is one of the major interests of a rural community. Farmers are keen supporters and many of them on hunting days keep a horse saddled in the field in which they are working so that, should the hounds come their way, they can join in. Foot followers are numerous, enthusiastic and knowledgeable. Posted on a suitable hill, their experience of the sport and their intelligent anticipation of the deer's tactics often enable them to share fully in a day's hunting. The vast majority of those who live on and around Exmoor believe that the Hunt performs a useful function: they know that it brings pleasure into their lives, and they regard this pleasure as wholly justifiable.

These facts are unpalatable to those who believe on moral grounds that deer hunting should be abolished. The humanitarian argument is advanced with sincerity and strong emotion, but there are important aspects of Exmoor hunting with which the reformers must reckon if they are to present a fully reasoned and, therefore, acceptable case. Too often, the abolitionists are ignorant of the conditions under which hunting is carried on. They do not realise that if they succeeded in abolishing the Staghounds they would probably destroy the deer *as a wild species.**

That statement must now be justified for, to many, it will appear both novel and obnoxious. First, it has to be understood that the numbers of the deer must be maintained at a tolerable level. By 'tolerable' is meant

* See footnote on page 61.

that level at which they exist and breed in sufficient quantity to ensure biological survival as a species, but do not increase to the extent that their food-gathering raids become economically unacceptable. As has been shown, they do considerable damage to the bordering farms by trampling and eating stored and growing crops. The stags are particularly destruct-ive, for they do not trouble to eat the whole of a root but take one bite out of, say, a turnip, then cast it aside and start on another. Nor should even a townsman have much difficulty in envisaging the damage done to a field of growing crops when a stag settles in it for the night, his heavy body couched on the ground while he bites off the tops. When he has cleared the area round him, he moves to a fresh position and starts again. It is not economically possible to fence farms and fields against deer. Such is their strength and their agility that the cost would be prohibitive. The farmers in the Exmoor National Park tolerate the raids of the deer because they receive a measure of compensation from the Hunt and because they enjoy hunting. While hunting continues, the balance between an intolerable amount of deer damage and the existence of a flourishing wild species is held, the Hunt keeping the deer at that precise level. If hunting were stopped, guns would be used indiscriminately against the deer. Since it is difficult to see them in their wooded coverts, shooting would involve rousing them with man, horse or hound, and once on the move they would be difficult targets—far too difficult for any but first-class marksmen. Many would be maimed and would die a much more painful death than is inflicted on them by the gun or humane killer used on the bayed deer by the huntsman: a method of killing which humanitarians accept for the thousands of animals slaughtered daily in public abattoirs.

When the Hunt flourishes the deer maintain their numbers and the health of the herds, for hunting—as will be shown—takes note of the deer's seasons and culls the herds in a biologically sound manner. When-ever hunting has declined, the deer population has dwindled to a dangerous level. This happened in both world wars and in the troubled years from 1825 to 1855. Only about sixty were left when Bisset's Mastership began. In the black years deer carcases were as common as pigs' in the farmhouses round the moor, and newly-dropped calves were killed by barbarous methods.

The argument is often advanced that the deer suffers an extremity of terror during the chase. There is no evidence at all to bear this out, and plenty to controvert it. Often, the hunted deer will stop to feed or to 'soil' until the pack is almost upon them. This suggests a disinclination to be caught by hounds, but a lack of fear of them at a 'safe' distance. Aboli-tionists usually transfer their own emotions into the mind of the deer. This is very misleading. The deer does not know that it is 'running for its life'. It is afraid of the noise and the smell and the appearance of man and hounds and tries to keep them at a distance. Animals live in the present: a deer which has thrown off its pursuers does not suffer psychologically. Once hounds are shaken off, it has no torturing recollections or anguished forebodings. It is quite unproved that an animal can envisage death.

The abolitionists' charge of cruelty is too facile. They forget, or do not know, that only 'warrantable' stags are hunted, that for nearly half the year no hunting takes place, that the deer has a good chance of escape—its fleetness, cunning, and mastery of the difficult terrain ensuring this—that the end is as swift and humane as possible, and that the followers of stag-hounds are not bloodthirsty monsters, but ordinary human beings neither more nor less cruel than their fellows, who hunt because they like the excitement of the chase, the battle of wits, the companionship, the risks, and the gruelling exercise.

It is sometimes argued that Exmoor should be turned into a deer park, but this is impossible. The deer population would still have to be controlled to ensure that it remained at a tolerable level. A corps of 'forest rangers' expert in woodcraft and marksmanship would thus be needed; full-time officials maintained at public expense. The roads that cross the moor and the tracks that farmers and walkers use would be a problem if these rangers were to keep the deer down with rifles. The inhabitants of Exmoor going about their daily business, visitors, and the cattle, sheep and ponies would all be endangered. If Exmoor is to be a gigantic deer park it must be depopulated first. Nor is the proposal that a small area of the moor be enclosed for the purpose any sounder. Nothing like the present number of deer could be supported in such a park, and those that were would cease to be the *wild* red deer. It is difficult to believe that any lover of the deer really wants to shoot three-quarters of them and put the survivors in what could only be a glorified zoo.

The blunt fact—however disagreeable—is that hunting has been essential to the preservation of the wild red deer of Exmoor. Unprejudiced observers who take the trouble to inform themselves about the species and its way of life are driven to this conclusion. If hunting were abolished the deer would not last more than five years at the outside.*

Until the passing of the Deer Act in 1963, deer in England and Wales were officially classed as 'vermin', receiving no more protection under law than rats. Those who are most bitterly opposed to deer hunting do not perhaps realise that the chief deer protection measures embodied in that Act had been voluntarily practised on Exmoor for many years. This fact, of course, does not imply that the Act was superfluous. It was a much-needed

* The bill for the abolition of deer hunting now (May 1968) before Parliament proposes elaborate methods (including the use of helicopters) for culling the deer herds, performing thus the same functions as those now performed by the hunt, but using different and very expensive means.

measure affording protection to fallow, roe, and sika, as well as to red deer. The fact that the wild red deer of Exmoor had been little troubled by the barbarities practised elsewhere was due to widespread enthusiasm for the Hunt; but that did not make the Act unnecessary. The prohibition of night shooting and of the snare and the establishment of minimum calibre and shot sizes for deer shooting were most welcome, even though comparatively few instances of the inhumanity that these provisions outlawed had occurred in this hunting region. The close seasons established by the Act were very similar to those that had been in force on Exmoor for very nearly 100 years —a tribute to the scientific (and humane) policy of the Devon and Somerset. Big stags are hunted in the autumn; hinds in the winter; and young stags in the spring—a hunting cycle corresponding to the life cycle of the species and observing the needs of mating, birth and mewing seasons.

The question "to whom do the deer belong?" is often asked. Since they ceased to be the Crown's property their legal ownership has often been in dispute. The law is complex, but the answer is "to the owner of the land on which they are standing": a legal point that reinforces the fact that the Hunt could not function without the goodwill of the inhabitants of Exmoor.

The techniques of hunting are complex, for the deer is a herd animal whose first instinct is to return to the herd. To keep hounds on the line, preventing them from switching to a fresh quarry, demands knowledge, endurance and patience from huntsman and hound alike. Again, each season presents different problems. In the autumn the big stags lie close in the thick undergrowth and must, therefore, be 'harboured'. Harbouring the stag calls for woodcraft of the highest quality, for the harbourer—a Hunt official upon whose skill the success of the whole operation initially depends—must find where a warrantable stag has lain up after coming in from night feeding and make sure that he is there in covert when hounds are brought up. As Collyns described it:

> It is said technically that a stag *harboureth* where he makes his bed or lair. The chief duty of the harbourer is to inform the master of hounds where a warrantable deer is to be found, in the neighbourhood of the fixture, on a hunting morning; to attend the huntsman at covert side, and assist him in 'rousing' that identical deer.

The preliminary work may have to be done without ever seeing the stag. Some time before the hunting fixture the harbourer will be looking for the evidence he needs, and working on this and his long experience of the habits of the deer, he narrows the area down to a particular covert. On the hunting day itself he is out very early, working to gain certain knowledge of the stag's whereabouts without disturbing the animal. Evidence comes

from browsing traces: oat stalks from which a whole ear is missing point
to a hind; if several have half the ear or less missing then a stag has been
feeding. The covert is approached against the wind as the harbourer
searches for the entry, where slots will tell him what he wants to know.
(That great harbourer, Goss, always judged by the fore-slot, which is
generally the larger and, because it carries the greater weight, leaves a
clearer impression.) Having examined the slots he works his way round the
covert to make sure that the stag has not gone out at the other side. Satisfied
that a big stag is there, he reports to the Master at the meet and the field
then moves towards the chosen covert, but while still some distance away
the pack is kennelled in a convenient farm building or in horse-boxes and
only the 'tufters' are taken into the covert. The whole pack cannot be used
to draw the covert, for hinds, calves and stags harbour together and if the
pack got in amongst them there would be complete confusion.

The tufters are up to four couple of steady, experienced hounds and they
and the Hunt officials draw the covert together. This is one of the most
skilful and exciting phases of the hunt: the wits of men and hounds
confronting the resources of the deer. The big stag practises every trick to
avoid breaking covert, putting up hinds and young deer and lying low
himself. The proceedings are sometimes protracted. The watchers outside
the covert hear the tufters give tongue; the wood echoes, sticks snap and
branches sway. A deer breaks, the tufters hard behind; but once in the
open the huntsman's horn rings out and the tufters leave the hind, now
heading fast for the open moor. They head back into the covert to work
again. More waiting; then another challenge, more movement in the wood.
This time, a heavier body crashes into the open, pauses for a moment, then
makes his point for the moor. A warrantable stag has been roused. Then,
and only then, can the rest of the pack be brought out and laid on the line,
and the hunt proper begin. A quotation from Collyns perfectly illustrates
the unchanging pattern of stag-hunting:

> *September 30th.* Cloutsham, celebrated, and justly so, as one of the best
> meets, was fixed for this day's sport. The stag did not hang long in covert
> after being found by the tufters, and the pack was soon got on him, when a
> most brilliant run to Brendon Barton occurred. The deer saved himself by
> mixing with the herd on Scobhill, when the hounds divided in all directions,
> and drove the deer into Farleigh brake, from which at least 20 hinds broke,
> but the old cunning stag would not leave the brake, and thus saved himself.

In the winter, when hinds are hunted, harbouring is not necessary, for
the undergrowth has died down. At the meet there is ample local information about the herds and any adult hind is the quarry. The hinds usually
break away in groups and half the pack makes the initial pursuit, the other
half being brought on when the group has split up and one hind has been

isolated. Except for the tufting problem, hinds are much harder to catch than stags. They are very swift and extremely clever in their use of terrain. Again, having no antlers, they are difficult to distinguish from each other and only the most experienced eye can tell a fresh hind from one that has been run already. If hounds switch to a fresh hind they have little chance of a kill.

When the big stags are shedding their antlers in the spring, young stags (about three years old) are hunted. The harbouring is not difficult, partly because the undergrowth is low and the trees and bushes are bare, and partly because the young stag does not lie as close as the big stag. The hunting is much more straightforward at this season, for the spring stags are easily roused and they lack the cunning of old stags or of hinds. Seeming quite certain that they can outdistance hounds, they run straight. The swiftness in which they trust provides hunts run at great speed and with comparatively few checks.

The Devon and Somerset has been fortunate in its huntsmen. The work requires qualities of skill and endurance not easily found, and it is remarkable that the office has been so ably filled for so many years. A few names stand out: Joe Faulkner, a genius who was frequently discharged when drunk and as frequently re-engaged when sober; John Babbage and Arthur Heal, both of whom carried the horn with great distinction; Anthony Huxtable, steady and reliable; Sidney Tucker, able in the field and a brilliant breeder of hounds. His successor, Ernest Bawden, may have been the greatest. He gave up farming for the Hunt and was whipper-in to Tucker. Since the sale of the great pack (see page 57) the Devon and Somerset had relied largely on drafts from other kennels and after the first world war such reinforcements were hard to come by. During Bawden's regime (under Colonel Wiggin's Mastership) the huntsman improved on Tucker's work and bred a pack upon which his pre-eminence in the field was securely founded. The original hounds had been famous for tongue but later generations were comparatively quiet, the energy expended in the chase making such demands that even well-tongued draft hounds from other kennels soon fell silent on Exmoor. Bawden consistently bred for tongue, finally achieving his ambition and producing a pack that ran with a fine cry and a better head.

Ernest Bawden became legendary in his lifetime, so superlative was his work. Not the least of his services was to build a team of hunt officials who not only saw the Devon and Somerset through the difficult years of the early twenties but who influenced its fortunes long afterwards. A link with that great team was snapped when Sidney Bazeley retired in 1961. Bazeley served under Bawden and became huntsman after Alfred Lenthall retired in 1950. In his fourth season as huntsman he broke his neck in a fall, but recovered and later established a reputation little lower than that of his mentor. His knowledge of the deer, control of hounds, and cross-country work were in the Bawden tradition. Bazeley, like Bawden before him, passed on his knowledge, for he was succeeded by William Lock, who had been his whipper-in. Such continuity is, of course, essential to the fortunes of the Devon and Somerset, and no account of Exmoor would be complete without mention of at least some of these men whose work will be woven into the Exmoor scene as long as the red deer flourish as a wild species.

CHAPTER FOUR

The Exmoor Ponies and Some Other Wild Creatures

REFERENCE has already been made to the antiquity of the Exmoor pony, a little wild horse directly descended from the original wild horse of pre-historic times. The Exmoor is native—indigenous—and exhibits a remarkable degree of genetic stability and instinctual continuity. Its average height of twelve hands corresponds with wild horse skeletons found in prehistoric deposits. Its colouring is perfectly adapted to blend with the Exmoor scene, and its wild shyness sends it galloping over the moor out of man's sight and scent. It throws a protective screen round its young when unidentified quadrupeds approach, as it did in the days when the wolf was loose on the moor.*

The first mention of the Exmoor pony occurs in the Domesday Book, and what was true of it then is true today, its way of life for uncounted centuries being accurately summed by this description written in 1795:

> . . . The Forester (Warden) has an annual sale for the small horses which are bred on the surrounding hills . . . these (in the whole upwards of 400) are not taken into better keeping, nor to more sheltered grounds during the severest winter; when the snow covers the Forest to the depth of many feet these hardy animals are seen in droves, traversing the little valleys and sheltered parts, getting their scanty fare from the banks of rivulets and small springs.

In ways and looks the Exmoor pony is closer to the wild original stock than any other breed. The true colouring is a variety of brown: bay (reddy-brown); dark brown; or dun (smoke-brown). The underparts and the insides of the legs are light and mealy, and the mane and tail are black. The mealy muzzle and the eye-cingle are the most characteristic feature; there is no true Exmoor without these. The foals—born in June—are light-coloured, darkening as they grow. The frame is strong and the legs, but for a small fetlock-tuft, are clean. The tail is carried low, the ears are short and pricked, the eye bright. The coat shines in summer, but in winter thickens to a protective rug that no storm can penetrate. The deep jaw is charac-

---

* See *The Exmoor Review*, No. 4, p. 56.

teristic of its prehistoric forebears' and perfectly adapted to cropping the scanty moorland herbage. The head is strong, straight-nosed and broad. The nostrils flare.

The herds roam the moor throughout the year, up to forty and more of mares and foals and one stallion to the herd. Wild, they have no use for man's society, though the broken pony brings an unequalled endurance, strength and courage to his service. Cross-breeding of any kind diminishes the hardiness. Only the true Exmoors survived, unfed by man, the terrible winters of 1947 and 1962–3.

When the Forest was sold all the ponies were rounded up and disposed of, but Sir Thomas Acland removed about twenty pure-breds to his estate at Ashway where the greatest trouble was taken to increase the stock and to maintain its purity. Between then and 1886 there were always eighty to one hundred pure Exmoors running on Winsford Hill, fifteen to twenty being sold each year at Bampton Fair. When the Acland Herd was dispersed in 1919 there were eager buyers of the 'Ashways' bearing the famous anchor brand, so that at the formation of the Exmoor Pony Society in 1920 there was a nucleus of breeders and owners to save the breed from dying out. The Society's work, assisted by an annual grant, has ensured that domesticated Exmoors flourish today, some forty to fifty foals being inspected and registered yearly.

The wild ponies gradually moved back on to the moor. John Knight abandoned his Arab-crossing experiment (see Chapter Two), but crossing of course was always likely, especially on the northern commons where a variety of ponies were turned out for grazing. To this day the expression 'Porlock pony' is used to signify a crossbred. The finest and purest wild herds are those running on Withypool Common and Withypool Hill, many of the ponies there being of Acland descent.

The wild ponies who, like the deer, belong to the owner of the land on which they are standing, are still rounded up once a year, selected specimens going to be sold in October at Bampton Fair. The rest are sent back onto the moor to be untroubled by man again for another twelve months. They are a fascinating element of Exmoor's wild life, prized for their utility and giving delight by their beauty, roaming freely over the moorland, their age-old home.

It would be beyond the scope of this book to attempt a comprehensive description of Exmoor's wild life, but to provide information about certain species which, for various reasons, merit special mention is the object of this Chapter. The blackgrouse must come high on such a list, for the bird—once plentiful—is in decline on the moor. "It seems certain that if the Exmoor blackgrouse are left to their own resources the species will soon disappear from the hills which they have inhabited since time immemorial."* The chief reason for the decline appears to be the intensive farming that in recent years has made such inroads into typical blackgrouse country, diminishing the supplies of heather and whortleberries. The best areas now are Brendon Common, Molland Moors, Winsford Hill and Dunkery, in each of which there is still plenty of heather of all ages and types, and wild valleys, small trees, water and worts. The popularity of these areas in the summer does not upset the blackgrouse, since there is space in which they can escape from intrusion.

The blackcock is a strikingly handsome bird, big and blue-black. He flies higher and faster than the red grouse and in flight shows his remarkable 'lyre-shaped' tail when climbing or turning steeply. The black head has scarlet markings over the eyes. The now-rare hen is quieter: soft brown with speckles of white, black and yellow. The comparative rarity of the hen is stressed by Coleman-Cooke's observations over a recent ten-year period in which he recorded annually an average of twenty-seven cocks and seventeen hens. The need to introduce new stock into the best areas is clear from these figures when compared with the hundreds of blackgrouse that were reported as a common sight in the nineteenth century.

The cocks gather in packs, feeding and roosting together. Tree-roosters elsewhere, on Exmoor they spend the night on heather clumps. Their 'lekking' is perhaps their most noteworthy habit. A rhythmic cooing in an April dawn announces that the lek is beginning, though the numbers now involved are sadly small. As they coo the birds display, and adopt grotesque attitudes, lowering heads and raising lyre tails, the white under-feathers bobbing as the hopping ritual dance takes place—advance and retreat succeeding each other for hours on end. To the victors go the hens—what few there are. A devoted group of Exmoor ornithologists is attempting to conserve the species by introducing young stock into selected areas. Upon the success of their efforts the survival of the species now depends; and though the argument is sometimes advanced that if wild life cannot survive by its own efforts it should be allowed to die out, since it is man's interference with the habitat that threatens the existence of the blackgrouse it seems fitting that men should make some effort to save this beautiful and interesting bird.

Many who know Exmoor well would think of the buzzard as its most characteristic bird: a symbol of the free life of the wild moors, planing and soaring majestically over the wooded combes. Its numbers have fluctuated dramatically; at times, dangerously. In 1897, W.H. Hudson wrote that it was "almost unknown in England", and early in this century there were no more than a very few breeding pairs in the whole of Devon and Cornwall. By the later thirties, however, it had recovered and was common all over

---

* See "Blackcock on Exmoor": John Coleman-Cooke, *The Exmoor Review*, No. 5. The substance of this section is derived from Coleman-Cooke's original work.

Exmoor. After the war myxomatosis almost wiped out the rabbit and many ornithologists feared for the buzzard again, but it proved to be far less dependent upon that source of food than had been thought. Mice, voles, beetles, worms and frogs were still available. A more serious threat was the use of pesticides, the increased ploughing and cropping of once-wild moorland bringing that menace ever closer to the Exmoor buzzard with a resultant decline in its fertility. The position has improved somewhat since limited controls on the use of pesticides were introduced, and the buzzard is again breeding in the combes.*

Together with the kestrel, the sparrow hawk, and the raven, the buzzard is the commonest of the larger and more dramatic birds of the moor. A few of the rarer species, however, can be seen. The peregrine, that large falcon, blue-black above and white beneath, swift as the wind in pursuit and swifter when it 'stoops', has bred intermittently along the Exmoor coast since the war. Its small cousin, the merlin, breeds in the eastern combes but migrates from the moor in September, lingering sometimes on the Minehead coast until winter. The female merlin is slightly larger than the male, and brown, not slate-blue, above. Both have buff underparts. They are swift and thrusting in flight and may sometimes be seen on the open moor in hot pursuit of small birds such as meadow pipits. An even rarer bird—the sickle-winged hobby—scarce summer visitor though it is, has bred on the moor in recent years (six recorded breedings since 1954)† and may be less rare in future. It can easily be confused with a small peregrine, but the chestnut markings on its upper legs and beneath its tail are a distinguishing feature.

The red kite, once so common and such a deadly raider that the church-wardens in Exmoor villages paid out money for its corpse, is now very rare indeed. Specimens have been sighted occasionally on the moor in recent years, probably straying from their breeding ground in south-west Wales, their last refuge. It is possible that the red kite may re-establish itself on Exmoor and visitors who are interested in the rarer birds of Britain should look out for it. It is not unlike the buzzard, but soars on flatter spread wings using its tail more in changing course. It is generally of a lighter colour too, and has pale patches under its wings. The marsh harrier bred regularly on Exmoor up to about 1850 but, though three sightings have been reported in recent years, there is little reason to suppose that it will return from its East Anglian haunts. Far less common on Exmoor at any time was the hen harrier—the last recorded nest was taken in 1906—but sightings are frequent in January, March, and October on passage migratory routes. Whereas the hen harrier is a winter visitor, Montagu's harrier comes in the summer, and occasional sightings are made most years

* "Survival": Richard Perry, *The Exmoor Review*, No. 9.
† D.K. Ballance: *The Exmoor Review*, No. 4, p. 25.

between April and June. Identification by experts makes it certain that both the hen harrier and Montagu's harrier are visitors, though even experienced observers can confuse the female hen harrier with a Montagu's.

Mention has been made of these rarer birds, but for most visitors the abundant life of the coast, the high moorland streams and the lower woodlands will prove sufficiently rewarding. Guillemots, razor bills and fulmar petrels are plentiful, Lynmouth being an especially favoured spot. Spotted and pied flycatchers and the ubiquitous dipper haunt the streams. Nuthatches and tree-creepers abound in the woodlands, where the willow warbler outnumbers the chiff-chaff. Larks and curlews soar over the moorland plateau on the slopes of which the brown hare and the hill fox have their homes.

The topographical surveys in later chapters describe the characteristic life and qualities of the Exmoor sub-regions, but this brief introduction must single out one remarkable feature of the East and West Lyn valleys— a unique area for the botanist—where northern species such as Welsh poppy and Irish spurge may be found. The fact that Exmoor escaped glaciation has resulted in other rarities in the National Park: and in its high heartland may be found the only extensive area of deer sedge in the whole of England.

CHAPTER FIVE

Physical Features of Exmoor

THE boundaries of the territory that is the subject of this book were laid down in 1954 when the Exmoor National Park was designated by the Minister of Housing and Local Government under the provisions of the. National Parks and Access to the Countryside Act of 1949. The northern boundary is the coast from Combe Martin in the west to a point just short of Minehead in the east. From that point the line loops south-east round the Brendon Hills and then runs south-west to include Dulverton and Anstey Common before returning on a north-west bearing to its starting point at Combe Martin (see map on page 23).

The longest north-west, south-east diagonal measures 32 miles. The longest north-south vertical measures 14 miles. The total area is 169,900 acres (about 265 square miles), and approximately two-thirds of the Park lies in Somerset and one-third in Devon.

Within the Park lies the Forest. The heart of Exmoor is the ancient Royal Forest; and the term 'Forest' (which no longer has legal significance) should be applied solely to the 20,344 acres and twenty perches enclosed by the old boundary and not to Exmoor as a whole. Perambulations of the Forest—necessary in medieval times when Forest Law was in operation, during later centuries when the Warden of the Forest held sole sway, and in 1815 when preparations for the sale of the Forest were in hand—have again been undertaken as walkers in the National Park have begun to discover the lonelier parts of Exmoor. Such explorers should note that although the Forest boundary as such is not shown on the new one-inch 'Tourist' map of Exmoor (Ordnance Survey, 1967), that map does show the boundary of Exmoor Parish, which is co-extensive with the old Forest.

To aid would-be perambulators—and there is no better way of reaching the heart of Exmoor than walking the Forest boundary—the map on page 23 shows the boundary line; and a detailed description of the route now follows, for the parish boundary line is not always easy to trace on the one-inch map and some of the topographical features prominent on the journey are named only on the six-inch maps.

The boundary runs from Alderman's Barrow, on the western loop of the Exford-Porlock road, south-westwards until the road bends sharply east of south. At this point the boundary leaves the road and continues in a straight south-westward line to the headwaters of Spraccombe (sometimes known as Orchard Bottom and unnamed on the one-inch map, but identifiable thereon as the eastern fork of Rams Combe). It follows the course of Spraccombe until this stream joins Rams Combe, when it passes through the confluence and crosses the Exe, proceeding then in a straight south-easterly line over Red Stone Hill. Some of the small boundary stones mentioned in the surveys of 1678 and 1815* may still be found along this section of the route, and Red Stone Hill itself takes its name from the Red Stone or Ridge Stone, one of the larger boundary stones. Here, as on the Edgerley Stone to Wood Barrow section (over Broad Mead, north-west of Pinkworthy Farm), the explorer of Exmoor may still take pleasure in navigating from stone to stone; the certainty thus gained of being precisely on course is ample compensation for the slow progress entailed by the search for small, half-buried, boundary or 'mearestones'.

Red Stone Hill crossed, the boundary meets the Exford-Simonsbath road (B 3224) and turns due west, running along the road past Red Deer Farm until it swings south (down Gipsy Lane). It continues south over White Hill (east of Picked Stones Farm) until it meets the Barle, runs for a short distance by the side of the river (upstream) to Sherdon Hutch (where Sherdon joins the Barle) at which point the boundary follows Sherdon Water upstream to Sherdon Rock where it climbs southward over Dilla-combe Hill. In its passage up Dillacombe it crosses the Sandyway-Landacre road and then marches south-east, dividing the Forest from Withypool Common, until it reaches the Hooked Stone on the Sandyway-Withypool Road. Here, it heads south for Willingford Crossing, at which point it turns due west up the stream called Litton Water (the upper reaches of Dane's Brook).

From this point the old Forest boundary, the Exmoor Parish boundary and the Devon-Somerset County boundary coincide for many miles. Bold marking on the one-inch map and a succession of prominent landmarks make detailed route description unnecessary as far as Mole's Chamber. A reminder of the landmarks each of which—scenically or historically, or both—is of importance will suffice. From Sandyway Cross the boundary follows the ridge road running north-west. Two Barrows are just inside the Forest boundary, and Five Barrows just outside. Beyond Five Barrows the boundary leaves the ridge road (which loops south-west) and proceeds straight through Setta Barrow, rejoining the ridge road half a mile beyond the mutilated tumulus and following the road to Mole's Chamber.

From Mole's Chamber to the Hoar Oak Tree mearestones are the only guides over much of the route, but a few of them—the Sloley Stone and the Edgerley Stone, for example—are prominent; and the diligent searcher

* See E.T. MacDermot: *The History of the Forest of Exmoor.*

Withypool Common—a view from the neighbouring Withypool Hill.

Landacre Bridge—not far away from where the Swainmote met (see Chapter One).

A gate across the Harepath—near Mole's Chamber.

The Harepath—the great prehistoric trackway along which the Saxons moved men and supp

At the foot of Hoccombe—and a break in John Knight's great wall.

Hoccombe Water and the Forest Wall—heading east for Badgworthy.

The Longstone—the most impressive standing stone on Exmoor (see Chapter Nine).

The Hoar Oak Tree—the most famous of the Forest's boundary marks.

will be able to identify many small ones between the Edgerley Stone and Wood Barrow, provided that he traces accurately the sharp westward angle made by the boundary as it leaves the Edgerley Stone (set in the north bank of the B 3558 road) and before it swings almost due north to cross Broad Mead. Wood Barrow, and its nearby Gate are easily identifiable, and from here the Forest boundary maintains its northern course to Saddle Gate. This is a turning point and used to be marked by the Saddle Stone, a large boundary stone shaped like a pack-saddle and standing somewhat north of the present gate. There is, for Exmoor, a large number of stones here-abouts, and in recent years I have investigated several claims that the Saddle Stone has been found. None that I have seen has answered in size or shape the descriptions given in Perambulation Surveys, and I am still of the opinion that the Saddle Stone has disappeared, probably having been broken up for road-making in the 1860's.*

At Saddle Gate the boundary turns east and descends first Ruckham Combe (unnamed on the one-inch map); then, having crossed Thorn Hill, drops into Binchinny Combe (again unnamed on the one-inch map, but identifiable as the eastern fork of Ruckham). Precipitous combes are a feature of this part of the route which, though tiring, is perhaps unequalled in scenic splendour. A northward curve across a spur of Benjamy (Bin-chinny) Hill leads into Warcombe (see map on page 23), and from that valley curves south-east across another spur of Benjamy to Gammon's Corner; then south-eastwards again to cross Hoaroak Water, east of which it reaches the most famous of all its landmarks, the Hoar Oak Tree. What may have been the original Hoar Oak Tree was famous as far back as 1658, when it fell "with very age and rottenness". It was replaced in 1662 by a new tree which survived until 26 December 1916.† Two or three saplings were then planted a little higher up the combeside, and the survivor of these is now painfully adding to its inches despite a climate that is particularly trying to oaks.

Between Hoar Oak Tree and Brendon Two Gates the boundary is easy to follow, crossing as it does only one sizeable combe (the upper reaches of Farley Water) and being marked by John Knight's Forest Wall (see Chapter Two). Age and the weather have reduced the height of the wall but there are notable stretches (immediately east of Hoar Oak, for example) where it runs straight and true, an impressive line cutting across the heather slopes that drop away to the north. The contrast between the heather moorland outside the Forest and the grass moor within (a feature discussed later in this Chapter) is particularly striking here.

From Brendon Two Gates eastward, Hoccombe Water is the boundary until Hoccombe meets Long Combe and the two streams unite to form

---

* Unpublished letter. E.T. MacDermot to H.C.N. Bond: 9 May 1934.
† MacDermot: *History*; and letter to H.C.N. Bond, 1 July 1934.

Badgworthy Water. From the confluence the boundary line ceases to coincide with the County Boundary (which follows Badgworthy northwards) and proceeds up Long Combe for about a quarter of a mile. It then leaves the combe and pursues an erratic course over open moorland. North-east of Tom's Hill it changes direction and runs due north to Stowford Bottom (the western fork of the headwaters of Chalk Water), enclosing on its next eastward turn the upland known as Kittuck—a name derived from Kite Oak, mentioned as a landmark in the reign of James I. From Kittuck to Black Barrow the Forest Wall again makes the route clear; and Black Barrow itself is easily identified by the prominent stake driven into its mound. Though the wall ends when the boundary turns slightly east of south at Black Barrow, half a dozen mearestones between there and Alderman's Barrow will help the walker to trace the ancient boundary line back to the point at which this itinerary began.

Such were the boundaries of Exmoor Forest when, after nearly a thousand years of royal ownership, this "ancient demesne land of the Crown of England" passed into private hands. For many years after the Conquest its extent had been much greater, including much of the parishes of Oare, Lytenore (Culbone), Luccombe, Stoke Pero, Hawkridge, Withypool, Winsford, Exford, Porlock, Cutcombe, and Dulverton; but at the Perambulation of 28, Edward I (1300), these areas were disafforested* and so freed from the operation of the harsh Forest Law. In the next hundred years the area between the Badgworthy—Black Barrow line and County Gate was also disafforested and so, by 1400, the Forest had assumed the shape that it still wore when it was sold in 1818. No part of the Forest lay in Devon.

So important has the Forest been in the history of Exmoor, and so outstanding is its scenery, that a knowledge of its boundaries and a thorough exploration of this barren heartland are essential to the Exmoor traveller.

An aerial view of Exmoor from above Chains Barrow, in the most desolate part of the Forest, reveals the anatomy of both the old Royal Forest and of the whole National Park.† The centre is a high plateau on which rise the moor's chief rivers, the Exe and the Barle. Their sources are two miles apart and both rivers flow south of east through deepening valleys—bare at first, then wooded—to their confluence south of Dulverton on the borders of the Park. The northern edge of the plateau is cut by northward-flowing streams which break the high ground with their deep combes and find their way to the sea through the Lyn valley, east and west of which stretches the superb Exmoor coastline. High, hog's-back cliffs with the

---

* James Savage: *History of the Hundred of Carhampton in the County of Somerset*; and MacDermot: *History*.

† See map on page 77.

bold jut of Foreland Point and the fertile Vale of Porlock forming the chief landmarks in this coast noted for its wild beauty, it is flanked on the east by the Selworthy Hills and on the west by the more rugged heights known as the Great and Little Hangman. Eight miles east of Chains Barrow, Exmoor's highest point—Dunkery Beacon—is the centre of a spectacular hill and valley system where wooded combe and moorland height provide a striking contrast to the sombre undulations of the western moor. On the eastern side of the Dulverton-Minehead road the Brendon Hills repeat, but on smaller scale and in gentler manner, the Dunkery pattern. They form the eastern fringes of the National Park. Three miles due south of Chains Barrow Hill lies Five Barrows Hill, 1,618 feet high, the main eminence on the long ridge that stretches fourteen miles north-west from Dulverton, terminates at Shoulsbarrow Common, and forms the southern rampart of Exmoor.

The map on page 77 makes this Exmoor anatomy clear, and the description just given, together with the map, will enable the traveller to take a bird's eye view of a territory which, though not large in extent, can bewilder the uninitiated by its variety and swift contrasts.

This variety of scene and land-form is perhaps the unique quality of the Exmoor National Park. There are, as the Introduction to this book states, many Exmoors, and each visitor will have his own vision of a 'characteristic' moorland scene. For those who best know the Park, however, the view from the summit of Chains Barrow (1,599 feet), in the north-west part of the Forest, may well represent what is most 'typical' of this varied landscape. Mile upon mile, the celebrated 'moor lines' heave in sombre beauty. The rounded hills are now dark in shadow, now golden in the sun. Nothing is static here. The curving contours rise and fall in an illusion of movement, perfected on a sunny day by the cloud shadows skimming over them, driven by the wind that always blows over the Forest. In stormy weather the dark mounds of the barrows and the crests of the ridges loom blackly like the gathering waves of an angry sea.

Three hundred and fifty million years ago—dates such as these are, of course, approximate—Exmoor lay under the Devonian ocean. To the north, hot suns beat down on the peaks of the Caledonian mountains; rains lashed them; winds swept them; night frosts cracked them; rivers collected the resultant debris and deposited it in the Devonian sea. For seventy-five million years the silt piled up on the ocean bed. Then came a titanic upheaval of the earth's crust. Widespread fracturing caused a tilting and folding of the strata and the high central plateau was thrust up out of its age-old resting place. Apart from the New Red Sandstone rocks near Porlock, Minehead, Dunster, Wootton Courtenay and Timberscombe, some recent alluvium in river valleys, and Triassic shales, clays and limestones near Selworthy, the rock system of Exmoor is wholly Devonian and the complete sequence of Devonian rocks from the oldest in the north to the youngest in the south can be identified. In later Cretaceous times a sea invasion deposited newer rocks, but the action of streams, the sea, wind and rain, and particularly the 'permafrost' period of 25,000 years ago (when the mean annual air temperature was fifteen degrees centigrade lower than it is now) has removed those later deposits and formed the soil and shaped the moor that we know today.

The soil* is basically of two kinds: freely-draining, brown, loamy soils on the lower hills and in the valleys; wet, peaty soil on the higher moorland. The 1,300-foot contour is the approximate dividing line. The moorland soil has a surface layer of hill peat—which, though attaining considerable depth on the Chains and at the heads of the combes, is usually shallow— brown, spongy and little decomposed in the wetter areas; black and heavily decomposed in areas where the water gets away. Below the peat is a sparse soil layer (from two to four inches deep) and immediately below this is a thin iron pan, about a quarter of an inch thick. The iron pan usually forms a continuous and impermeable layer and no drainage of the wet lands can take place until subsoil ploughing has broken the pan. Below the 1,300-foot contour line there is a useful topsoil of about ten inches of friable, brown loam resting on a rather shaly orange-brown silt. In the steep-sided valleys there is little soil on the upper slopes, and the shaded side is heavily covered with sphagnum which thrives on the wet, dark-grey loam. Even the good soil is deficient in lime and requires generous dressings.

Although there is much heather moor in the Park, there is little within the Forest boundary, where purple moor grass or flying bent (*Molinia Caerulea*) is the dominant plant. This striking feature—so marked that many miles of the Forest boundary line coincide with the division between heather and *Molinia*—has been the subject of much conjecture. C.S. Orwin,† quoting Professor Stapledon, put forward the most likely explanation. For over 700 years the Royal Forest was used for intensive summer pasturing of sheep and cattle, and it is known that heavy and prolonged grazing will destroy heather-heath and let in grass. It is very probable, then, that the grazing of the Forest (MacDermot's researches showed that in some years as many as 30,000 sheep were summer-pastured on it) is responsible for the present-day vegetation.

Speculation concerning the 'original' vegetation of Exmoor has been much clouded by popular misconceptions about the meaning of the word 'Forest'. As was shown in Chapter One, Exmoor was once called a

* For a detailed description of Exmoor soils see an article by L.F. Curtis in *The Exmoor Review*, No. 3, pp. 16–18.

† C.S. Orwin: *The Reclamation of Exmoor Forest*.

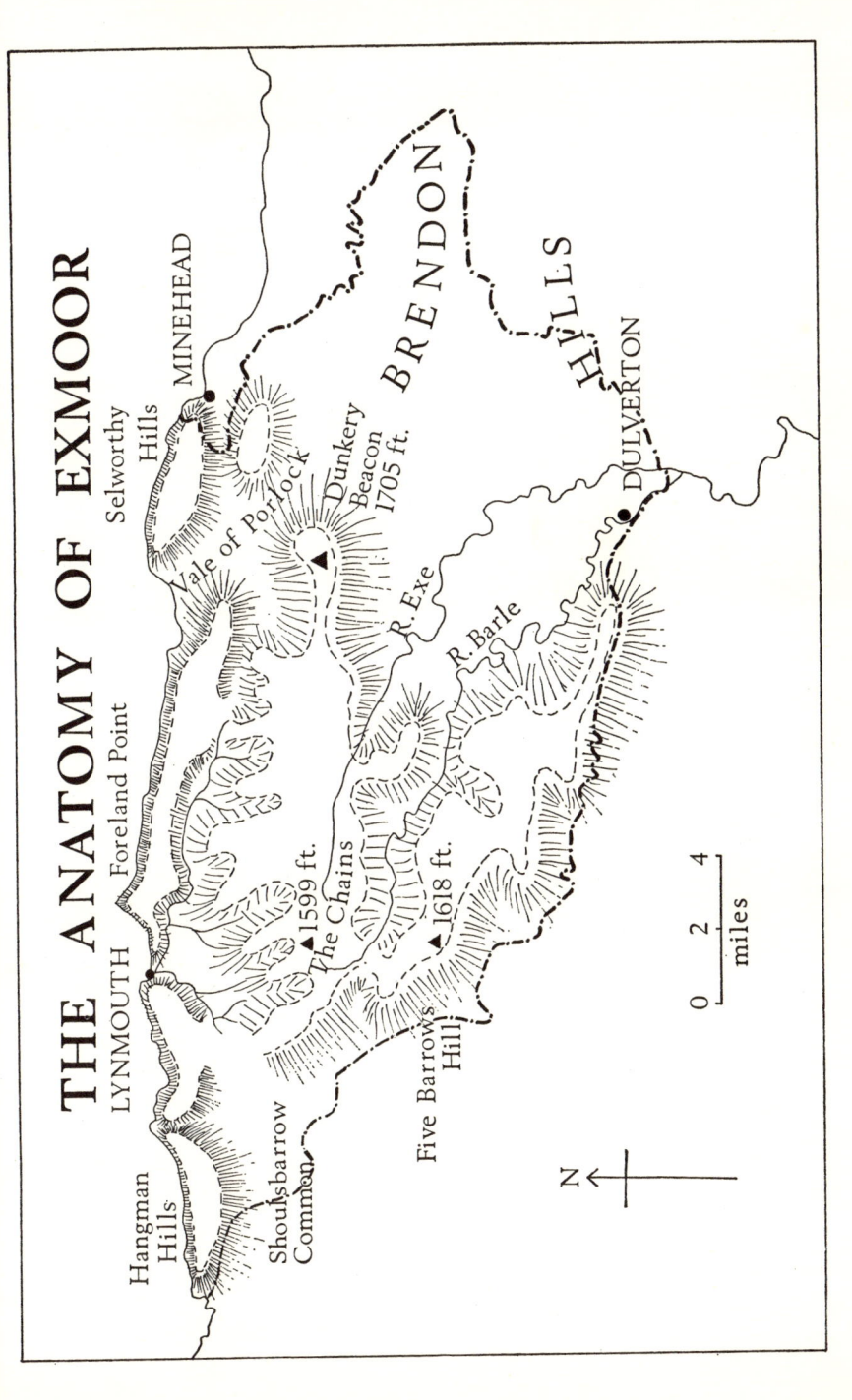

THE ANATOMY OF EXMOOR

Hangman
Hills

LYNMOUTH   Foreland Point

Selworthy
Hills   MINEHEAD

BRENDON

Vale of Porlock

Dunkery
Beacon
1705 ft.

R. Exe

HILLS

DULVERTON

R. Barle

▲1599 ft.
The Chains

▲ 1618 ft.

Shoulsbarrow Common

Five Barrows
Hill

0   2   4
miles

N

'Forest' not because it was wooded but because it was a royal game preserve; and there is no doubt that through all recorded time it has been a "Baren and Morisch Ground".* Domesday Book has little to say about Exmoor beyond recording that in Harold's time the royal manor of Mollenda (Molland) had toll rights over the rents charged for pasturing on the moor. The valuation of the forests of Somerset (1289) is more to the point. It states that North Petherton and Selwood yielded annual sums through the sale of wood and the letting of hog pasture ('pannage'), thus proving the existence of woodland in these royal lands; but the record shows no such items for Exmoor whose most lucrative yield is the annual £10 for "herbage in the said forest". Witnesses from Porlock in the reign of James I (testifying as to Forest boundaries) stated that the Kite Oak was the only tree of any size on the moor—they unaccountably omitted the Hoar Oak—and all available evidence, as well as the inexorable facts of altitude and climate, combines to disprove the idea that there was any appreciable tree growth within the Forest. In 1689 the heart of Exmoor was described as "a very barren place and very full of Bogges", and the surveyors who drew up the report of 1814, prior to the sale of the Forest, counted thirty-seven trees, excluding the Hoar Oak; and these were all growing round Simonsbath House.

And today, the Forest proper is effectively treeless. A belt of beechwoods and pines round Simónsbath; thorns and rowans (or 'wicking'—witching —trees) in some of the combes; a struggling successor to the Hoar Oak Tree on the windy slope of the valley; a pine plantation by Cow Castle— but on the plateau itself hardly a tree to interrupt the interminable undulations of the grassy hills. The beeches planted by the Knights as windbreaks do something to soften the austerity of the scene on the fringes of the farms they made, but 'out-over' the Atlantic gales sweep unopposed across a bare upland.

In 1965 the Exmoor Society (see Chapter Thirteen) commissioned Geoffrey Sinclair (now Chief Field Officer of the Second Land Use Survey of Great Britain) to complete the Land Use map of Exmoor and to contribute all the technical information to the publication entitled *Can Exmoor Survive?* (1966). The detailed description of the natural vegetation of the National Park that now follows is derived from Sinclair's original work and his annual reviews.

First, however, clear understanding of the term 'natural vegetation' must be established. In considering plant life in relation to its environment, ecologists make use of the concept 'Climatic Climax'. This refers to a vegetation cover derived solely from natural physical factors, reaching

* John Leland (1506?-1552): his *Itinerary*—from which the quotation is taken—was first published in 1710.

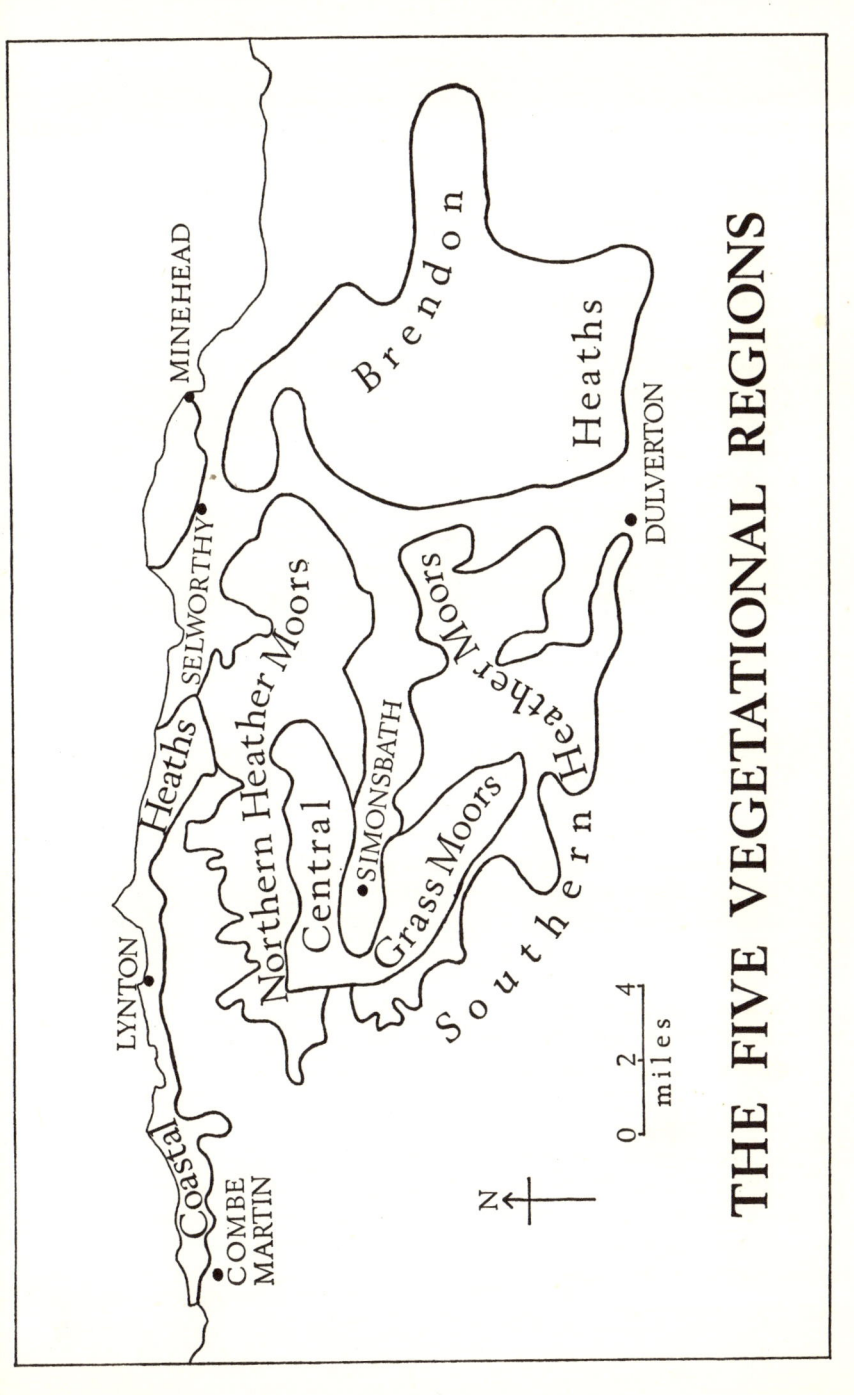

THE FIVE VEGETATIONAL REGIONS

eventually a stable balance; which balance sustains and is controlled by an indigenous animal population. Expert opinion holds that the Climatic Climax (or 'original vegetation') of Exmoor was peaty bog on the highest land, scrub in more sheltered but still exposed situations, and woodland in the lower valleys.

With the arrival of man the balance of plant and animal life altered. Selective killing and domestication of wild animals, draining, grazing, and burning of the vegetation brought about big changes in the environment, to which changes the zoological and botanical life-forms adapted themselves. This post-Climatic Climax stability is represented by what we refer to as 'natural vegetation'. Rather less than one-third of the Exmoor National Park is in this so-called 'natural' state, a state for which human activities have been very largely responsible.*

The Park can be divided into five regions,† each individualised by its topographical and vegetational characteristics. The *Coastal Heaths* extend to the coast north of a line from Combe Martin through Parracombe, Lynton, Brendon, and Malmsmead to Oare Post. Though separated from the main coastal belt by the Vale of Porlock, the Selworthy Hills are part of the Coastal Heaths. Topographically the region consists of rocky hills averaging 900 to 1,000 feet, covered mostly with heath (*Erica Cinerea*) and gorse. On their sheltered sides they grow bracken and stubby oaks. Natural vegetation (in the form of gorse and heath) often persists down the seaward slopes of the hog's back cliffs from hill-top to sea level. The flatter uplands support Fescue heaths—pasturable, but plentifully invaded by heather, gorse and bracken.

The *Northern Heather Moorland* backs the Coastal Heaths. Its northern boundary runs from Challacombe Common through Woolhanger, Ilkerton Ridge, Cheriton and Malmsmead to Oare Post, extending eastwards through Porlock Common and Stoke Pero to Crawter Hill. It is bounded on the east by Luccombe and Dunkery Gate; and its southern boundary runs through Hillhead Cross and Red Deer to Warren Farm. From Warren it loops back eastward again to Alderman's Barrow, returning to the southern edge of Challacombe Common via Brendon Common and Butter Hill. This rolling upland lies between 900 and 1,400 feet, its shallow peat and stony soil supporting dense heather (*Calluna Vulgaris*) interspersed with moor rush (*Juncus Squarrosus*) and deer sedge (*Scirpus Cespitosus*) in its wetter areas. Then northward-running combes (Ruckham, Farley, Chalk, and Weir Waters, for example) are grassy at their heads but grow bracken, gorse, thorns and rowans as their valleys rapidly deepen.

The boundaries of the *Central Grass Moorland* have been traced earlier

* See—earlier in this Chapter—the discussion of the vegetation of the Forest. See, too, Chapter Thirteen.
† See map on page 79.

in this Chapter: they coincide with the Forest boundary, enclosing that peaty upland plateau of central Exmoor that was once Crown land. As has been stated, the chief vegetation is purple moor grass or flying bent, but in higher, wetter areas—notably the Chains—this gives way to deer sedge. On the peatier areas cotton grass is abundant. There are fewer valleys here than in the heather moors and they grow less bracken and more coarse grass—poor quality fescues and bents with extensive areas of matgrass (*Nardus Stricta*), and rushes.

The *Southern Heather Moorland* borders the Central Grass Moorland from Mole's Chamber, Kinsford Gate and Sherdon to Simonsbath. The boundary line then runs through Hereliving and Chibbet Post to Hoe Farm (near Wheddon Cross). The rivers Quarme and Exe then mark the eastern boundary as far as Miltons (south of Bridgetown). The southern edge is formed by South Hill and Varle Hill; and at Northmoor the boundary of the southern heather moorland coincides with the National Park boundary, following this north-west—by Molland and Twitchen—up to Barcombe Down (above North Molton). What is left of Fyldon, Wester, Bray and Shoulsbarrow Commons completes this region of Exmoor. As will be seen in Chapter Thirteen, the western half of the southern heather moorland has suffered dramatic changes in recent years.

The *Brendon Heaths* are found east of the Dulverton-Minehead road (A 396) and form the eastern fringes of the Exmoor National Park. Widely-spaced bracken-filled valleys separate isolated remnants of heather and gorse moors. The gentler slopes have all been reclaimed, and many of the steeper areas have been afforested.

The climate of Exmoor—except on the coastal fringes and in the Vale of Porlock—is wet and severe. In describing it, there is no reason to change the words of the Parliamentary Commissioners who surveyed the Forest in 1651:

> Memerandum that the said Chace is a Mountenous and cold ground much be Clouded with thick Foggs and Mists, and is vsed for adjisting and depasturing of Catle, horses, and sheepe, and is a verrye sound sheepe pasture, but a verrye great part theirof is overgrowne with heath, and yeilding but a pore kind of Turf of Litle vallue their . . .

The rainfall is heavy. The records over the past seventeen years (some of the vital gauges have been in existence only for that period of time) show that annual rainfall in the Exmoor National Park varies from thirty-five inches in some coastal areas (the eastern boundary of the Park, near Minehead, for example) to the upper seventies at Chains Barrow and Winsford. (The gauges at these two places in fact averaged over eighty-one inches between 1951 and 1960.) As C. H. Archer—the leading authority on

Exmoor rainfall—stressed, however, volume is but one of two significant factors in rainfall; the other being intensity. In 1960, for example—regarded by the Meteorological Office as the wettest year since 1872—Exmoor was not particularly wet up to the last day of September. In a year when England as a whole received 131 per cent of the 1916–50 average, the first nine months on Exmoor were but 4 per cent above average. In October, however, all weather stations in the National Park recorded more than ten inches. In November Dunkery recorded over ten and Chains Barrow 14·6 inches. On 3 December over four inches fell in the day from Dunkery all the way to Longstone Barrow, Dunkery itself receiving six inches in the course of that day. The month's total was again over ten inches all over the moor. West Dunkery achieving the highest total of 14·1 inches. Nor did the first month of 1961 bring any respite, for Simonsbath recorded twelve inches.

These figures for 1960 have been quoted—though, surprisingly, that year's *total* rainfall was not particularly heavy *for Exmoor*—because they emphasise the intensity factor, a topic to which Chapter Twelve must again direct attention.

Page*stated that "it always rains on Exmoor" was a proverbial saying in his day (1890); and "Exmoor the tea-pot: Tiverton the spout" is still quoted. Certainly no explorer of the Park should fail to equip himself with good boots and waterproof clothing. Nor is it solely on the high moor that such protection is needed. On 18 December 1964 I walked ankle-deep on the road from Hawkcombe Head to Lucott Cross and might as well have been wading through a high moorland stream in spate for any advantage the road could offer. But it is, of course, on the open western moor that climatic conditions can test endurance almost to breaking point. Open to the Atlantic winds, western Exmoor is often lashed by gales of great velocity which drive rain into the walker's face with a venom that must be experienced to be credited.

Even more trying, because there is no trace of exhilaration in *this* experience, is a chill mist, sometimes persisting for days on end and very wetting. Such mists come down with frightening rapidity. On 27 November 1947 I was caught in one of these on my way from Winsford's Wambarrows to Great Bradley, crossing the open moor south of, and parallel to, the track. I know the route well, but within seconds visibility was down to feet and I had to return to the road by compass. The lack of warning and the muffling, distorting effect of being trapped in such a mist accounts no doubt for some of the Exmoor superstitions, notably that of the Yeth Hounds—the moor's equivalent of other demon packs. Certainly, it is this chill dampness—which is, of course, most prevalent in winter—that holds spring back on Exmoor.

* *An Exploration of Exmoor and The Hill Country of West Somerset.*

On the other hand, except when the mists form, the air is fresh and heady. Even in high summer a breeze blows over the plateau and it is rare to become overheated when walking; but the precipitous combes shut out the wind, making their exploration warm work in summer and gratifyingly comforting in winter. I have sat with my jacket off in Farley Valley on a sunny mid-December day, yet several layers of clothing were essential for comfort once the shelter of the combe was left behind.

Snowfalls on Exmoor are spectacular because of the immense drifts encouraged by the strong winds and open surface. The combes are buried brink-deep and the roads are impassable. Long after the higher land throws off its wintry cover snow persists in the valleys and in the lee of the wind-breaks. Readers of *Lorna Doone* will remember Blackmore's description of the great snow through which Jan Ridd journeyed to seek Lorna:

> There was nothing square or jagged left, there was nothing perpendicular; all the rugged lines were eased, and all the breaches smoothly filled ... Not a patch of grass was there, not a black branch of a tree (in the Doone Valley); all was white; and the little river flowed beneath an arch of snow; if it managed to flow at all.

Those who saw Exmoor in the snows of 1947 will not accuse the novelist of exaggeration in *that* part of his romance. He drew his material from records of the 1676* winter which—with 1564-5 and 1962-3—appears to have been the most severe in England as a whole and on Exmoor in particular.

There is evidence† of a cyclic pattern in winter severity. We know of a climatic deterioration in the late Bronze Age when, about 750 B.C., the worsening conditions drove the settlers off the uplands. It seems that the winters between 1896 and 1937 were milder than those of any other comparable period since 1300. Between 1938 and 1957 the winters reverted to a hardness comparable with what was usual in the nineteenth century; and since 1958 there has been a trend back to the extremely severe conditions that persisted from 1564 to 1740. What such winters mean on Exmoor is difficult for the summer visitor to imagine. Drifting occurs not only during the blizzards, for the continuous cold produces a drift-surface, thus ensuring that even light showers of powder snow drift immense distances whenever the wind is fresh and block the roads and tracks that have been laboriously cleared. Communications are maintained, if at all, over open fields or moor, on foot, by horse or tractor, or—as in 1962-3— by helicopter, the use of which saved many animal and some human lives. In that dreadful winter the cold began on 23 December and lasted until 3 March and during those seventy-one days the mean day temperature on

* Blackmore dates it as 1686, but this cannot be verified.

† C.H. Archer: *The Exmoor Review*, No. 5, pp. 12-14.

the moor was 26·4 degrees fahrenheit. Even today, when electricity, the telephone and the internal combustion engine can do much to alleviate distress, such a winter is a terrible ordeal. Memories of it will persist until the next great freeze drives it from men's minds.

The scenes just depicted and the figures quoted suggest a grim setting; and it would be misleading to minimise those features of climate and structure that challenge and may sometimes dismay the explorer of Exmoor. The rewards, however, are great: not the least of these being the colours of the moorland—subdued but wonderfully varied. Bracken in the combes marks the passing of the seasons, from the vivid green of spring to the golden brown of autumn. Each boggy patch on the higher moor presents its changing tones: green sphagnum, golden patches of bog asphodel, nodding tufts of white cotton-grass. On the drier hillsides in midsummer the coarse grasses yellow under the sun until an eminence like Trout Hill appears a restless golden sea. On outer Exmoor—on the Grabhurst range, for example—the colours are more vivid: purple heather challenged by the flame of gorse, short upland cropped turf bearing misty clusters of the wort, and in the combes the 'beadbonny ash' burning red among the gnarled black branches. These are the bold colours. Closer attention reveals the pale pink of cross-leaved heather among the purple of its more prolific relatives, and the tiny gold star of tormentil blooms by the diminutive blue of the milkwort, white-starred heath bedstraw and yellow lesser spearwort.

Despite rumour, there are no dangerous bogs on Exmoor; but there are many wet lands where the walking is bad and where even boots topped by gaiters will be insufficient protection if the walker takes an unwary step. Bad patches, such as Duckypool at the top of Bray Common, will provide a nasty wetting; but the worst going of the lot is on the Chains, with the Pinford Bogs, between Exe Cleave and Badgworthy, coming a close second. Mole's Chamber has an evil reputation. According to one story, Farmer Mole met an untimely end here on his way home from Market. Page records that two versions of the story were current in the nineties, one saying that Mole perished while hunting, and the other stating that he deliberately rode into the bog to prove that it was harmless. More matter-of-fact people have denied the existence of Farmer Mole and they believe that the name refers to the River Mole. Certainly the bog is tame enough now and has been for many years. On the other hand, the bog at the head of Farley Water was bad enough in the nineties to kill a horse, its rider throwing himself off just in time to avoid death.* Another bog to achieve fame was 'The Prince of Wales's Bog' at the head of Land Combe, a stream running into Badgworthy north of the Deer Park. King Edward

* Letter from Ernest Bawden (famous Devon and Somerset huntsman) to H.C.N. Bond: 13.10.39.

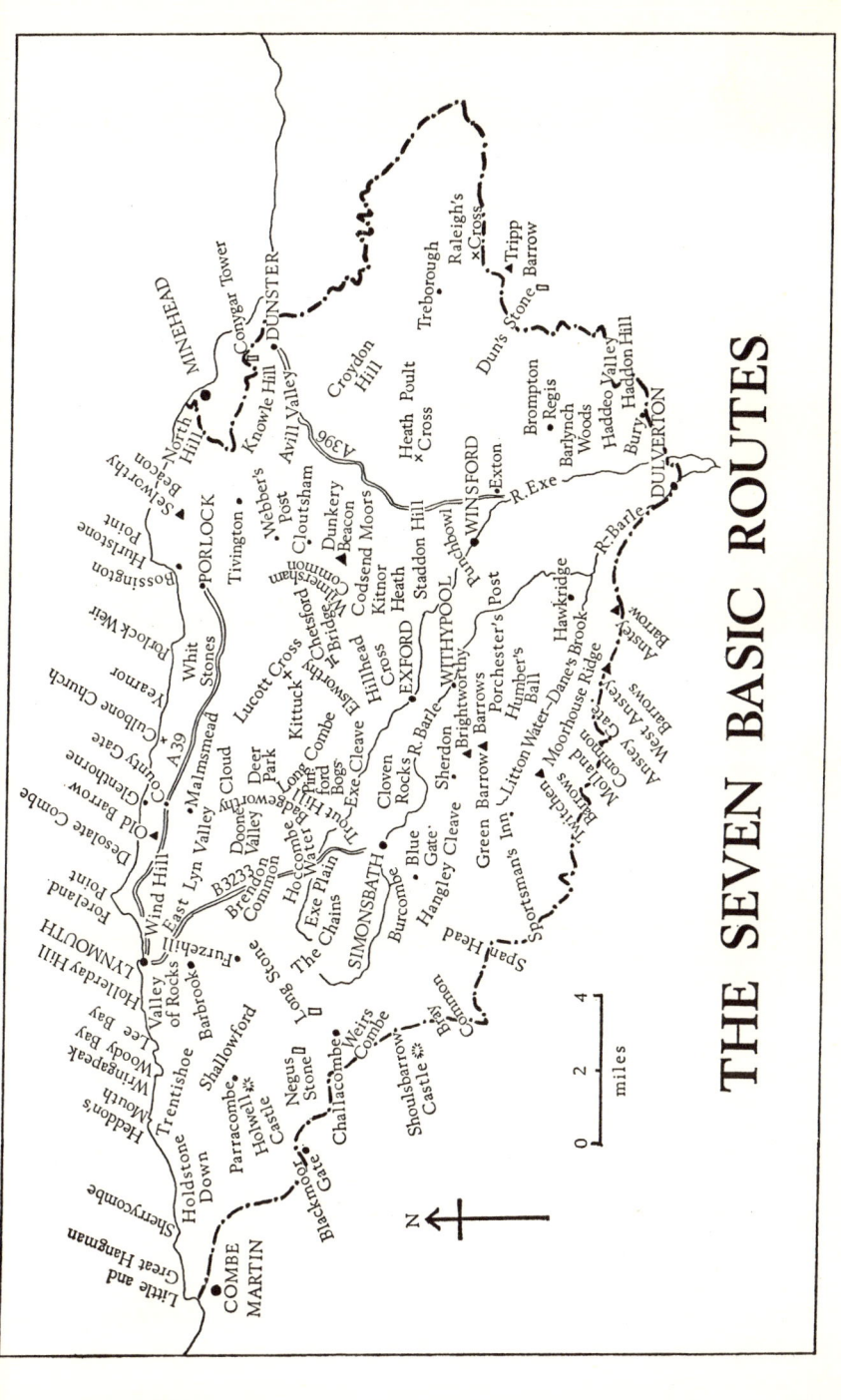

THE SEVEN BASIC ROUTES

VII, when Prince of Wales, was unhorsed there while hunting with the
Devon and Somerset. The second world war produced a cherished story
to the effect that a tank was swallowed up during night exercises. Diligent
enquiry has not elicited precise details, and the legend should be classed
with that of Farmer Mole. It must be borne in mind that the character and
location of the moorland bogs can change considerably over the years.
During and after the exceptionally intense winter rainfall of 1961–2, and
earlier—in the cataclysmic downpour of August 1952—the deepening of old
bogs and the creation of new ones has been recorded. Ironically, storms of
this power can also result in the disappearance of bogs, for the force of
run-off sometimes channels out drainage paths that did not previously
exist. And though it is only after exceptional rain that comparatively rapid
change occurs, the steady action of water erosion and the fluctuation of the
water table produce results, imperceptible from year to year, but considerable in their cumulative effect.

.   .   .

The varied structure of Exmoor has been stressed and an attempt has been
made to clarify this by describing the 'anatomy' of the Park (see pages 74
to 75 and the map on page 77). The description of the vegetational sub-
regions (see pages 80 to 81 and the map on page 79) was intended to provide
a similar clarification of a variety that newcomers or, indeed, frequent
visitors often find bewildering, delightful though it is. Long experience has
shown, however, that a different division of the territory is necessary for
thorough and methodical exploration of Exmoor. While bearing the
structural and vegetational regions in mind, the walker or rider bent on a
mastery of Exmoor needs a grasp of the basic routes to be followed.
Knowledge of these gives shape to his Exmoor travels and provides the
indispensable framework for further study. Here, then, are the seven basic
routes* that open up the whole of Exmoor:

1. The southern ridge
2. The Barle valley
3. The Exe valley
4. The Chains and the area west of the Simonsbath-Lynton road
5. Badgworthy and the area east of the Simonsbath-Lynton road
6. Dunkery and the Brendons
7. The Coast of Exmoor

* See map on page 85.

CHAPTER SIX

The Southern Ridge

THE southern rampart of Exmoor is a narrow ridge stretching fourteen miles in a north-westerly direction and extending from a point just south of Dulverton to Shoulsbarrow Common. It rears abruptly out of the lower Barle valley two miles north of the confluence of the Barle and the Exe and, gaining height as it goes, reaches its extreme elevation of 1,618 feet at Five Barrows. Beyond that point it drops to Setta Barrow (1,556 feet) and Mole's Chamber (1,396 feet), but rises again on Shoulsbarrow Common which climbs to 1,564 feet. The ridge is everywhere above 1,000 feet and, for the most part, between 1,200 and 1,500 feet. All along its southern slope steep valleys descend south-west to the broken hills of the north Devon farmlands. Its northern slope at first drops swiftly to the wooded valley of the lower Barle; later, as the higher reaches of that river swing north, the ridge is bordered by the Barle's principal tributaries, the Danes Brook and Sherdon Water. At its north-western termination the ridge again slopes down to the Barle whose course is once more roughly parallel with it along the Five Barrows to Shoulsbarrow Common stretch.

This upland provides the easiest walking on Exmoor, for a very fair road runs along the crest from Five Crosses (just east of Anstey Barrow, the first notable landmark) to Two Barrows—a nine-mile stretch of excellent country from which, equipped with one-inch map, compass and binoculars, the Exmoor explorer can familiarise himself with the chief topographical features of much of the National Park. East of Two Barrows the ridge road swings south but rejoins the old Forest boundary at Kinsford Gate. A mile further west, just beyond Five Barrows, it repeats the manoeuvre but comes back to the boundary again beyond Setta Barrow, following it to Mole's Chamber. Here, the ridge rises and splays out its base, its high termination being the bleak plateau of Shoulsbarrow. Unfortunately, the agricultural developments of recent years have resulted in a good deal of ploughing and fencing over the last four miles of this route. From Fyldon Common westwards it is no longer easy to enter the moor for close inspection of some of the more remarkable antiquities, and the character of the moorland vegetation has been much altered by reseeding. In some areas even the satisfaction of seeing improved land is denied to the fenced-out walker, for the essential follow-up work has been neglected and what was once open moor is now enclosed rush and scrub of lower agricultural value than the moorland it replaced. It is only fair to add that such wanton destruction of the moor is the exception on Exmoor. Most reclamation has been properly managed, with resulting improvement of the pasture. The irony of the situation lies in the fact that 'rush growing' gets the taxpayer's subsidy in as full measure as the carefully planned and laboriously continued operations of the conscientious farmer.

At the eastward point of the ridge Anstey Barrow lies between the ridge road and the lane that drops down to the Danes Brook before climbing to Hawkridge. Like the West Anstey Barrows a mile or so further on, it is large and prominently sited. All the barrows and other landmarks along this southern stretch of the moor make admirable navigational aids for the walker or rider deep in the central moor. It is easy, for example, to pin-point one's position when skirting the South Chains Wall (Chains Barrow itself not always being in view) provided the ridge landmarks have been memorised. Some hold that these round barrows of the Bronze Age, almost always placed on a hill top, were sited thus as way-marks; but their sepulchral function makes this unlikely. Their chief purpose was clearly to contain and to memorialise the remains of the mighty dead: it was natural then to lift them skywards. Barrows of the size of these must have occupied in their construction all the able-bodied men of a tribe for several days— and who now knows what rites were necessary at successive stages of the work? That their lofty positions made them useful to travellers was incidental.

In later times, particularly in Saxon days, they were regarded with fear; a fact reflected in the name that country people in more recent ages gave them—'the graves of the giants'. This was an unintentional irony, for their bulk concealed cremated remains in an earthen or metal vase hidden in the tiny stone chamber of their hearts; or else a skeleton hunched up tight—the human embryo in the great earth womb.

From Anstey Barrow the ridge road runs straight to Anstey Gate, passing on its way a memorial of more modern times—the Froude Hancock Stone. This large granite block, to the north of the road, was placed in position in 1935 in memory of Froude Hancock, a notable stag-hunter. Weighing thirteen tons, it was brought from Marsh Bridge on a steam lorry which broke down several times on the steep gradients before it finally conveyed its massive burden to the moorland plot marked out as a suitable site by the dead man's friends and admirers. The methods and materials were different, but the motives and the choice of site were strikingly similar to those of Bronze Age man. The inscription is fading in the unfriendly weather, and to the casual passer-by the Froude Hancock Stone may some day seem as mysterious as a round barrow.

At Anstey Gate a good track leads north to Lyshwell farm in the Danes Brook valley. This pretty river, which is called Litton Water in its upper course, is one of those rapid Exmoor streams whose steep-sided valley seems far too big in summer for the volume of water passing swiftly over the pebbly bed. In winter, swollen with flood water, the Danes Brook needs all its space as it rushes fiercely, a brown foam-covered torrent, to join the Barle. For the last mile and a half its banks are heavily wooded in striking contrast with the bare moorland where the austere outlines of Clogg's Down, Moorhouse Ridge and Humber's Ball look down on its banks. The clear stream and the company of dippers, herons and kingfishers make this a delectable place on a hot summer day.

Beyond Anstey Gate the road crosses Molland Common before it reaches Cuzzicombe Post, where the Devon and Somerset often meet, as they did in Collyns's day. It was here that on 10 September 1816 a fine twelve-pointer was viewed as it ran to soil in the Danes Brook: a sight as typical of Exmoor as the brooding barrows and the bare hills that surround the Post, whose origin is now forgotten. A landmark, of course, but in 1897 the people of Molland celebrated the Jubilee by erecting a new Post to replace the old one. The operation was accompanied by festivities that suggested some dim inarticulate memory of the bygone significance of the landmark. Barrels of ale were taken to the site and drunk around the new Post: an interesting example of the commemoration of boundaries in modern times long after the significance of the ceremony and of the boundary itself had been forgotten. On an unfenced waste such as Exmoor, boundary stones and posts were for centuries of great importance. At perambulations, boys accompanied their elders to the marks, where, not only were the bounds—and the boys—beaten, but heated boundary stones were sometimes used to impress young memories with precise locations.

From Cuzzicombe (or Cussacombe) Gate, half a mile east of the Post, a road runs due south to Molland—well worth a visit for its church* and its inn. The church is mainly fifteenth century but is unusual in having largely escaped the well-meant interference of Victorian restorers. Its furnishings are mainly Georgian: horse-box pews (some with hat-pegs), three-decker pulpit and early Georgian screen. The Courtenay monuments are fine examples of seventeenth and eighteenth century work and typically frank in their acceptance of the more brutal facts of death: stone roses wreathe grinning skulls; a double heart-stone is a symbolic receptacle for the squire and his wife. But the overall effect is of rural peace and a mingling of the elegant with the rustic. The parson's desk and the clerk's desk are on the same level—the latter a tiny, cramped cell—preaching desk above, and the whole surmounted by a splendid sounding board where an angel holds a trumpet. The delightful screen is pierced by a wicket-gate, and above the screen, on the plastered tympanum, higher even than the royal arms, big letters tell us that these arms were painted by one Rowlands in

* A. Elliott-Cannon has an interesting article on Molland in *The Exmoor Review*, No. 8.

1808 when L. Mogridge was Churchwarden. Local worthies are rarely afflicted with false modesty.

It was just four years earlier that Parson Froude became vicar of Molland and Knowstone. Believed by many to be the original of Parson Chowne* in Blackmore's *The Maid of Sker*, Froude acquired an unenviable reputation as a tyrant and was said to maintain a private army of tenant farmers and grooms to perform such services as rick-firing or beatings-up when he wanted to terrorise an enemy. His legendary encounters with the Bishop of Exeter invariably ended with the total discomfiture of his lordship against whom Froude employed the rough humours and rustic cunning with which he was plentifully endowed. The Froude stories are still remembered locally, and it is not easy to separate the man from the myth; but his appearances in Molland pulpit have left a vivid—if vague— impression of Satanic manifestations.

The London Inn is near the church. It was the scene of a dramatic episode in Frederic Knight's day when his miners, happily drinking away their week's wages, were driven out by their angry wives who had marched in a righteous army from Simonsbath. In the brief and decisive battle they are reputed to have used the overflowing chamber-pots so beloved of eighteenth-century novelists. Legend is silent about the source of supply. The inn would hardly provide so many. Did they carry their missiles across the moor? It is a quiet spot nowadays; low, oak-beamed rooms, old settles, good beer, and outside, a remarkable menagerie which has included foxes, badgers, deer calves, parrots and monkeys.

Beyond Cuzzicombe Gate the ridge road runs due north to White Post and then west past Twitchen Barrows perched high above Litton Water, a lovely valley. The moorland north of the ridge is easily accessible and should not be missed. The best route opens up at Sandyway Cross, where John Knight's North Molton to Withypool road crosses the ridge. The road to Withypool leads past the Sportsman's Inn to the Cross, from which a good track drops down into Sherdon Water, a swift stream running through some of the barest yet most varied scenery in the whole of the Park. In this broken country lie three of the finest farms that Frederic Knight made: Horsen, Wintershead and Emmett's Grange, as well as Woolcombe and Sherdon. The humps of rounded hills roll northwards to the Barle, their bases separated by the clear streams that swell the growing river. There are big flocks here, shepherded by the hill farmers on their sturdy Exmoor ponies.

Further on, having skirted Green Barrow, the road drops down to Knighton Combe, a fine valley running right up to the roadside. The

---

* The identification has been disputed, but it seems likely that Blackmore's fictitious character owed a good deal to the lurid Froude *legends*. The only certainties are that Froude was a hunting parson and that Knowstone parish during his day was said to be "infamous and notorious to all the western parts of this kingdom". (*Western Times*, 5 June 1841.)

combe head provides an excellent view of a characteristic Exmoor phenomenon: the tight interlacing of wild moorland with cultivation. A few moments of careful observation here will do much to inform the visitor about the problems facing those who are trying to reconcile amenity and agricultural interests in the Exmoor National Park.

Both Withypool Common and Withypool Hill, between which the road now passes, are barrow crowned. Brightworthy Barrows on the summit of the Common command a magnificent view of the southern moor and, like the ridge road, should be used as an observation point by those who wish to study the moorland anatomy and master its basic features. The Hill, a little lower than the Common, has a good tumulus on top, but its most noteworthy feature is the stone circle, 200 yards south-west of the barrow. This is the finest Bronze Age circle on the whole of Exmoor. Below the circle, near the base of the hill, a clearly-marked right of way leads to Porchester's Post, dips down into the Danes Brook valley, and then climbs up to the ridge at White Post, thus completing a picturesque moorland circuit. Porchester's Post, a boundary marker between Hawkridge and Withypool parishes, was erected by the Carnarvons after they acquired Hawkridge by the marriage of the second Earl with the Acland heiress in 1796. From the Post, Old Barrow can be seen to the south-east and readily identified by a stake standing crookedly on the mound: a useful landmark for the walker who is aiming across country for the Hawkridge road.

Beyond Sandyway the ridge road travels through a sad stretch of country. The problems of the National Park—discussed in Chapter Thirteen—are nowhere more apparent than here. What was once open moorland is mostly enclosed and reseeding has been extensive, though with varying results. The restricted access is the more grievous because so many important landmarks lie off the road and, behind their fences, must in future remain unseen by many who would wish to develop an informed interest in the moor.

Two Barrows is another good viewpoint for the serious explorer of the Park. Northwards, the descent into Hangley Cleave—the deep valley of Kinsford Water—is immediate and swift. Emmett's Grange, one of the most handsome of the moorland farmhouses and for long the home of Robert Smith, is on the further slope. Beyond are Blue Gate and the bare hills, varied by the Simonsbath woodland. Fine though these views are, the panoramas from the Span Head and Five Barrows vantage points are more highly rated by many. Five Barrows is a most impressive sight, the eight-barrow complex covering an area 2,000 feet long and 500 feet wide. (Paradoxically, the name 'Five Barrows' is not as misleading as it sounds: though there are eight barrows in the group, only five can be seen from a distance from most moorland viewpoints.) Leland called the place by its old alternative names of Span Head or the Towers, but the moorland people, with logic derived from their own knowledge of the moor, have stuck to 'Five Barrows', and the Ordnance map rightly reserves the name 'Span Head' for the source of nearby Lyddicombe Bottom:

> A place callid the Spanne, and the Tourres; for ther be hillokkes of yerth cast up of anncient tyme for Markes and the Limites betwixt Somersetshir and Devonshir, and here about is the Limes or Boundes of Exmoor Forest.

The coincident County and Forest boundaries do indeed run 300 yards north of the tumuli, but Leland was quite wrong in describing the 'hillokkes of yerth' as mere boundary markers: they were there before Devon and Somerset had their names and before the Forest was marked out. They are undoubtedly sepulchral and linked in prehistory with the other barrows that crown each eminence on Exmoor's southern heights. The Bronze Age men who made them gave to the blind eyes of their dead an awe-inspiring vision: the tors of Dartmoor loom up in the southern sky, while to the north-west over empty moor and north Devon farms the Atlantic coast dominates the horizon.

The road dips beyond Five Barrows and passes through another fine cluster of round barrows. They form an irregular triangle; two widely spaced to the north of the road make the base, three close together to the south form the sides and the apex. Due north of this group lies Setta Barrow, neighboured by the squelchy patch called Duckypool. The County and Forest boundaries run through the barrow, and so does the deep furrow that—in callous disregard for the monument—was once driven to mark the boundary. Despite its mutilation Setta is worth the effort to see, not merely for its great size and lofty position but because, most unusually for an Exmoor barrow, the circle of retaining stones at the base of the mound is clearly visible. This giant, with its two satellites, is the last tumulus on the ridge itself, though there are two more on the north and east slopes below the Shoulsbarrow plateau in which the ridge ends. Like other barrows on Exmoor, some of the ridge mounds have been fruitlessly plundered for the mythical treasure they were once believed to contain. On Dartmoor the 'crock of gold' with which legend endowed each barrow has caused much destruction; its Exmoor counterpart, 'a steyn o' money', has been equally damaging. Barrow plundering was practised for centuries. The Romans were perhaps the first offenders, and though in subsequent ages superstitious dread acted as some deterrent to would-be treasure hunters, many barrows were violated. The romantic antiquarians of the later eighteenth century did much damage too, but fortunately some of Exmoor's best barrows were too remote to attract their attention. This remoteness, however, has had its disadvantages: scientific excavation has been thoroughly understood for many years, but few of the Exmoor barrows have been properly explored.

Mole's Chamber lies in a dip between Setta Barrow and Shoulsbarrow. The evil reputation of its bog is, as has been seen, far in excess of its possible performance; yet it is a desolate place with a heap of grassy rubble to indicate the ruins of the Acland Arms. This was an inn erected during the mining period of Frederic Knight's rule to enable the Cornham Ford workers to combat the loneliness of the moor. It had no very enviable reputation, and when the mining ended its only callers were the wind and the rain. On a grey day this is as dreary a spot as Exmoor affords. The track from Mole's Chamber running north-east to meet the Challacombe-Simonsbath road (B 3358) is of great interest. It is a section of one of the most ancient trackways in Britain: a trade route of immense importance that ran from the Midlands, through Gloucester and Bristol, over the Quantocks to Exford and Simonsbath, and thence to Barnstaple and on into Cornwall. As mentioned in Chapter One it was used by the Saxons for their penetration of the moor and, entering the National Park at Elworthy Barrow on the Brendons, it leads to Summerway Cross above Cutcombe, sometimes followed by the modern roads but more often appearing as a farm track or—as in this Mole's Chamber section—as a rutted way. Its moorland route still demonstrates its military advantages: by taking it over, the Saxons could dominate the uplands on which they had no wish to settle but to which their occupation of the valleys was driving the Celtic farmers. Men and supplies could be moved along the Harepath to strike with comparative speed at clustering remnants of the dispossessed tribesmen or to make surprise outflanking attacks on valley farms or villages expecting frontal assault from forces moving up the rivers. Between Mole's Chamber and Driver Cott the track presents a classic illustration of trackway transport. Where boggy ground occurs, parallel rutways can be seen. In the thousand years of use before the Saxons came the pannier trains and human bearers made no attempt at road-construction. A contoured route was sufficient, and where mud and water made the going hard alternative ways higher up the slopes were beaten out by the passage of men's and horses' feet.

At the Mole's Chamber end of the track the old Forest boundary diverges northwards on its way to the Edgerley Stone. This short section is picturesque and interesting. Between Mole's Chamber and the ruined inn stands the Slolely Stone, erected in 1742 to mark the boundary between High Bray Common and Gratton Manor Common. The inscriptions can be read, though with some difficulty: on one side, "William Longe Oxenham Esquire Lord of the Manor of Highbray 1742"; on the other, "Christian Slowley Lady of the Manor of Gratton". The Stone once stood further to the north, at the head of Lew Combe. Between the Sloley Stone and the Edgerley Stone (set in the north bank of the B 3358 road) there was once another prominent mearestone, but patient searching as long ago as 1935* failed to discover Broadbarrow Stone. It probably suffered the same fate as the Saddle Stone (see Chapter Five), but that is no reason for calling off the search. Its discovery would be a minor but gratifying triumph and might throw new light on the mysterious wanderings of the Sloley Stone.

The southern ridge ends with what is in some ways its most striking and enigmatic feature. Beyond the Mole's Chamber depression it rises to the Shoulsbarrow plateau, on the south-western slope of which lies the 'Castle'. This bleak spot is little visited, for the sunken road running from the Chamber round the base of the Common gives little indication of the interesting historical and scenic features to be discovered once the steep wet land on the slope has been climbed. Yet there are few more intriguing sites on Exmoor than this.

> Shoulsbury (or Shoulsbarrow) Castle is a nearly square ramparted enclosure of between four and five acres, round two and a half sides of which there is an outer rampart. This fort seems to have no close affinity with any other in the area and is probably unfinished.†

Though just below the flat top of the hill, the fort stands high—over 1,500 feet up—open to the winter gales, a fact that does little to explain the mystery of its function. Nor do its constructional features make the guessing easier. Its main enclosure is an almost square area with rounded corners. East, south, and west the rampart runs straight and true; but on the north follows an irregular curve. A ditch adds to the defences on all sides except the south, where the ground falls steeply away. It could be argued that there is no ditch here because the lie of the land provided sufficient defence and made the labour of ditch-digging unnecessary. Archaeologists, however, are unwilling to be so positive, arguing that other features indicate an unfinished state. For example, an outer rampart covers the ditch on the east and north but extends only half way along the west side. The outer defences are at varying distances (between thirty-one and seventeen yards) from the inner rampart; the main enclosure measures 144 yards from north to south and 146 yards from east to west; there is an undoubtedly original entrance in the middle of the west side, and another —but probably later—entrance in the east. The ramparts, which are not very high (a maximum of eight feet from ditch bottom to rampart top), contain a good deal of stone rather haphazardly added as a strengthener.

These unusual features have made experts cautious about Shouls-

---

* H.C.N. Bond: Correspondence with MacDermot.

† Charles Whybrow: "Some Multivallate Hill-Forts in Exmoor and North Devon", *Proc. Devonshire Archaeological Society*, 1967.

barrow,* particularly when discussing the 'Roman' associations with which it has been endowed by legend. One of the myths may be dismissed at once. Towards the end of the nineteenth century what were popularly supposed to be Roman swords were found at the fort, and the subsequent discovery that they were seventeenth-century rapiers did nothing to weaken the belief that the Romans built Shoulsbarrow. A stronger basis for this belief is provided by the three rectilinear sides—an improbable shape for an Iron Age camp or fortress. In the absence of precise guidance from trained archaeologists there is no harm in a little guesswork. The moorland tribes, we know, gave the Romans no trouble, but we also know that Silurian pressure demanded a Roman military presence on the coast (see Chapter One). The conquerors may well have thought that it would do no harm occasionally to send a detachment from Exeter to show the Eagles to the moor folk. Shoulsbarrow was already the site of a hill fort and the Roman soldiers squared it up for their own purposes. Spells of duty in this unpopular station served the double function of toughening the troops and of reminding the tribesmen of Roman might, and since occupation was occasional there was no need for the more elaborate living quarters provided at the signalling stations on the coast.

The other Shoulsbarrow legends are more romantic and less probable: King Arthur is supposed to have had a 'castle' here—but there is hardly a hill top in the West Country which his ghost does not haunt; and King Alfred is credited with a successful defence of Shoulsbarrow against the Danes.

Whatever the truth about the mysterious fort may be, the views it affords are among Exmoor's best. To the north-west the jagged shape of the Hangman adds drama to the skyline. Lundy is faint but identifiable, and Bideford Bay seems near. Northwards, fold upon fold of moorland roll splendidly away. This is another of the high points from which the Exmoor explorer may establish a thorough knowledge of the moor's landmarks.

A little over half a mile north of Shoulsbarrow, where the slope of the southern ridge quickens to its ending, is an Exmoor curiosity to which has been grafted a story in comparison with which the most extreme Shoulsbarrow myths seem like sober statements of fact. Just beyond Weirs Combe a little stream rises, and to the south of this lies Chope's Well. Mentioned in 1658 in connection with a perambulation which established the boundaries of Challacombe Regis Manor, the Well was then described (by Ambrose Dallyn of Challacombe) has having three names: Chopehill, Heath Delight and Dulverton's-well. In the thirties the Well received

---

* "Although it seems probable that Shoulsbury Castle was some sort of a collecting centre for cattle and other livestock depastured on western Exmoor, there is really no convincing explanation of the outer rampart." Charles Whybrow.

some attention in a book called *Egypt on Exmoor*, the theory of an Egyptian settlement of the moor being bolstered by the assertion that 'Chopes' was a corruption of 'Cheops'. It need hardly be added that there has been little scholarly enthusiasm for either the etymology or the theory it was supposed to support.

CHAPTER SEVEN

The Barle Valley

THROUGHOUT its moorland course the Barle is a more impressive river than the Exe, and nowhere is this fact more obvious than at its source. John Knight's great dam is imposing, especially when seen from the south, and the lake which it forms by ponding back the head-waters of the Barle makes a dramatic beginning for this beautiful river. Pinkworthy Pond —an irregular triangle, curving at its north-west extremity and splaying out at the north-east—fills a depression in the desolate Chains of Exmoor. The water can sparkle on a bright day; but the peaty bottom and marshy banks, the windy uplands and cloudy skies, more often harmonise with the chill greyness that is its dominant mood and colour. This is a lonely spot: Chains Barrow to the east and Wood Barrow to the west; and the top of the Pinkworthy dam merging with the South Chains wall, along which a careful walker may proceed with dry feet across two miles of solitude until he reaches the marshy hollow where the Exe rises.

Appropriately, a ghost haunts the Pond—the sad wraith of a young farmer who drowned himself there in 1880. The hat and coat of the missing man were found on the bank, but as dragging did not discover the body an age-old device was tried: a candle floating on a loaf. However, the wind was too strong to allow the candle to be lit, and the loaf failed to come to rest over the corpse. Divers were then brought from Cardiff, but they could not work in the clouds of peat sediment stirred up by their heavy movements. It was, one of them said, like searching in a pool of ink. Finally, the Pond was drained, and the body was found close to the bank in shallow water.

Pinkworthy had to be emptied again in 1913, again in search for a suspected suicide, though this time without result. The herons from miles around had great sport in the mud, and the Pond was left empty for some time in the hope of draining the Chains. So many sheep and cattle were 'stogged' that the outlet was stopped and Pinkworthy filled again, but it was not this time restocked with the trout that used to be one of its main attractions.

On the sides of the Pond, in striking contrast to the coarse grass of the Chains, whortleberries, ling and bell heather grow in abundance. In the dampest parts the pale pink of cross-leaved heather may be seen. There is little of the yellow tormentil so common over much of the moor, but ivy-leaved bell flower and an occasional golden patch of bog asphodel make the marshy ground attractive.

Yet few would care to linger at Pinkworthy after dusk. It is such a quiet, brooding place, and the human mind can play strange tricks when daylight fails and only the grass rustling in the wind relieves the heavy weight of silence.

Between Pinkworthy and the bridge on the Simonsbath–Challacombe road (B 3358) the Barle flows through marshy land, Pinkworthy Allotment to the east and Broad Mead to the west. The valley deepens and tributaries from the waterlogged Chains add to the flow. A quarter of a mile away stands Pinkworthy Farm, made by Frederic Knight and typical of his work —grey and substantial, a massive windbreak to the west, the improved 'in-fields' greener and smoother than the moorland wildness that surrounds them. In many ways Pinkworthy epitomises the problems and achievements of the Knight era.

Beyond the bridge—a favourite picnicking spot—the river returns to the moorland and though, for a mile or so, the road is near, the bare hills silence even the summer traffic, imposing their quiet authority and deep peace upon the scene. Before Cornham is reached half a dozen streams from the Chains and the folds of the Southern Ridge foothills have made the Barle a sizeable river, deepened its valley, and added to its power and speed. Many consider this the finest moorland stretch of the river, rivalled only perhaps by the Simonsbath–Landacre section.

Cornham is another Knight farm—every farm in the Forest or on its southern fringes was made by them—standing high above the river with tracks connecting it with the Simonsbath road to the north and the Kinsford Gate road to the south. The southern track leads to the ford, where there is a substantial footbridge. Cornham Ford is one of the mineral bearing areas on which Frederic Knight set such hopes, and it was here— developing one of the old surface workings—that the Dowlais Company drove their main adit into the hillside. The opening is still there, but rock falls and dripping water discourage the exploration that a barrier is rightly intended to prohibit. Only the foolhardy would attempt to enter the passage that Knight's miners drove nearly half a mile into Burcombe Hill. Burcombe itself, a pretty valley, is a vivid reminder of the apparently sure foundation on which Knight's plans rested. The rocks through which the stream has cut its path gleam red with the iron he hoped to mine. And higher up the hill, at Blue Gate, another abandoned shaft proves that— though Knight was disappointed with its effort—the Dowlais Company did not give up lightly.

Heading back for Simonsbath, the Barle is joined by a considerable tributary, Bale Water, before it reaches the hamlet. The moorland capital is a fascinating place. Its name—nearly lost in the nineties, when its postal address was simply 'Exmoor'—is said to derive from an outlaw named Simon who was in the habit of bathing in the deep pool up water from the bridge. The tradition is vague as to any further details and must be dismissed as typical and obvious 'folk etymology'. The finest building is Simonsbath Lodge, for so long the only house in the Forest (see Chapter One). Its connections with Boevey and the Knights make it of the greatest interest to all students of Exmoor, and its sheer loveliness appeals even to the casual visitor. No trace now remains of the great mansion that John Knight planned, and we may be thankful that it was not built, for it would have dwarfed the Lodge.

Up the hill, beyond the roadside cottages where miners once lived, is The Exmoor Forest Hotel where, in delightful surroundings, much may be learned of Exmoor life and history; and higher up still, the vicarage and the church are visible monuments to the Knights. Both were built in 1856 and though the church has no pretensions to beauty, the vicarage is a pleasant-looking house. They afford, in fact, a striking contrast architecturally, showing what the Victorians could do and what they were incapable of. The parsonage is a comfortable dwelling house: it succeeds. The church got the usual dose of vague 'ecclesiasticism': it is a mess. And yet, the drab slates, the colour-washed walls, the pitch-pine pews, cannot prevent a certain admiration. The astonishing thing about it is that it exists at all. But for the courage and energy of a remarkable family it would not be here; and nor would the community it was built to serve. Sir Frederic and Lady Knight and their ill-fated son are buried in the churchyard of St. Luke's, Simonsbath; their true memorials lie all around them.

Nowadays Simonsbath is not isolated as it was when its first incumbent, the Rev. W.H. Thornton, wrote his reminiscences while experiencing the problems of raising a growing family with no doctor nearer than eleven miles away. His memoirs are disappointing historically—he could have recorded much valuable material—but they provide a picturesque account of lamp-lit rooms on winter evenings, little pools of light and warmth amid the darkness of the Forest. They give the feel of life there in what were still pioneering days. And even today, once the snow begins to swirl off the moor onto John Knight's roads, Simonsbath returns to its loneliness until the snowploughs break through.

Below Simonsbath, the sheltering trees soon thin away and the prospect is wild indeed. The river winds rapidly through its steep-sided valley, a paradise for the fisherman and the naturalist. About a mile from Simonsbath it makes a big curve southwards and in the semi-circle so formed, on the north bank, rises the steep and grassy hill of Flexbarrow, a sudden and surprising sight. It is somehow too dramatic to be natural, but there is no evidence to show that it was made by man. A furlong away, there is evidence of man's work: the Wheal Eliza Cottage, built for the miners who worked the Wheal Eliza shaft. The cottage is grim and derelict, slate roof falling in, windows gaping, grey spoil heap between it and the river—spanned here by a footbridge. The mine was opened for copper and the shaft was driven down 250 feet. No copper was found, but the discovery of good iron ore raised hopes of a different reward. As at Cornham, the deposits were too thin to be economically worked.

The Wheal Eliza is notorious as the place chosen by a murderer for the concealment of his victim's body. Lower down the Barle, on the banks of one of its tributaries, the White Water, there once stood a cottage inhabited by a man named Burgess, a widower. Wishing to marry again, he discovered that his daughter—his only child—was hated by the woman he loved, and he decided to remove this obstacle to his happiness. He killed the child and buried her on the moor. It was the practice of sheep-stealers then to bury the carcase of a stolen sheep until such time as it could safely be removed, and two of Burgess's acquaintances, finding the newly-made grave, informed the wretch that they had discovered a prize and arranged with him to remove it that night. The panic-stricken man disinterred the body and flung it down the Wheal Eliza shaft, fleeing to Wales immediately. The discovery of fragments of cloth and hair in the grave on the moor occasioned a search for the poor girl and, so tradition says, mysterious blue lights hovering over the shaft* guided the searchers to the body. Burgess was arrested in Wales and having confessed was hanged at Taunton in 1858. I once talked with the grandson of one of the policemen who brought Burgess back from Wales—in an open boat. He reported his grandfather as saying, "We knew we'd a murderer on board by the way the waves leapt at the boat and tried to drag it down."

Cow Castle is the next feature of especial interest. In the angle formed by the junction of the White Water and the Barle, three steep hills rise out of the valley. On the middle and highest of these stands the most impressive Iron Age fortress on Exmoor. Close study reveals the principles of siting and fortification practised by the energetic and violent people who thrust up the Exmoor valleys to dispossess the Bronze Age men, already turning away from the uplands in the climatic deterioration from about 500 B.C. A rampart, in places ten feet high, surrounds the summit of the hill, and round the wall except on the north-west, where the ground falls precipitously, there is a considerable ditch. There is a fine entrance, defended with some elaboration, and the circumference of the outworks is over 1,000 feet. In places the dry walling forming the core is clearly visible. The view from the rocky summit in the interior of the Castle is magnificent. South-east is a knoll, called the Calf. Below, runs the silver thread of the Barle, twisting

* There is an obvious and unpleasant explanation of this.

between lofty hills. Upstream, a glimpse of the moor lines beyond Simonsbath is caught when the sun shines on them, though the hamlet itself is
hidden by a fold in the ground. In the opposite direction the broadening
river flows in widening curves past Sherdon Hutch and on to Landacre.*

North of Cow Castle, the triangle formed by the White Water, the main
road and Gipsy Lane is full of interest. Three Knight Farms, Winstitchen,
Honeymead and Picked Stones ('Pickst'ns'), are within its boundaries, and
at the head of the White Water Valley is Cloven Rocks bog which some
have imagined to be where Carver Doone met his unpleasant death. A
track from Picked Stones connects with Gipsy Lane, up which the Forest
boundary ran, and leads out to the main road and Red Deer farm house,
once known—when an inn—as Gallon House.

South of Picked Stones is the one blemish in scenery that is aesthetically
and historically satisfying. A vigorous conifer plantation marches in
regimented lines up the hillside. Planted with good intentions—as covert
for the deer, they say—it now obscures the splendour of the fortress as Cow
Castle is approached upstream. Until it is felled the newcomer to Exmoor
will not easily appreciate the strategic instincts of the Iron Age men; and
in any case the trees are utterly alien to the spirit of the place.

The bare grandeur of the moorland is left behind once Landacre Bridge is
reached, for the Barle flows under its graceful arches into cultivated
enclosures on its way to Withypool.† The earliest known reference to
Withypool is the Domesday entry that mentions Dodo, Almer and Godric,
three 'foresters of Widepolla'. As was seen in Chapter One, Withypool has
had a long and close connection with the Forest, and this reference to
Saxon foresters shows that even before the Norman Conquest Exmoor was
used as a game preserve, though it was the Normans who systematised
previous custom, introduced the full harshness of Forest Law and, under
Robert de Odburville, first Norman Lord of the Manor and probably first
Warden of Exmoor,‡ employed Withypool men on clearly defined Forest
duties and created the Free Suitors. Their duties and privileges (outlined
in Chapter One) lasted as long as the Forest: and until James Boevey, for
his own devious ends, moved the Swainmote Court to Simonsbath it was
held in Landacre fields or the Withypool inn, thus marking Withypool as
the moorland 'capital' until the second half of the seventeenth century.

These long-gone events add considerably to the interest of what is
undoubtedly a pretty and well-sited village, clustering mainly on the north
bank of the river and backed closely by the sheltering hills. Though not

---

* Pronounced '*Lanacker*'.

† A very detailed account of the village and its common may be found in *The Exmoor Review*,
Nos. 7, 8 and 9.

‡ There are doubtful points, closely discussed by MacDermot in his *History*.

old, its bridge is a fine feature; and the parish church of St. Andrew combines a variety of architecture in pleasant fashion. Some have considered that its curious arcade was a local attempt to copy the one at Winsford. The total effect is typical of the moorland—low, grey, weather-beaten. The inn and the Post Office (general stores and petrol too) provide a centre, and the bright houses and gardens, the excellent fishing and superb scenery ensure success with visitors. But, like all the moorland villages, Withypool has a declining population and its future as a thriving community is imperilled. Primary industry—farming, forestry, quarrying—needs less manpower as mechanisation develops, and the crafts and small industries that once provided secondary employment are in decline. In 1963 the Exmoor Society, using a grant from the Dartington Hall Trust, commissioned a survey of Exford, Winsford and Withypool to investigate present problems and to look for possible solutions. Copies of this report—most ably conducted by Captain Philip Gibbs, R.N. of Winsford—were lodged with the County Planning Department at Taunton and in the archives of the Exmoor Society; and in *The Exmoor Review*, No. 8, Victor Bonham-Carter discussed in some detail the steps that must be taken if the moorland settlements are to be revitalised. Basing his suggestions on the facts revealed in the Gibbs Report he argued for the establishment of new forms of secondary employment to take the place of the old crafts and small industries, adducing the example of Switzerland and Germany, where village workshops in such trades as tool-making, electronic components, watchmaking, bookbinding, textiles and cabinetry play an important part in the national economy. His plea for research into the problem and the establishment of a pilot scheme on Exmoor is worth urgent consideration for, as he put it, "social vitality is closely linked to economics" and villages cannot long survive in a vacuum. Visitors to Withypool—and many return year after year—who take pleasure in identifying themselves with the life of the community as well as in relaxation, scenery and sport could find added interest and purpose in their holidays through an informed concern not only with the village's history but with its future, too.

Dominating the village to the south-west is the huge dome of the Common, capped by Brightworthy Barrows. The moorland vista from the summit is superb, and many would rate the Common and the adjacent Withypool Hill (1,306 feet; also barrow-crowned and the site of a magnificent stone circle) as among Exmoor's finest scenes. It would be difficult to find an area that more strikingly embodies characteristic scenery, more vividly symbolises Exmoor history from prehistoric to modern times, or more sharply presents the problems that—while being to some extent inherent in rural life in an industrial age and, therefore, endemic throughout rural Britain—are particularly acute in a National Park. Nobody who wants to understand Exmoor can neglect the Withypool area, preparing himself by a careful reading of "Withypool Common: A Study in Depth", *The Exmoor Review*, No. 9. The problems of Exmoor as a National Park are discussed in Chapter Thirteen of this book. Here, it is sufficient to quote the words of Geoffrey Sinclair in the 'Study' just mentioned in which he takes Withypool Common as typifying the dilemmas, and in carefully surveying its present use draws conclusions about policies that are desirable for the future:

> At present, faced with declining profits, the hill farmer tends to do one of two things: either he fences and cultivates open moorland; or he concentrates on his in-bye land and reduces expenditure on the hill. In the first case moorland begins to vanish; and in the second it deteriorates agriculturally. Further, if hill land is actually abandoned it soon reverts to scrub or swamp, which is useless to farmer and public alike. But the multiple use of moorland can be achieved, if hill farming and amenity on Exmoor are recognised as being mutually dependent.

In the family records of the Miltons of Withypool the life of several generations of Exmoor people is revealed. The family goes back to the seventeenth century, and Fred Milton of Weatherslade has made available some fascinating information about past times.* The story he tells depicts the struggle of the moorland farmers through centuries of adversity and endeavour: a battle conducted by tough and self-reliant men whose courage and humour reduced the odds against them, and whose individualism—necessary for survival—rarely prevented them from contributing both time and money to the welfare of the little community whose life they shared. Fred Milton's own activities epitomise the lives of his ancestors. He has lived and farmed in Withypool parish all his life. The oldest member of the Commoners' Association, he played a major part in re-establishing Commoners' rights and duties after the upheavals of the second world war, and he is a noted breeder of pure Exmoor ponies. His own words about the hard times of the thirties might have been spoken by his great-great-grandfather who became tenant of Landacre in 1807 "just in the prime of life for hard work":

> In 1930 prices fell badly. Sheep and lambs fetched only a few shillings, two-year-old Devon cattle £10–£12, and Exmoor ponies £2–£3. In the depression that followed, it was very difficult to make a living at farming. But we survived it all.

So little does the breed change.

South and east of Withypool, between the Barle and the Exe, the fine

* *The Exmoor Review*, No. 9, pp. 63–8.

expanse of heather moor called Winsford Hill rises to 1,404 feet at its summit and is conveniently explored either from Withypool or Winsford. At its west and south sides it falls sharply to the Barle which, below Withypool and all the way to Dulverton, is heavily wooded. The hill is National Trust property and deservedly popular with visitors, for it is itself magnificently picturesque and commands extensive views in all directions. Crossed by the modern B 3223 road, it is laced with a network of ancient tracks and these, as well as the numerous antiquities, argue the existence of a considerable and flourishing population in prehistoric times. The Wambarrows at the summit have a vague reputation of being haunted: all three have been despoiled, a fact that may have something to do with this cloudy tradition. They certainly provide an excellent viewpoint. All the landmarks on the Southern Ridge are easily identified and several of Dartmoor's northerly tors can be clearly seen. North-west, the twisting Barle can be followed into the heart of the Forest; slightly east of north, Dunkery stands up boldly.

To the east of the barrows a track leads to the Punchbowl on the north face of the hill. This striking hollow, 200 feet deep, contrasts vividly with the bleakness of the surrounding moor. The rim is pronounced, a narrow circular platform from which to view the Punchbowl, in the basin of which a little stream rises, its banks grass-covered for a few yards before they merge with the rowan- and thorn-covered sides of the Punchbowl. This is a good place for deer. Indeed, the whole of the Winsford Hill area offers considerable delight—ponies, deer and blackcock being prominent—to those who are willing to leave their cars and explore quietly on foot.

A mile along the road from the Wambarrows, near Spire Cross, a track leads to the mysterious Caratacus Stone, officially listed as "an inscribed stone of the Dark Ages".* The stone is five feet three inches in length, one foot three inches being in the ground. It is about six inches thick and over one foot broad and is set at an angle, leaning towards the west and eight degrees out of plumb towards the south. It weighs about seven hundred-weights. It is possible that the stone was erected hundreds of years before it was inscribed and the existence of an ancient trackway alongside, leading to the Barle, strengthens this possibility. But, like most things about the Caratacus Stone, this is guesswork. It was mentioned as a landmark in the Perambulations of 1219 and 1279, but appears to have attracted little attention until John Lloyd Warden Page began his researches in 1890. In the previous centuries a certain amount of folk lore had clustered round it— buried treasure; ghostly horses and waggons rumbling towards the Stone at midnight—but there had been no attempt to uncover its archaeological secrets. Page was baffled by the inscription for a long time but, with the assistance of Professor Rhys, he eventually established it as:

* There is a monograph by Alfred Vowles: *The History of the Caratacus Stone.*

CARAACI

EPVS

Deducing, correctly as was later proved, that 'N' was missing from the beginning of the second word, where a fracture was visible in the Stone, and reading Ā as AT, Page and Rhys arrived at *Carataci Nepos* as the answer. This most probably means 'Kinsman of Caratacus', though 'Nephew' and 'Grandson' have been suggested. In 1908 the fragment bearing the missing 'N' was discovered and restored to its proper place.

There is no evidence that the Stone is sepulchral, and what precise interpretation should be placed upon it is not known. It is very unlikely that whoever had the Stone inscribed was either the grandson or the nephew of the great Silurian leader, but the fame of Caratacus was clearly being invoked for a purpose, and what little is known of conditions in the Dark Ages permits a fair guess. The withdrawal of Roman power left the Dumnonii of Exmoor exposed to the pressure of Saxon invaders. Sometime in the fifth century the local chief inscribed the Stone in Latin and proclaimed himself 'Kinsman of Caratacus', thus at once laying claim to the inheritance of Roman might and the courage of a British leader. We cannot know for how long the gesture was efficacious.

The shelter now protecting the Stone prevents further weathering, though many regret its shape and consider it quite unsuitable for this intriguing monument.

The road south-west from Spire Cross leads to Tarr Steps, another of Exmoor's mysteries, though in this case the function is plain enough. The dispute centres on the age of this ancient bridge, some experts maintaining that it is prehistoric, others that it is medieval. Even those who deny its extreme antiquity concede that it cannot be later than the thirteenth century; and all agree that it is probably the finest bridge of its type in England. Comparison with the famous 'clapper' at Postbridge on Dartmoor is highly favourable to the Exmoor example. The Barle is 120 feet wide at this point (there is evidence to suggest that it was considerably wider when the bridge was built) and the 'Steps' have seventeen spans consisting of flat stone slabs supported on piers laid on the river bed. The slabs average seven feet in length and about four feet in width. One of the larger ones weighs about two tons, a figure that gives some idea of the immense labour involved in the construction. The up-stream piers are protected from the rushing current by sloping stones, resting on the river bed at one end and angled against the piers at the other. Including the paved approaches, the bridge is about 180 feet long and stands some three feet above the surface of the river.

The name 'Tarr' may derive from the Celtic 'Tochar', a causeway—in some ways a more accurate description of the structure than 'bridge'—and certainly it was sited to link ancient trackways, chief of which is the

Winsford Hill ridgeway, dropping down past Liscombe and ascending again on the other side of the river to Hawkridge and Worth Hill. But both banks of the Barle at this point, and the sloping hills above them, are rich in prehistoric remains, testifying to a long period of population and continuing needs of travel and trade.

Twice within the last twenty years Tarr Steps has sustained serious damage. In 1947 an immense tree trunk moving at high speed down the swollen river rammed the central pier and then swung broadside on. Other debris then piled up until the pressure carried away a section of the bridge. Repairs were carried out with great skill by a local Territorial R.E. unit. In 1952, the year of the Lynmouth flood, the damage was much greater.* All but one span was swept away. A stone weighing about a ton was carried 157 feet downstream and, such was the turbulence, another weighing three-quarters of a ton was swept thirty-five feet transversely across the river. Most of the other dispersed stones lay within thirty feet of their original site, to which they were patiently and carefully restored by the Bridge Engineer of the Somerset County Council whose detailed survey of Tarr Steps, once it had become the Council's responsibility, enabled every stone to be identified.

Below Tarr Steps, at the foot of Hawkridge, the Barle and the Danes Brook meet in thick woodland. The confluence is a wild romantic spot. Above, towers the ridge, its sides wooded, its top bare. The hamlet is well-named, perched high on its hill, and its church must have one of the finest Norman doorways in all Somerset. The ridge track leads down through the woods to the two 'castles' that guard the valley: Brewer's and Mounsey. Where a 'clammer' now spans the water there is an ancient ford, a sufficient explanation for the siting of these earthworks. Both are grown over now and hard to find. Mounsey, on the north bank, is the more impressive: age-old when it got its Norman name. Its rampart can be traced for part of its course round the hill top—some of the core stones are huge—but, like Brewer's, the fort can no longer be appreciated as a stronghold, choked as it is with bracken and saplings.

Past New Invention—where a laundry was once established—the winding, wooded river hurries into Dulverton. The riverside track can be followed into the town and is greatly preferable to the road, picturesque though that is. The walker is now down at water level, now raised so high above the river that he looks down on the tops of trees growing by the bank: an incomparable riverside walk for the Exmoor visitor who wishes to learn about the animals and plants of the Park.

Dulverton itself has considerable charm, making an excellent base for Exmoor travel. The big church is impressively sited at the top of Fore

* See "The Lynmouth Flood of August 1952": published by The Institution of Civil Engineers, 1953. Further reference is made to this paper in Chapter Twelve.

Street, but it was, unhappily, the object of more than common zeal when the Victorians destroyed so much beauty and called the process 'restoration'. The light spaciousness of the interior and the fine proportions remain.

It is an old joke that in Dulverton the 'Lamb' lies down with the 'Lion'; a happy if improbable circumstance. These two inns are among the excellent amenities of a town which contrives to cater for the needs of its many visitors without losing its sense of identity. The shops are stocked surprisingly well for so small a place in such a rural setting, reminding the visitor that, as in Blackmore's day, Dulverton is the metropolis for the hundreds of countryfolk who come in from the moorland parishes. A central space by the Town Hall provides manoeuvring room for cars, but the main impression is of narrow streets and cottage architecture of quiet beauty.

Two miles from Dulverton, just north of Exebridge, the Barle and the Exe meet at last. Born so close to each other in the heart of the Forest, the two rivers sweep east and west round the base of lofty Pixton Hill (site of the fine Herbert house called Pixton Park) before the Exe rather unfairly captures the Barle just south of the boundary of the Exmoor National Park.

CHAPTER EIGHT

The Exe Valley

FROM Coppleham Cross down to its confluence with the Barle the river
Exe flows through a wooded valley. With the Minehead road (A 396) as its
neighbour it divides the Exmoor hills from the Brendons, marking the
contrast between these two adjacent but strikingly different sub-regions of
the National Park. A belt of combe land on the west bank hides the bare
moorland from the traveller, but the open spaces are not far away,
whereas to the east woodland and cultivation predominate and comparatively little moor survives. The whole of this section of the valley provides
harbouring for the deer, herds of twenty-five being common, though their
excellent camouflage conceals them from the hasty or impatient gaze of
visitors who expect them to be on show. Even casual observation, however,
will note three features between Dulverton and Coppleham Cross: the
large deer sanctuary in Barlynch Woods; the lovely remains of St.
Nicholas's Priory now incorporated in the walls of Barlynch Abbey; and
the fine structure of Chilly Bridge. Just north of the bridge, at well-named
Bridgetown, the Rock Inn and the delightful river-skirted cricket ground
(where even moderate hitting can interrupt play for a lost ball) evoke an
authentic village flavour, rare in these hill and valley hamlets. Above, and
on the Brendon side, Exton is a most picturesquely-sited place whose
church is well worth visiting for its Norman traces.

At Coppleham Cross the river makes a right-angled bend southwards
after a twisting and partly-wooded course down from Winsford, claimed by
many as the prettiest of the moorland villages. There are six bridges, for
both the Exe and the Winn brook—from which the village takes its
name—find it hard to go straight hereabouts. The church has several
notable features, the nave and aisles being under one external roof (an
uncommon sight in Somerset) though inside they have separate waggon-
roofs. There is a Norman font and it may be that the fifteenth-century
arcades were cut out of the lower part of Norman walls, though the earliest
identifiable work in the fabric seems to be the thirteenth-century lancet
windows in the chancel. The aisles are early fifteenth century, and the
tower, a fine, tall, battlemented structure with a staircase turret, was built
late in that century. There is a magnificent painted panel of the royal arms
of James I, dated 1609, and the Jacobean pulpit and altar rails are con-

sidered to be very good. Winsford was clearly a prosperous place in the early seventeenth century.

With its cluster of bridges—the best is the packhorse bridge by the Vicarage—and the excellent Royal Oak, Winsford makes a good and attractive base for exploring the eastern fringes of the moor, and particularly for visiting the two camps with which the courses of the Exe and Larcombe Brook were defended. Road Castle stands on the highest point of Road Hill; a belt of trees now interposed between the earthworks and the Exe and a track running down to Lyncombe Farm complete a pleasant site, to which is added the interest always inherent in these antiquities. Little serious investigation of Road Castle has yet been made, but its near neighbour on Staddon Hill was thoroughly surveyed by Charles Whybrow in 1965. The Staddon fort lies on a spur between the converging valleys of Larcombe Brook and of another, but anonymous, stream. The combined rivers then join the Exe near Kemps Farm on the south-eastern slopes of Staddon Hill. The main part of the fort is just over 1,000 feet up and the sides of the spur fall steeply to the two streams. Southwards, the land rises steadily to the crest of Staddon Hill. This siting seems to suggest a defensive purpose chiefly concerned with possible penetration from the north, a guess made more probable by the fact that the Staddon camp commands a clear view of the strategically important Harepath, which runs just north of the ramparts. The main defences take the form of a single-walled enclosure, roughly oval and measuring 150 feet from east to west and 135 feet from north to south. The entrance is on the west, and two crossbanks to the south of the fort complete the protection, the outer of the two being much more formidable than the inner. As is common, the Staddon fort presents some enigmatic features. These Exmoor hill camps usually survive in sufficient detail to enable a fair guess to be made as to their approximate date and general purpose, but peculiarities of construction or siting prevent the modern investigator from offering confident and full interpretations. At Staddon the two southward crossbanks end on the brink of the westward valley, where the fall of the land renders further man-made protection superfluous; but between their eastern terminations and the Larcombe Brook valley there is a considerable space of more or less level ground. This appears to be a most vulnerable and obvious gap in a defensive system to the making of which much thought and labour had been devoted. Whybrow's survey discovered no evidence of protective works to guard the undefended space and so—as in the case of Shoulsbarrow—we must question whether Staddon was complete. If it was, we shall never know the reason for the gaps: if it was not, the search for a reason for the sudden termination is at once baffling and intriguing.

Recent spruce plantations on the Staddon spur will in time make further investigation difficult. The main fort and the inner crossbank have not been planted: they are still grass and bracken covered as they have been for many years. But the outer crossbank has been included in the plantation, and damage to the earthwork seems inevitable as the roots grow and spread.

These two hill forts are midway between Winsford and Exford, the next and last village in the valley of Exe; beyond, lies the open moor. The church is high up on a steep hill, and is now known as St. Mary Magdalene's but was formerly dedicated to St. Salvin whom the Revd. Prebendary Chanter identified (in the *Proceedings of the Somerset Archaeological Society*) with a famous West Country saint—Selyf. If he was right, this is another interesting example of Celtic survival of the Saxon invasion (see Chapter One). Perhaps the most interesting feature of the church is its lovely screen. Restorations took place in the 1780s, and again in 1869, with ruthless destruction of the old furnishings. Parts of the original rood screen were lying in the Rectory outhouses for many years, but nothing was done to preserve them and they disappeared. Between 1928 and 1930 a subscription was raised to secure a suitable screen for the church, with the happy result that may now be seen. At St. Audries, near Watchet, a fine fan-vaulted screen of the typical West of England design had been removed when the church was rebuilt in 1858, and though attempts had later been made to replace it the extensive rebuilding prevented that. At considerable expense the beautiful screen was skilfully repaired and moved to Exford.

Another interesting object is the memorial to Robert Baker with its eulogistic, and apparently deserved, epitaph:

... (he) came from Hawkridge young, laboured, thrived, married, and settled in this parish, and changed this life for a better, April 25th, 1730, aged sixty-eight... his extraordinary virtues deserve to be had in everlasting remembrance. His life was a pattern of piety towards God, and integrity towards man; of industry without covetousness; liberality without pride; charity without ostentation ...

A hundred years after Baker's death stories of his good deeds were circulating in Exford* and he established charities in both his native and his adopted parishes.

In Baker's day and for many more afterwards Exford was noted for its 'Revel'. Held on the Saint's Day of the parish, this was the occasion for rejoicing and festivity of an almost Maltese intensity. However, the wrestling-ring, not fireworks, provided the chief attraction. Savage (see footnote) says that the play followed the Devonshire pattern, except that the wrestlers did not pad their legs.

Today,† the village is—despite the extent (6,300 acres) and nature (800

* See James Savage's *History of the Hundred of Carhampton*, 1830.
† There is a good account of present-day Exford in *The Exmoor Review*, No. 7, pp. 41–3.

to 1,550 feet above sea level) of the parish terrain—a close-knit and comparatively thriving community. It exists chiefly on sheep-farming, tourism and hunting. The Devon and Somerset kennels are here and over twelve per cent of the population depends on the employment either directly provided by the Hunt or by the farriery, grooming and horse-hiring required by hunting visitors. (This employment is distinct from the holiday hacking demanded by other visitors.) The two hotels and the guest house (employing full- or part-time about twenty people) have a very long season, due mostly to the hunting. Facts such as these emphasise the part that hunting plays in the life of the National Park.

There is an excellent Youth Hostel, one of four given to the Youth Hostels Association to further the aims of the National Parks Act.* In 1964 the Somerset County Council bought Exe Mead with the aid of a seventy-five per cent grant from the Ministry of Housing and Local Government, later selling it to the Y.H.A. for £10. The main house was repaired and an annexe built (with the help of a grant from the Department of Education and Science) to provide accommodation for fifty hostellers. This very popular hostel makes an excellent base for moorland exploration and with its loose-boxes and paddocks it is ideally equipped and sited for the 'adventure holidays' that appeal to pony-trekking members.

A little-known feature of Exford should attract more visitors than it does. The chapel contains two Burne-Jones windows, presented by Cyril Scott, a composer who lived at Exford during the second world war, and given in memory of two of his friends: T. Holland Smith and Bertram Binyon, neither of whom appears to have had local connections. The windows were put in soon after the war and are an astonishing embellishment of what is in all other respects a typical Nonconformist chapel. They and their setting are well described by Peter Hesp in 'Angels of Exford', *The Exmoor Review*, No. 8.

The best route from Exford to the open moor is along the valley road that leads west and forks at Edgcott, the right-hand branch climbing steeply towards Hillhead Cross and Codsend Moors, the left-hand branch keeping close to the river and swinging due west beyond Downscombe. Here, the road enters the first really spectacular stretch of the great Cleave through which the Exe flows from Prayway Head in the west to Exford in the east. As far as Westermill Farm the steep sides of the valley are enclosed and cultivated; coppices grow here and there, and lanes wind up and down the hills, linking Westermill and Riscombe, Hill Farm and Wellshead with the valley road. There is some arable farming here, and stock raising, and wintering for the moorland flocks. For even in this part of the valley,

* The other three are in the Pembrokeshire, North Yorkshire Moors and Peak National Parks, and further hostels are planned.

which the labour of generations of farmers has snatched for the use of man, there is a perpetual awareness of the wasteland brooding on the western hill tops. A dozen streams hurrying to join the Exe fill the valley with their music, the thin notes of summer deepening to a hoarse roar as the autumn rains begin to fall on the moor.

Beyond Westermill the eastern arm of Rams Combe, down which the Forest Boundary ran, provides the walker with his first extensive moorland prospect. To the north, Long Combe twists through bare hills on its way to Badgworthy, and the rounded summits of Swap Hill, Trout Hill, the Deer Park and Brendon Common can be identified. West, the Cleave of the Exe makes a deep wedge in a tussocky plain; and further on, the western moor is glimpsed when light falls on Dure Down and Hoaroak Hill. To the south, the Southern Ridge rears up, Five Barrows black against the sky; and at its feet the breaking waves of the undulating land south of the Barle.

Surrounded by this magnificence, Warren Farm is splendid in its loneliness. Fronted by the deepening Cleave, the house is linked to the Simonsbath road by a long and skilfully-engineered track that edges laterally across the northern slope of the Cleave, crosses the Exe by a substantial bridge, and contours the southern and higher wall before straightening on the gentler ground to come out of the moor between Cloven Rocks and Honeymead. Warren is an excellent example of a Knight-built farm, substantial within its windbreak, in-fields green and improved, and all around—no less vital to its economy—the moorland grazing for its flocks. It was a common saying once that Warren had the largest dairy in Somerset, but it is hard to understand why this should be since only 'house' cows are kept. Few homesteads in England can rival Warren in the romantic appeal of its setting. Faced by the steep walls of the valley, backed by one of the loneliest and loveliest stretches of the moor, the farm is Wordsworthian in its austere grandeur; "alone amid the heart of many thousand mists".

Not far west of Warren, where the Cleave narrows even more until the southern bank shuts off the distant prospect, is Ravens' Nest. This narrow, scree-strewn cleft in the south wall reaches from the valley bed to the rim of the gorge. Its name is well deserved, for these big birds can often be seen and heard here, the valley echoing their ominous croaking and the fierce western wind buoying their tumbling flight. Further on, the ground is lower and marshy; frequent drainage channels impede the way without perceptibly diminishing the morass. The Simonsbath-Lynton road (B 3223) is just ahead, flanked by Dure Down and Prayway Head. Along this route for centuries the Free Suitors drove the sheep and cattle, and here Frederic Knight's railway was to bring iron from Cornham to the sea.

The Exe is now a very small stream running in a boggy land. It is bridged above Prayway where the spectacular Cleave is left behind. A gate below

Blackpits leads into its 'Plain': its upper course from source to Cleave being so known. Cotton grass and flying bent are the dominant vegetation on the flat wet surface, though the upper slopes of Dure Down, beneath which the river runs, have good, grazed turf. The soil is black, acrid, peaty. Westwards and then south, the track runs by a dwindling river. Another track comes in from Long Chains Combe and, beyond a gate, where in a dozen places water oozes to the surface, with marsh all around and where the path to Hoar Oak crosses the boggy land, the Exe is born. For many the source of the river is a disappointment. They hope for a clear spring and find instead a black bog in a shallow depression: the South Chains Wall runs west across the solitude until it joins the Pinkworthy dam; the hump of Chains Barrow swells up slightly north of west; and all around lies the silence of the innermost moor. The scene at Exe Head has a grandeur of its own.

CHAPTER NINE

The Chains and the Western Moor

PRECISELY to define the area of Exmoor called the Chains is not easy. Identification depends more on vegetation and terrain than on landmarks and boundary lines. It is the largest expanse of level ground on the moor and ranges in altitude from just under 1,500 to nearly 1,600 feet. The Barle, the Exe, the West Lyn and Hoaroak Water all rise on its perimeter, and a not inaccurate description of its extent would be arrived at if a line were drawn on the map connecting these rivers—source to source. Within the area so delimited there are no streams, but an artificial water course—dug for drainage, but not noticeably effective—links the Barle with the West Lyn.

The iron pan (see Chapter Five) is very near the surface of the Chains; drainage is, therefore, restricted and the water table lies at or near ground level. The soil is extremely acid and this fact, coupled with high altitude and rainfall, low temperatures and strong winds, has resulted in a remarkable vegetation. The blanket bog covering the Chains supports the largest area of deer sedge (*Scirpus Cespitosus*) in Southern England. Experts consider that this vegetation represents the climax moorland vegetation of the Chains and that it has been virtually unchanged since the climatic deterioration of the later Bronze Age. Deer sedge, thriving on the rigours of the weather, tolerating the acidity of the soil, and withstanding grazing, has the Chains in practically sole sway.* Only on Chains Barrow itself, higher and drier than the bog, is there much variety of vegetation.

The walker intent on a thorough exploration of Exmoor will cross the Chains and will find the sense of achievement ample compensation for the laborious passage. It is heavy going. Even in summer the land is soggy, and though no danger is involved a wetting is likely. It cannot be too strongly emphasised that nobody should attempt the Chains in mist or after dusk, for even in full daylight each new foothold must be tested, and the firmer tussocks are often too far apart for an easy stride and must be jumped for. Mist comes down with alarming rapidity: one moment the skies are clear; seconds later, the first ominous swirls rise in the west and the traveller is enveloped in the wet opacity before he has time to do more than take a

* For a detailed account see *The Exmoor Review*, No. 2.

hurried bearing on one of the few available landmarks. Then he must use his skill, indeed. The compass will get him back to some identifiable spot from the nebulous world into which he has been plunged, but only experience, agility, and a good deal of luck will save him from plunging knee-deep into the pitfalls that surround him.

Fenwick Bisset characterised the rigours of the Chains neatly at a hunt dinner. Contrasting the delights of hunting with the pains of legislation he said, "I assure you that I would far sooner be anywhere on Exmoor, *except the Chains*, in the thickest fog, than in the House of Commons".

The best route (from the east) to Chains Barrow is along the South Chains Wall until the mound and its triangulation pillar are in opposite view. Then the comparative security of the wall must be left and the walker proceeds in a straight line to the barrow. (There are no 'easier' routes inside the Chains, so there is nothing to be lost by walking along straight lines.) The moorland views from the barrow amply reward the determined explorer. Immediately to the north lies Long Chains Combe (the western arm of the forked valley of Hoaroak Water), a superbly wild rift, running under the massive dome of Hoaroak Hill. From east to west a succession of northward-flowing streams can be identified: Farley Water and Hoaroak, separated by Cheriton Ridge; Binchinny Combe divided from Ruckham by Thorn Hill, at the northern foot of which the two streams unite to form the West Lyn. These steep-sided valleys cut deep clefts into the north front of the Chains, jagging the plateau into a hill and valley system of some complexity and great beauty.

To the south, the valleys of the Barle tributaries similarly etch the opposite termination of the Chains: Lime Combe in the east; then Tang's Bottom and its big western fork; and two unnamed combes running into the Barle at Driver and Pinkworthy farms.

Chains Barrow, in fact, is in the centre of the watershed that separates the tributaries of the East and West Lyn rivers in the north from those of the Barle in the south; a fact that accounts for the scenic splendour commanded from the barrow summit—a panorama of the heart of Exmoor treasured in the recollection of all who make the pilgrimage through the Chains.

Westward from the barrow, the further moor unfolds; and nobody who has seen this distant view will be content until he has penetrated the Chapman Barrows area, richest of all, perhaps, in archaeological interest.

The South Chains wall leads straight to Pinkworthy Pond, and from there it is a simple matter to reach Wood Barrow Gate, an opening in one of the beech barriers planted in Frederic Knight's day to provide shelter from the killing winds. Just west of the gate is Wood Barrow, standing on the old Forest and the present county and parish boundaries. In Thomas Westcote's *A View of Devonshire in MDCXXX* he tells of a 'conjurer'—

such preternaturally wise men (and women) have ceased only within living memory to flourish on Exmoor—who divined that there was a 'brass pan full of treasure' in the barrow. Persuading some Challacombe men to accompany him—and arranging with them a satisfactory division of the spoils—he began to open the mound. When the centre was neared a deadly faintness stole over his assistants. This appears to have been a common hazard of barrow-rifling, and the conjurer kept his head better than the others, due no doubt to his professional poise. Even he, however, was overcome when a loud clap of thunder resounded and a shaft of lightning arrowed into the very heart of the barrow. When the treasure-hunters recovered they saw an empty 'brass' pan, green and corroded save for a shining spot in the bottom where the treasure had been. The conjurer told his terrified associates that he had seen the treasure but, as the thunder roared and the lightning flashed, 'they'—presumably the spirits guarding the barrow—had snatched it away.

From the top of Wood Barrow—where a sunken circle indicates that digging has taken place, though we are not thereby bound to accept Westcote's account—Longstone Barrow is in view, and further on, the Chapman Barrows. Unless the explorer knows exactly where to look it is better to use Longstone Barrow as the lookout post for the Longstone itself, since it is difficult—except in very favourable light—to pick it out from Wood Barrow. Even from Longstone Barrow, the weird, crooked figure is not always easy to find. The Longstone is the most impressive standing stone on the whole of Exmoor. It is a nine foot high slate menhir, its greatest breadth being two feet, eight inches, though its thickness nowhere exceeds six or seven inches. Its widest face is in the north-east and south-west plane, a fact that may throw light on the enigma of its siting.

There is general agreement that the Longstone is contemporary with the nearby barrows, and it is difficult to doubt that the menhir had a phallic significance—its shape hardly permits of any other interpretation, and in this respect it is strictly comparable with stones elsewhere (in Transjordan, for example) about which there is no controversy. What has always been a matter for dispute is why this particular site was chosen, for the Longstone stands in a shallow depression which makes it much less conspicuous from a distance than would otherwise be expected from its height and the labour expended in transporting and setting up so large a stone. A people who were willing to undertake so difficult an operation, who attached religious importance to the stone, and who selected prominent sites for their burial mounds, appear to have chosen the site for the Longstone with remarkably little care or skill. So it has always been concluded, and so the writer of this book believed until exploration of Swincombe provided him with an explanation.

A little to the south of the Longstone a combe leads almost due west, deepening rapidly before it joins Swincombe at a point where the course of the latter is north-south. The river Bray flows through Swincombe and at and below the junction of the two valleys there is a striking outcrop of slate. From this rock pile a direct view up the tributary valley is obtained, and beyond the combe-head the Longstone stands up clear, a thin black line on the rim of the moor. This is by far the most impressive distant view of the Longstone, a fact made the more significant by the nature and structure of Swincombe Rocks themselves. For the rocks are the obvious source of the Longstone: not much surface quarrying would be needed to strike out other menhirs from the exposed strata, the layers of which would split naturally and readily into masses corresponding in size and shape to the megalith now standing on the moor. These two deep combes were quite clearly the homes of the people who set up the stone. Here, they found not only their altar, but shelter from storms, wood for their fires and huts, and water in abundance. On the skyline of their little world they erected a symbol to propitiate their fertility gods, placing it to the north-east where it would flame in the rising sun. The outline of the stone was clear enough for the valley people to be aware of it as they went about their tasks; its site was close to the route that the hunters took to the open moor; and the way up was easy enough for the whole community, young and old alike, to gather there for the festivals and ceremonies.

Between Swincombe and the Longstone combe is a hillside called Radworthy. Crossing it on foot, one comes across low, crumbling stone walls enclosing rectangular 'fields', though pierced by big gaps. Looking down on these relics from the elevation of the Rocks the fields stand out clearly as in an aerial photograph. This was the site of the farm and farmhouse built by Walter and Jeffery Lock in the late seventeenth century. Boevey brought one of his innumerable law suits against the brothers, alleging that they had no pasturing rights and that, as Warden, he could claim dues from them for their grazing on the commons, though their farm was west of the Forest boundary. It was a typical Boevey manoeuvre when he was harrying the little men whose property lay close to his empire. It is known that he lost his case, but nothing more is known of the Locks and of the house they built in so wild a spot. In all probability, though they won, the expense and worry of protracted litigation, spun out with all Boevey's resources of money, influence and cunning, proved too much for them.

Though there is a direct and easy route from Swincombe Rocks to Chapman Barrows, a circular approach, taking in Challacombe with its pleasant inn and—at Challacombe Mill, right on the National Park boundary—its intriguing church is well worth while. The parish itself merits study, and Westcote's account of the strange happenings at Broken-barrow throws light on the mingled greed and superstitious awe excited in bygone years by the many archaeological remains of the district. Broken-barrow, as the name clearly shows, is an opened tumulus, near which stood a cottage built by the man of whom this story was told:

A daily labouring man, by the work of his hand and the sweat of his brow, having gotten a little money, was desirous to have a place to rest himself in old age, and therefore bestowed it on some acres of waste land, and began to build a house thereon, near, or not far from, one of those barrows, named Broaken Barrow, whence he fetched stones and earth to further his work; and having pierced into the bowels of the hillock, he found therein a little place, as it had been a large oven, fairly, strongly, and closely walled up; which comforted him much, hoping that some good would befall him, that there might be some treasure there hidden to maintain him more liberally, and with less labour in his old years; wherewith encouraged, he plies his work earnestly until he had broken a hole through this wall, in the cavity whereof he espied an earthen pot, which caused him to multiply his strokes, until he might make the orifice thereof large enough to take out the pot, which his earnest desire made him not long a-doing; but as he thrust in his arm, and fastened his hand thereon, suddenly he heard, or seemed to hear, the noise of the treading or trampling of horses, coming, as he thought, towards him; which caused him to forbear, and arise from the place, fearing the comers would take his purchase from him (for he assured himself it was treasure); but looking about every way to see what company this was, he saw neither horse nor man in view. To the pot again he goes, and had the like success a second time; and yet, looking all about, could ken nothing. At the third time he brings it away, and finds therein only a few ashes and bones, as if they had been of children, or the like. But the man, whether by the fear, which yet he denied, or other causes, which I cannot comprehend, in a very short time after lost senses both of sight and hearing, and in less than three months consuming died. He was in all his lifetime accounted an honest man; and he constantly reported this, divers times, to men of good quality; with protestations to the truth thereof, even to his death.

Even though Westcote was intelligent and well-informed, his contemptuous reference to 'a few ashes and bones' reveals total ignorance of the true nature of the 'treasure'—an ignorance typical of centuries of barrow-digging during which incalculable harm was done.

The lane to Withecombe Farm and the track beyond the farm lead to Chapman Barrows, the most striking group of tumuli on the moor. There are eleven in all, eight of which mark the boundary between the parishes of Parracombe and Challacombe. This western moor must have supported a considerable population in the Bronze Age for it has a remarkable density of prehistoric remains: the Chapman Barrows, Longstone Barrow, the

Longstone, and Wood Barrow, closely neighboured by stone monuments on Challacombe Common and the Longstone Allotment, with two good standing stones on Lyn Down.

The site of the Chapman Barrows is superb. Eastwards lies the whole of Exmoor, the rolling moor lines seen nowhere to better advantage than here. Dartmoor looms up to the south; and to the west the eye can travel over the hills and villages of north-west Devon, backed by the shining Severn Sea. At all seasons, in calm and in storm, this is a wonderful piece of Exmoor.

But neither the magnificent setting nor the massive bulk of the mounds has protected the barrows from mutilation. The next to the westernmost was opened in 1885 by one Thomas Antell at the direction of the farmer for whom he was working.* Their original quest was for fencing stones, but when they came upon the circle of retaining stones at the base of the mound and the stone chamber in the centre, they at once agreed upon terms for the division of the spoils. Inside the chamber they found a 'steyn' (urn) covered over with a flat, thin stone. They broke open the urn, which was two feet high and one foot, six inches in diameter, to find only bones inside. Antell, when interrogated by archaeologists, maintained that the bones were those of a sheep, and said that he had seen enough sheep bones in his time to know what he was talking about. He may have believed this, but a disinclination to admit to tampering with human remains is common enough, and there is of course no doubt that the steyn was a funereal urn.

In 1905 the Rev. J.F. Chanter, a local and very active antiquary, opened another of the barrows. The mound was nine feet high and 100 feet in diameter. In the centre was a burial place containing human bones and teeth, from the evidence of which the occupant was deduced to be an adult well past middle age.

There is, then, ample proof—though the barrows await full investigation by modern skills—that the Chapman tumuli are the memorial of a forgotten race who buried their notable dead on this swelling upland and who, in all probability, also raised the crooked Longstone. The dead whose remains lie in the great mounds once knew the meaning of that weird menhir and took part in its rites.

The Negus Stone is a modern memorial in the vicinity of the Chapman Barrows. The fast-fading inscription on the granite block tells that it was erected to the memory of Robin Negus, a boy 'who loved this place'. The memorials of Exmoor are in great need of the hammer and chisel of a twentieth-century 'Old Mortality', such havoc do the gales and rain wreak on any lettering.

* See *Transactions of the Devonshire Association*, Vol. XXXVII.

North of the barrows the bare moor merges into the hills and valleys to the rear of Lynton. The scenery in this area is extremely fine, and in striking contrast to the rolling lines of the inner moor. Ilkerton Ridge is an especially lovely hill with beautiful valleys to the east and west of it. Shallowford lies on a track worth following through splendid scenery to Barbrook, and from there another road leads south along the slopes of the West Lyn Valley past Stock Castle to Furzehill. This area is incomparable walking country, though the steep combes are tiring. Over Furzehill Common and into Hoaroak Water is a route that all lovers of Exmoor should take, not only for the scenery but to make a pilgrimage to the most celebrated of all the Forest boundary marks, set on a slope of one of Exmoor's most beautiful valleys. The present Hoar Oak Tree is the sole survivor of the half dozen or so saplings planted when the 'Second' Hoar Oak Tree fell in 1917. Photographs of the veteran show that it had attained no very great height or girth in its 254 years of life. Yet it was a remarkable tree for the moorland on which anything larger than a thorn bush is regarded with something like the veneration that Dr. Johnson said the Scots would have for his oak stick. The new tree is very small as yet and covered with a grey lichen which cannot be doing it any good. Even so, it is alive, though its growth must be slow and painful.

Between the Hoar Oak Tree and Saddle Gate, two miles to the west, some of the old Forest boundary stones still remain. To the east, there is a striking stretch of Forest Wall, straight and true, across Cheriton Ridge and down into Farley Water—a lovely combe. Bare, narrow, and steep at first, its eastern wall broken by side combes which carry tributary streams rushing furiously down valleys as precipitous as Farley itself, it is wooded in its lower course. All these streams are unbelievably clear—trout streams every one of them. Dippers flash over the water; stonechats, redstarts, chiffchaffs and wagtails abound; and even now blackcock occasionally make off in low, whirring flight across the moor, startling the walker who has climbed the lower slopes to avoid the boggy patches by the water.

From Farley Water Farm to Brendon Two Gates lies the finest stretch of moorland road in the Park, with the possible exception of the Exford—Whit Stones route. The B3223 should be walked, not driven over. It winds unfenced between the uplands of Farley Hill, Middle Hill and Pig Hill to the west and Shilstone Hill and Brendon Common to the east. As glorious an expanse of open moorland as the heart could wish for spreads out on either side of the walker who follows the hilly highway along which John Knight's carriage so often rolled in those early, optimistic days, the Forest kingdom that he set out to conquer spreading its wastes all around.

CHAPTER TEN

Badgworthy Water and The Doone Country

THIS part of Exmoor has as its western border the Simonsbath-Brendon road (B3223), and as its eastern limit the Exford-Porlock road. It is bounded in the north by the Porlock-Lynmouth road (A 39) from Whit Stones to Lynmouth, and in the south by the Exe Cleave from Westermill Farm to Prayway Head. Its most picturesque feature is the Badgworthy Valley which, with its side-combes and fishtailing headwaters, cuts deeply into the high, bare moorland; a pattern repeated on a smaller scale to the east of Badgworthy, where Chalk Water and Weir Water flow south to north before swinging due west into the deepening and wooded valleys of Oare Water and the East Lyn.

The best-known route into Badgworthy is from the north, by Malmsmead and Oare, but those who are prepared for a longer walk should choose the routes from Brendon Two Gates or from Warren Farm. The latter should not be attempted until the walker has built up a fair body of Exmoor knowledge—and should not be attempted at all unless a wet and quite tiring walk is of no concern. It is possible to detour the West Pinford bog and come onto Trout Hill by a reasonably dry route; but it calls for careful map-reading and a certain amount of luck, since the wet patches shift and vary greatly in difficulty from one visit to the next. The reward of perseverance is great: the walk along Trout Hill and down into Badgworthy commands some of the finest views on the whole of Exmoor. Rather than attempting a direct approach, try heading for Trout Hill from the north bank of the Cleave at a point directly opposite Ravens' Nest, for there is an excellent landmark here: a turf-grown bank that runs as sure as a Roman road from Exe Cleave across Trout Hill to Badgworthy Water. Close by the bank, and on it, the walking is firm, yet to east and west the slopes of the hill drop rapidly to the two Pinford bogs—not dangerous, but very wet and tiring areas to cross. Both of these marshes are threaded by streams that join Long Combe; streams that pursue no clearly defined courses in their upper lengths, but fill each depression with black, peaty water as they well sluggishly out of the uneven ground. Sprained ankles and wet feet are the worst that can happen in the Pinfords, but they are not very pleasant features of a walk.

Trout Hill itself has many moods. In full summer the yellow light that dominates the grass moor areas of Exmoor is more strikingly apparent here than anywhere else. The coarse vegetation wilts in the sun and the moor is bathed in a golden shimmer. From late autumn to early spring there is little juice in the grass, and when the west wind is tearing across the hill the brittle blades snap off and whirl away eastwards, blowing so thickly sometimes that the walker's head must be lowered against the assault of the flying bent.

The turf bank leads down a long decline, dropping sharply at last into Badgworthy and passing near to a fine stone row well worth seeking out, even though the search may delay entrance into what many have claimed to be Exmoor's finest combe. Badgworthy Water is formed by the junction of two considerable combes: Hoccombe Water flowing in from the west; and Long Combe flowing down from Larkbarrow in the east. The upper reaches of Badgworthy pass through bare, precipitous hills, but as the valley widens the lower slopes display a profusion of vegetation. Perhaps this contrast accounts for its fascination; and no visitor who makes the usual entrance from the north should fail to walk up Badgworthy at least as far as Badgworthy Lees in order to enjoy the wilder as well as the gentler aspects of this famous combe.

For Badgworthy is of course renowned not only for its beauty but as the heart of the Doone country. Thousands who visit Badgworthy every year come away convinced that the main combe is 'the Doone Valley'. This is not so, though there is little doubt that R.D. Blackmore drew on many features of Badgworthy when describing the Doones' home in his novel. The true Doone Valley lies at the lower end of Hoccombe Combe, a tributary that joins Badgworthy immediately north of Hoccombe Water, the two streams being separated by Badgworthy Hill. Those who have the curiosity to investigate the Doone Valley with a view to comparing it with Blackmore's description should bear in mind what the novelist himself said about his fictitious treatment of the scenery (the words are taken from a letter that he wrote to James F. Muirhead who compiled *Baedeker's Handbook of Great Britain* in 1887):

> When I wrote *Lorna Doone* the greatest effort of my imagination would have been to picture its success. If I had dreamed that it would have been more than a book of the moment, the descriptions of scenery—which I know as well as I know my garden—would have been kept nearer to their fact. I romanced therein, not to mislead any others, but solely for the uses of my story.

There is no doubt that anybody who visits the real Doone Valley, however delighted he has been with the grandeur of Badgworthy, will be disappointed by the contrast between Blackmore's description and the realities of the Valley itself. The question at once arises: "Then why not call Badgworthy Water the Doone Valley and forget about the far from impressive side-combe?" And the answer is that lower Hoccombe Combe must have provided the basis for the fictional Doone Valley, for it is there that the ancient Badgworthy settlement was placed; and it was there, if anywhere (a point soon to be discussed), that the Doones lived.

The antiquity of the Badgworthy village is very great. Charles Whybrow gives this account in 'Antiquary's Exmoor—II' (See *The Exmoor Review*, No. 9):

> There are in and around Exmoor a number of deserted medieval settle-ments *which probably originated in late Saxon times*, the houses being rebuilt in stone or cobb during the twelfth century and abandoned two or three centuries later, although the sites have sometimes been reoccupied on a small scale in comparatively recent years. The best known of these deserted settlements is at Badgworthy, where the so-called Doones' houses are in reality the ruins of typical medieval two-roomed long-houses of about the twelfth century. The room at the higher end of such houses was occupied by the owner and his family, while that at the lower end was the byre. There are about half-a-dozen long-houses at Badgworthy, as well as a number of barns, two of which contain corn-drying kilns, used for parching grain in the hope that it would keep until the next crop ripened.

After the Norman Conquest the Badgworthy settlement was in the possession of the Pomeroy family for about 100 years, but sometime before 1189 Henry Pomeroy gave "the land of the hermits of Baga Wordia to the Brethren of the Hospital of Jerusalem". One of the signatures to this deed of gift—'Roberto clerico de Bradeworda'—shows that there was a priest at the settlement. From the Hospital the Badgworthy property passed to Walter Bagworthy or Badgworthy, and when—in 1400—his son John passed the land to Robert Lord Harrington, Lord of the Manor of Brendon, we learn from his bailiff's accounts that there were cottages and a farm there. By 1430 the same accounts reveal that there was difficulty in letting the property, and between that date and the nineteenth century there are no records of occupation. A former inhabitant of Oare, however, told MacDermot—a man not readily impressed by mere hearsay—that his father remembered an old man named Tucker living there with his grand-daughter. Both perished in a blizzard on their way home from Simonsbath.

The remains of the Badgworthy buildings are not striking. The walls have crumbled to ground level and are overgrown with grass and brambles. The more prominent ruins further up the Doone Valley have nothing to do with the ancient settlement, being all that is left of a shepherd's cottage built in the 1860s. During the construction of this cottage—later christened by and commercialised under the name of 'Lorna's Cot'—stones were removed from the Badgworthy houses, hastening their decay to such an extent that it is impossible now to visualise the ruins as Blackmore knew them. Jan Ridd described his mother's glimpse of the Doone settlement in these words:

> . . . on either bank, were covered houses, built of stone, square and roughly cornered, set as if the brook were meant to be the street between them. Only one room high they were, and not placed opposite each other, but in and out as skittles are; only that the first of all, which proved to be the captain's, was a sort of double house . . . Fourteen cots my mother counted.

An indefatigable researcher, Alfred Vowles, identified exactly fourteen separate ruins in the Doone Valley, and though his count does not tally with Charles Whybrow's (see above) his monograph *The Doone Valley** left little room to doubt that the lower end of Hoccombe Combe was the setting of Blackmore's Doone Valley.

The next problem is the Waterslide, for there is nothing whatever in Hoccombe Combe which could have suggested this to Blackmore. Further north, however, a clue is found. Beyond the Doone Valley a stream called Withycombe Ridge Water (so-named on the six-inch map) flows down the hillside of Badgworthy Lees to join Badgworthy Water. Beyond (north of) this point the trees thicken and Lank Combe joins the main valley at the southern edge of the gnarled Badgworthy Wood where a path overhung with bushes leads up Lank Combe to the Waterslide. Nowhere near so dramatic as the feature described in the novel, this watercourse is nevertheless an interesting sight. Three smooth rock slabs extend for about thirty feet and then drop steeply, making a sharp division between the upper and lower courses of the stream. Even when the water is low its smooth, sliding motion over the slabs is worth travelling up Lank Combe to see. In spate, the fall is impressive; and powerful enough to remind the observer of Blackmore's words as he sees the 'long pale slide of water' coming smoothly towards him before pitching into the pool and completing its journey to Badgworthy in a succession of foaming bounds.

Apart from 'The Doones' War Path'—a track curving boldly up the east wall of Badgworthy—there is nothing else in this valley which may be specifically associated with the murderous outlaws, but a love of *Lorna Doone* and a little imagination will go a long way in Badgworthy Water, and we should at least do the author the justice of remembering that he was writing a romance and not a guide to Exmoor.

The contemporary success and continuing popularity of *Lorna Doone*— filmed and televised as well as read—have created intense interest in the

---

* Cox, Sons & Co., Minehead, 1929.

Doone legends, and there is much speculation about the degree of fact underlying the stories. Before turning to this topic, however, it is necessary to dispose of the widely-held belief that Blackmore invented the Doones. A.G. Bradley* advanced this theory with great confidence, describing how he and some friends when riding near Brendon Two Gates encountered the then Headmaster of Winchester, who asked to be directed to the Doone Valley. Completely baffled, they confessed their ignorance of any such place or any such people. Trying again, the tourist asked if they could tell him the way to Badgworthy Water: this they were, of course, able to do. Bradley comments that as far back as the early spring of 1870 nobody on Exmoor known to him had any knowledge at all of the Doones or of wild doings 'out over'. The Doones, he said, were Blackmore's creation, and any legends about them had sprung up after the publication of *Lorna Doone* in 1869.

But there is overwhelming evidence to prove the existence of a Doone tradition before Blackmore wrote his novel and to support his own contention (stoutly maintained in his frequent footnotes) that he was drawing on established legends widely circulated and commonly believed. Indeed, the wording of several of the footnotes (e.g. "... this vile deed was done beyond all doubt") shows that Blackmore himself whole-heartedly believed in the Doone stories that he used, though he was frank in admitting his own additions to them for fictitious purposes.

A summary of the evidence may be welcome. The Vicar of Lynton, the Revd. Matthew Mundy, collected many of the Doone stories and they were written out by the girls at Lynton National School in 1853. The Revd. J.F. Chanter stated that one of these manuscripts was in his father's possession. He added that when he first went to a boarding school in 1863 a boy whose home was on Exmoor used to entertain the dormitory at night with blood-curdling stories of the Doones' exploits. T. H. Cooper's *Guide to Lynton* (1853) has a section on the Doones of Badgworthy and so has the Revd. G. Tugwell's *North Devon Handbook* (1857). In 1848 the Revd. W. H. Thornton, then Vicar of Countisbury, was shown the famous long gun of Yenworthy and was told the story of how it had repulsed the Doones.

In the face of all this, it would seem that Bradley and his companions were singularly unfortunate in not having heard of the Doones; and it would certainly be unwise to accept Bradley's confident assertion that nobody else had until *Lorna Doone* became popular.

The more important question is the degree of truth underlying the Doone legends, of which the following outline conveniently presents the common core. In or about the year 1620 a number of desperadoes settled on Exmoor in the Badgworthy cots. They maintained themselves by

*Exmoor, Memories Metheun, 1926.

raiding the farms on the fringes of the Forest and by highway robbery. They abducted women from the farms and villages and they were responsible for several brutal murders. After a particularly barbarous deed at Exford in about 1699 the countryside rose against them and stormed their stronghold. The few Doones who survived fled from Exmoor.

Though there is much vagueness about dates and places in the several versions of each story, the legends were specific enough when recording the brutality of the outrages. The crime that finally brought retribution upon them was the murder of a child whose mother they carried off. As the child lay dying they laughed and joked, singing a rhyme which remains as perhaps the most vivid testimony to the violence and callousness attributed to the Doones:

> Child, if they ask who killed thee,
> Say it was the Doones of Badgworthy.

There is a macabre element, too, in another of the Doone stories. This used to circulate in slightly different versions, though the situation depicted in each was essentially the same. One account (printed in *The Athenaeum* on 26 August 1905) told how the Doones raided a farmhouse, knowing that the master was away. The mother concealed herself in a tub of feathers, but one of the villains seized her little girl and stabbed her, calling out as he did so, "Kill the calf and the cow will howlee!" The wretched woman at once emerged from her hiding-place and told the Doones where the household valuables were kept. Having taken these, the robbers killed both the mother and her child. In another version the same crime was said to have occurred at Parsonage Farm, Oare, and the mother, concealed this time in the bread oven, did not leave safety even though her child was stabbed to death. The words in this story were, "Prick the calf and the old cow'll mooee!" The fullest version was first written down by a Mrs. Tucker of Court Barton, Parracombe, in about 1908, having been told to her by her grandmother in 1857. In this account the scene is set in Badgworthy, but the Doones are not mentioned by name. After the household was in bed the robbers entered the shippon and pricked the bullocks to make them roar. A farmhand who came down to investigate was killed; a similar fate then overtook one of his fellows, and finally the master himself. The little boy then heard the robbers entering the house and hid up the chimney, while his mother hid in a tub of feathers, leaving her baby in its cot. An old woman accompanying the raiders spoke the traditional words, "Kill the calf and the cow will mooee!" and the child was then taken outside and murdered before the house was ransacked. The next day a great dog came and licked the blood. Neighbours threw a chopper at it, tracked it by the bloodstains it left behind and were thus led to the robbers, who were all taken. This grim story—with its obvious fairy-tale elements—was told as a children's tale for many years.

The story of the long gun at Yenworthy, already mentioned, recorded that the Doones when besieging the farmhouse were fired on by Widow Fisher to such good purpose that they broke off so warm an engagement. This victory over the hitherto invincible gang was supposed to have first set the Exmoor people thinking that it would be possible to take a full revenge for the many wrongs they had suffered.

From a tradition recorded by H. Snowden Ward, the editor of the great 'Dooneland' edition of *Lorna Doone* (Sampson Lowe, 1908), it appears that the Doones began their Exmoor career with expropriation and violence. He was told early in this century that it was generally believed that on the very night that the Doones 'comed in over' they seized a house and turned a farmer and 'his little maid' out into the snow. The next morning both were dead, 'one under a withy bush, and the other somewhere else'. It seems certain that in this case a Doone story has been grafted onto an historical event—the deaths of Tucker and his grand-daughter.

Where did the Doones come from when they 'comed in over'? Many theories have been advanced, and perhaps the commonest of these is that they were refugees from Sedgmoor; but this seems most unlikely since there was widespread support for Monmouth's cause in the West Country, and fugitives from the battle would hardly inflict a reign of terror on their sympathisers. In *Legends of the West Country* (1854) they were said to have been noblemen dispossessed at the end of the Civil War. This, while in conformity with the superior social origin often ascribed to the Doones, would give a later date to the beginning of their Exmoor life than most of the stories support. Another theory is that all the legends are based on folk memories of the brutality and rapaciousness of the *Danes*, and that *Doones* is the local corruption of the name. Dr. Francis C. Eeles, in *The Church of St. Dubricius, Porlock*, put forward another guess. Buried in Porlock churchyard is Adam Bellenden, sometime Bishop of Aberdeen and Chancellor of that University. He was presented to the living of Porlock by Charles I and died there in 1647. Near Dunblane in Scotland, a place with which Bellenden was connected for twenty years, is a village called Doune. Eeles suggested that Bellenden might have brought to Porlock with him a servant bearing—or known by—the name of the village. After his master's death this hypothetical servant would have found himself very much a stranger in a strange land. Alone and friendless, he might have 'gone native' and taken up the life of a freebooter.

This Bellenden theory is the merest speculation, but it has been given some space because there is a persistent tradition of a Scottish connection with the Doones, the most remarkable and detailed version of which appeared in *The West Somerset Free Press* in 1901. It was written by Ida Marie Browne, who signed herself 'Audrie Doon'. She expressed surprise at finding in *Lorna Doone* so plausible an account of the origins of the Doones from whom she herself was descended through her mother. Her family name was Doon, "subsequently spelt with a terminal 'E' for a few generations, and originally written Doune". They were exiled from Scotland in 1620 and settled in 'the Oare Valley' being "more or less hated and feared by the countryside until their return to Perthshire in 1699".

Having thus outlined her story she produced some interesting details. In 1618 Sir Ensor James Doone (or Doune), who had claims to the estates of the Earl of Moray, was imprisoned by the Earl and given the choice of life imprisonment or exile. Choosing the latter, he left Scotland accompanied by his wife and a servant named Beeton and travelled to London to seek redress from the king. The rebuff he received exacerbated a disposition already "vindictive, quarrelsome, and intensely proud", and Sir Ensor determined to be revenged upon a world that had so wronged him:

> In the valley of the East Lyn, a short distance from Oare Ford, they halted, and took possession of a half-ruined farmhouse . . . As time went on, other sons were born to the outlawed knight, inheriting the stern nature of their father and growing up to regard all men as their common enemies.

'Audrie Doon' then described the career of her ancestors in terms which reflected the horror and brutality of their deeds as recounted in the Exmoor legends. She also gave an explanation of their departure from the moor, telling how in 1699 the new Earl of Moray, repenting of the wrong his grandfather had done, invited the Doones to return and offered them reparation. The exiles accepted his offer and left Exmoor for ever. Her story was supported with quotations from the journal of Rupert Doone, who visited Exmoor in the 1740s. A typical quotation read:

> Sept. 3rd. 1747. Got to Oare and then to the valley of the Lyn; the scenery very bonny, like our own land but the part extremely wild and lonely. Wandered about and thought of the doings of the family when here, which I gather were not peaceable.

Associated with 'Audrie Doon' was a Mr. John William Beeton of Hunstanton. He was of Scottish descent and had in his possession many Doone relics, among which were: the journal of Rupert Doone; a large oil painting of Sir Ensor Doone, dated 1679; and a flintlock pistol which was engraved 'C. Doone 1681' on one side of the butt and 'Porlock C.D.' on the other. Unfortunately, in 1902, a fire destroyed several of the relics and most of the associated papers, none of which had been thoroughly investigated. H. Snowden Ward examined and photographed such relics as survived. His conclusions may be summarised in his own words: "they seemed, including their inscriptions, undoubtedly old". He went on to say that, unless Miss Browne and Mr. Beeton were to be accused of deliberate fraud, it must be accepted that there was a Scottish family named 'Doon', 'Doone' or 'Doune' with a *tradition* of exile on Exmoor.

All this, of course, falls far short of proof. It was 'Audrie Doon's' belief that Blackmore heard of the history of the *Dounes* from some Scottish friend and at once—and rightly—identified them with the Exmoor Doones, changing in his story the details of their flight from Scotland while preserving all the essential features of their exile. Research, however, has failed to corroborate 'Audrie Doon's' account of the quarrel between the Earl of Moray and Sir Ensor Doone and has, moreover, not succeeded in establishing that there was ever a knight by that name.

It appears then that the vexed problem of the Doones is far from being resolved but a few conclusions and several theories may be advanced with some confidence. First, it is certain that for many years before Blackmore wrote his novel, traditions of the Doones were circulating on Exmoor. Next, it is extremely probable that during some part of the seventeenth century the Badgworthy settlement was the home of a disreputable gang whose members *may* have come from Scotland and who *may* have had as their leader one Ensor or Sir Ensor. (The 'Sir' may well have been assumed: there would be few to challenge it.) Next, it is as certain as may be that these ruffians were known as 'the Doones'. Lastly, we may be confident that their exploits were enormously magnified in the legends and, of course, for the purposes of his novel by Blackmore. Sheep-stealing, robbery, and rape may well have been in their repertoire—Exmoor being so desolate a region they had every chance of getting away with a good deal of lawless behaviour—but it is highly improbable that they established the widespread reign of terror depicted in the legends and in *Lorna Doone*. In this connection MacDermot's acute observation should be remembered: they are supposed to have been lording it over Exmoor during the Wardenship of the redoubtable James Boevey. Depredations on the scale attributed to them would have had a very serious effect upon the Warden's revenues from the moorland pasturing, as farmers would not have sent their cattle and sheep into so unsafe an area. That would not have been a state of affairs that Boevey with his pugnacious temperament and his powerful friends at Court would have suffered gladly or for long. If the Doones were there in Boevey's day a much more likely guess is that he used them as his henchmen to put pressure on recalcitrant farmers and commoners; rather as, in the nineteenth century, Parson Froude of Knowstone may have had *his* iniquitous gang. If this happened, then the legends could make sense: hatred and fear of Boevey lingered on Exmoor long after his death.

One interesting tailpiece may be added. In the early 1950's the writer met David Ensor,* writer and farmer, who had been an able lawyer before turning to other occupations. Ensor told how an ancestor of his, when a pupil at the school kept in Dorchester by the famous poet and scholar William Barnes, was reprimanded by the irate master in these terms: "What else can be expected of one of the Doones!" Briefly, Ensor's family legends embodied the belief that the Ensors were descended from Carver Doone's little son Ensor, saved and 'bred up' (as Blackmore tells) by the magnanimous Jan Ridd. Though no lawyer, it seemed to me that there were weak links in a chain of very intriguing evidence; but at that time, at any rate, an intelligent man with a trained legal mind was prepared to argue forcefully that he was 'the last of the Doones'.

The lower reaches of Badgworthy Water flow through deservedly popular scenery, familiar to the thousands who visit 'The Doone Country' every year. Cloud Farm is tucked away beneath the steep side of Oare Common where bare moorland contrasts most satisfyingly with the now luxuriant Badgworthy growth. Malmsmead, 'gateway to Doone Land', offers welcome amenities to an ever-growing influx of summer visitors. It is easy to deplore the superficiality of most trippers' interest in the moor and to conclude that commercialisation is an inevitable and distasteful result of National Park publicity. In fact, nobody comes without seeking a very real enjoyment, even if it is based solely on hazy hearsay about the Doones or a natural wish to see the more accessible and obvious features of the lovely scenery. The work of such bodies as the Exmoor Society and of the information departments of the National Park Committees will in time spread a more informed interest and so deepen enjoyment.

Oare, a mile to the east, is the goal of many of the tourists: something like 50,000 a year now visit the church. The parish, one of the largest in the Williton rural district, is the home of a widely scattered population of less than 100. It has a long history reaching back to and beyond the days when Matthew, parson of the church of 'Ar', was fined twenty shillings for harbouring his son Walter and his servant John Elyot who had brought out of the Forest a hind that John Scrutenger had shot with an arrow. In medieval times Oare's life was closely affected by Forest Law. Farming, of course, was and is the way in which Oare people got their living and the parish records tell a fascinating tale of rural life and customs through the ages. Apart from the church (the chancel has been added since Blackmore's day; a fact that explains away the apparent impossibility of Carver Doone's attempt on Lorna's life, as described in the novel) the other notable building is the Manor, for so long the home of the Snows. It was here that the Prince of Wales was entertained to tea when he visited Oare in 1863,

* Now—May 1968—M.P. for Bury and Radcliffe.

and it was here, too, according to an often-told story that 'a little loving cup' was kept—presented to Nicholas Snow by Blackmore in reparation for his not wholly complimentary treatment of the family in his novel. MacDermot, who knew Snow very well, asserted that the story was false.* Snow, he maintained, would never have accepted any present from Blackmore whom he disliked and—making insufficient allowances for the demands of fiction—referred to on every possible occasion as 'a darned liar'.

Both east and west of Badgworthy there are superb stretches of wild and open moorland. Tippacott Ridge, to the west, may be reached by ascending Lank Combe. From the spring where the stream rises a good track leads along the ridge which separates the enclosures and provides a very pleasant moorland walk into Brendon, that pretty hamlet on the banks of the East Lyn the spectacular course of which is known to thousands of visitors and dozens of artists. East of Badgworthy, a delightful way into the moor is via Oareford with its fine farmhouse—Plovers' Barrows?— and then up Chalk Water, which leads through a wonderful moorland right up to Three Combes' Foot. Here, Chalk Water is born and here, too, is one of Exmoor's best 'stells' or pounds. It was made when Tom's Hill and Larkbarrow were built: a circular wall with a ring of beeches inside the wall to give additional protection from the wind and to break the drifting snows. Such stells have saved the lives of hundreds of wintering sheep.

The moorland between Badgworthy and Alderman's Barrow is very highly regarded by lovers of the wilder moor. The basic exploration route is from Alderman's Barrow (on the western loop of the Exford-Porlock road) along the Forest boundary to Black Barrow—at least six of the old mearestones can still be seen, and there are one or two more 'doubtfuls'. Black Barrow—a great place for seeing ponies—is easily identified by the stake that is driven into the mound. From here there is a splendid walk down Weir Water to Oare Post, but those intent on knowing the interior will turn west and follow the Forest Wall past Three Combes' Foot to Kittuck, across Chalk Water, then due south almost to Tom's Hill before swinging west again to Badgworthy.

The return journey from Badgworthy to Alderman's Barrow is best made up Long Combe, a very wild steep valley. Two miles out of Badgworthy a track leads to the ruins of Tom's Hill. It is difficult to realise that this heap of grass-grown rubble, the haunt of owls, was once a thriving homestead, and even more difficult to reconstruct from the remains of Larkbarrow—half a mile further on—a picture of it as it was up to the second world war. On page 77 of *The Reclamation of Exmoor Forest* is a photograph of Larkbarrow in 1929. A sturdy farmhouse is flanked by

* Correspondence with H.C.N. Bond.

good shippons surrounding a large yard and enclosed by a stout wall. The now grass-covered track was a serviceable road. Behind and to the west of the farm a belt of beeches formed the windbreak. Now, all is down; even the beeches. During the war the area became a training ground. The inhabitants, of course, had to leave. Mortar shells damaged the farmhouse and its buildings, and the wind and the rain soon completed the destruction of the little world of warmth and light that Frederic Knight established on the bare moorland.

The track from Larkbarrow leads across Swap Hill and out to the Alderman's Barrow road. It used to be easy to walk, but recent reclamations have resulted in sometimes-padlocked gates.* (Access is now a problem in parts of Exmoor. Permission will often be granted, but it is not always easy to find the owners.) In freer days, the Larkbarrow track made a wonderful evening walk, for deer and ponies were often seen. As the light failed, however, it could be an eerie place: Mr. Lucott's malicious ghost used to haunt not far away and, even without recollections of long-gone legend, the ruins of the two farms threw a melancholy shade.

---

* A good alternative route may be followed by leaving the Larkbarrow track (where it swings south) and striking straight across the moor to hit Alderman's Barrow road where there is a stile at a gap in the beech hedge. (See *Waymarked Walks 2*, published by Somerset County Council.) In conformity with the very sensible policy of the Park Authority this particular route is not waymarked—see introduction to *Waymarked Walks*.

CHAPTER ELEVEN

Dunkery and the Brendons

THOUGH separated by the Dulverton-Minehead road (A 396) these two sub-regions of the National Park can conveniently be described in the same chapter, for they have features in common and lie in such close proximity to each other that many visitors will include both in the same day's travels. Not, of course, that it is possible to explore either properly in so brief a time: each—and especially the Dunkery region—amply repays repeated visits and detailed investigation.

Dunkery Beacon is Exmoor's highest point (1,705 feet above sea level) and commands magnificent distant views, a range of up to 150 miles—from the Malverns to Brown Willy—being possible in the right conditions.* The fascination of identifying both the near and the remote landmarks from Dunkery's summit makes a whole day spent there, or frequent returns in search of ideal viewing weather, abundantly worthwhile; to the south, Winsford Hill, the Punchbowl and the Wambarrows; beyond, the Southern Ridge of Exmoor and the Anstey Barrows, the Froude Hancock Stone (a black dot in a skyline dip), Two Barrows, Five Barrows and Setta Barrow. Further to the south, Dartmoor rears up; Hey Tor, Cawsand Beacon and Yes Tor are easy to identify. Further still, Brown Willy shows a head friendlier than the Dartmoor heights. To the south-east Hembury Fort and Sidmouth Gap are plain: east-south-east, the Wellington Monument is prominent on the Blackdowns, and the rolling downs of Dorset stretch into the distance. Due east are the Brendons and the Quantocks: due west, the humps of Rowbarrows, and beyond them the beckoning lines of the western moor with Chapman Barrows as its symbol. Immediately to the north lie the wooded valleys of Horner and East Water, the tiny settlement called Stoke Pero, the dome of Cloutsham Ball and, slightly east of north, the tree-covered hills round Webber's Post. Plain on the coast are Porlock Bay, Hurlstone Point, the Selworthy Hills, and North Hill above Minehead. In the Channel lie Flat Holm and Steep Holm, while from west to east on the clearly-visible Welsh coast Worms Head, Swansea Bay, Barry, Penarth and Cardiff are in view. The Welsh scene is completed by the Black Mountains, the Brecknock Beacons and the Sugar Loaf.

* I have been assured by a reliable informant that Snowdon can be seen, though I have not myself identified it.

The cairn on the summit of Dunkery is modern and the memorial stone set in its side commemorates the gift of Dunkery to the National Trust 'by Sir Thomas Acland Bt. Colonel Wiggin and Allan Hughes Esq'. The summit mound on which the cairn stands is not known to have sepulchral or other significance, but it is certainly not natural and has been there time out of mind. Savage noted that on an old map (dated 1687) Dunkery was shown capped with a tower, but there is no record that there ever was such a building and there are no signs of its foundations. The map-makers of those days were given to poetical flights. Page stated that an ornamental tower was planned for Dunkery in the late eighteenth century. Nothing came of this, either; but one of the same design—the Conygar Tower—was erected at Dunster.

According to Ekwall the name *Dunkery* means 'rocky hill' (*dun*: height, mountain, hill; *creic*: rock), and *Beacon* of course refers to its use as a fire-signal station from the fourteenth to the mid-seventeenth century. Collinson stated in his *History and Antiquities of the County of Somerset* (1741) that there were then on the top of Dunkery "the ruins of three large fire-hearths . . . the remains of the Beacons which were formerly erected on this elevated spot". Round the summit mound are the remains of other cairns and tumuli which have been so despoiled that their secrets can never be known. Vast quantities of stones have been removed from Dunkery even within recent years.

In summer time Dunkery is much visited, but solitude is within easy reach: the route westward from the summit is little used. A gently descending ridge leads towards Rowbarrows; seascape on the right, and on the left Codsend Moors sloping sullenly down to Kitnor Heath. The ridge-track itself provides quite firm walking but there are wet patches on both sides, where the dominant moorland vegetation—bracken, forest grass and ling—is diversified with spotted orchids, round-leaved sundew (an 'insect-eater'), ivy-leaved campanula and bog pimpernel. The plant-life of the Dunkery uplands is, in fact, unusually varied, largely owing to the geological characteristics of the area. The base rock is Foreland Grit, a practically lime-free, hard sandstone. The soil is a mixture of sand formed from the Grit and peat derived from decomposing plants. The peat depth and, therefore, the water-holding capacity of the soil vary greatly, thus causing marked vegetational variation.* Most of the common moorland plants can be seen, but in closer neighbourhood than elsewhere, and there are some interesting specimens, rare in their own right, or rare on Exmoor. For example, between the Beacon and Rowbarrows crowberry is prolific. This northern plant is very near its southern limit here. Another northerner, stagshorn moss, has been commoner than it now is. In recent years it has been seen only in the immediate vicinity of the Beacon.

* See *The Exmoor Review*, No. 1, for a full botanical description.

Little Rowbarrow is first reached by this ridge-track and then the stony mound of Great Rowbarrow, with two more barrows adjacent. Here, the bigger track from Dunkery Gate cuts the ridge-track and may be followed north-west across steadily dropping ground until it reaches the Cloutsham road, from which the most dramatic of all the possible views of Dunkery is obtained. Nowhere does the great bulk of the hill show to better advantage than here. The steep slope of its northern flank emphasises its height, and the contrast between its bare, heathy slopes and the thick woods of the Horner valley is most satisfying.

Half a mile south of the junction of the Dunkery track with the Cloutsham road another track leads across rough moor along Stoke Ridge, passing very close to the Stoke Ridge plantation. Soon the tower of Stoke Pero church is seen: a church set in a hollow so deep that the top of its tower seems level with the rim of the bowl. The church, nine farms, and thirty-two souls—that is all there is of Stoke Pero. It is the highest and most isolated settlement on Exmoor,* and the old rhyme—in whichever version—emphasises its loneliness:

> Culbone, Oare and Stoke Pero,
> Parishes three, no parson'll go to.
>
> Culbone, Oare and Stoke Pero,
> Three such places you'll seldom hear o'.

This is said to be the earliest Christian site on Exmoor, but the date and even the dedication of the church are lost. Elliott-Cannon suggested that the inscription 'sancta barbara' on a fifteenth-century bell might preserve the memory of the original dedication, and he commented on the surprising link thus established between the patron saint of miners in France and this remote Exmoor church.

'Stoke' comes from *stoc* (enclosure, settlement) and 'Pero' is derived from *Pyrow* or *Piro*, the family to which the land was granted after the Conquest. Apart from a fourteenth-century Rector who signed his name 'Perow', we know little more about the family. The list of incumbents is a long one, and Robert Thoryng is worth singling out for mention as perhaps the most remarkable of them all: in 1369 he abducted the wife of one of his parishioners—Alice from Buckethole. But apart from this unusual exploit the parsons of Pero have left little impress on local history.

The church was rebuilt in 1897, the earlier structure by then being in ruins. A few of the medieval features—a door, some window frames and stones—were incorporated in the present building, which was given an excellent barrel-beamed roof. All the timber for this was transported from

* See "Stoke Pero" by A. Elliott-Cannon, *The Exmoor Review*, No. 9.

Porlock by a donkey named Zulu. Restored again in 1958, the interior is
bright and pleasant; redolent, as Elliott-Cannon rightly says, of homeliness
rather than of antiquity. Yet the chalice and patten—Barnstaple-made—
have been in use in this little church since 1574, and the first-known
incumbent was instituted in 1242.

From Stoke Pero, Horner Wood may easily be explored, and the wonderful medley of bare knolls, deep valleys and swift streams that is the glory
of the Dunkery area will provide a walker with many hours of enjoyment.
This is a great place for deer; and Horner Wood is particularly renowned
for its varied bird life. Cloutsham, built originally as a hunting lodge by
the Aclands, and famous as the scene of the opening meet of the Devon
and Somerset, is one of the best places for an Exmoor holiday. South, it
looks over the steep valley of the East Water, with Dunkery's massive
northern slope frowning above. To the east there is the grassy mound of
Cloutsham Ball and the dense green woods of Horner. In October, these
same woods ring with the belling of the stags.

The woodland path from Cloutsham to Horner is a summer day's
delight. The hamlet takes its name from the stream which, says Savage,
derives from *hwrnwr*, 'the snorer'; and though in summer it makes gentle
and pleasing music, in spate the brown flood roars as it thunders through
the woods. The story is told of the rider who was thrown into the East
Water (Horner's tributary) in time of flood. His dead body was seen by
horrified and helpless observers as it was swept under bridge after bridge,
to be recovered at last from the sea at Bossington.

Less than a mile from Horner is another delightful hamlet. Luccombe's
name—'the valley shut in by the hills'—epitomises its scenery; and, apart
from its lovely setting, it has features that make it well worth visiting: the
picturesque cottages in Stony Street; the church of St. Mary with its fine
waggon roof and slender tower. Then a winding road leads to Blackford,
and a lane from there to Tivington, where a steep track comes out on
Tivington Common and Knowle Hill. There are splendid rides through
the Forestry Commission woodlands and onto the bare hills; a most
spectacular ridge this, seen at its best in late August or early September.
The sea breaks into lazy waves on a coast that seems spitting-distance
below. Part of Minehead is in view, the rest hidden beneath North Hill.
South, the three peaks of Dunkery are clear: the Beacon, Easter Hill and
Robin How. The ridge itself is heather-covered, the rich purple diversified
with the golden-flamed gorse and the lush green bracken and, when the
worts are ripe, misty black globes among the grass and ling. Then the
ridge narrows and the valley of the Avill is precipitous. The 'Goosey Path'
leads to the Giant's Armchair, high above the road along which toy cars
crawl. In the woods north of Dunster the Conygar Tower appears; and
then, like one of those enchanting cardboard castles in Olivier's *Henry V*,

Cottages at Luccombe.

A view of eastern Exmoor, taken from near Oare Post.

Luccombe Church and the Selworthy Hills beyond.

Dunkery from Webber's Post—bare moor and dense woods, typical of eastern Exmoor.

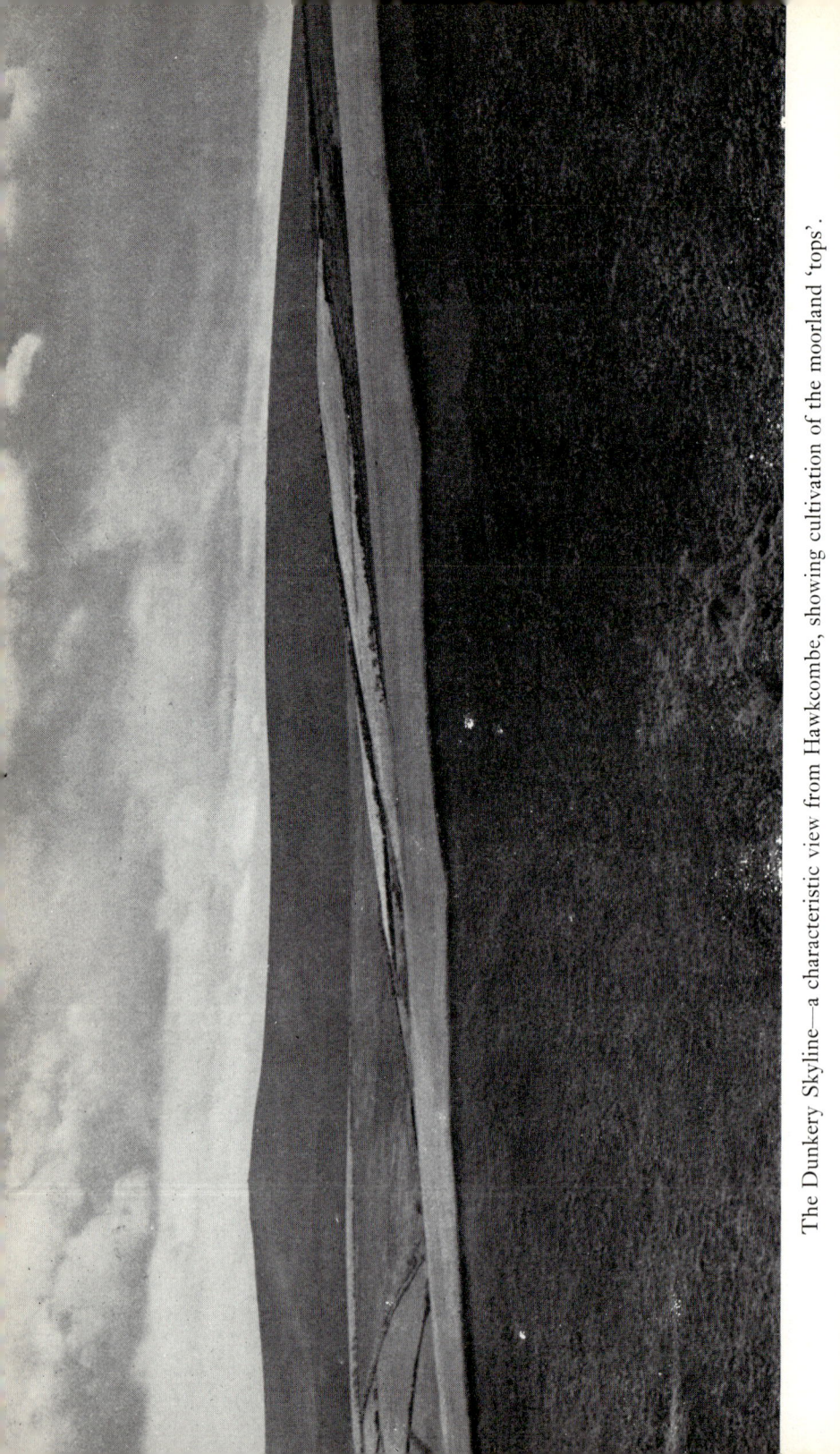

The Dunkery Skyline—a characteristic view from Hawkcombe, showing cultivation of the moorland 'tops'.

the fortress comes into view. Its towers rise thirty feet above the tops of the trees surrounding the mighty knoll on which it stands. At its feet cluster the houses and shops of the ancient town, and in the foreground of it all is St. George's Church, the finest in West Somerset.

The best way into Dunster ('the fortress on the hill'), though few take it, is down the steep side of Grabhurst or Grabbist Hill. Savage interprets this name as *graba* (moat or trench) and *hyrst* (wood); thus, 'the entrenched or fortified wood'. (Perhaps the reference was to the earthworks in the grounds of Dunster Castle.) At the very foot of the hillside is the church, a large cruciform building 168 feet long and fifty-five feet wide, dating mainly from the early fifteenth century, though with a Norman west door. The tower is ninety feet high. Inside this beautiful building are many fine monuments and an ancient font sculptured with emblems of the Crucifixion; but the outstanding feature is the wonderful rood-screen stretching the whole width of the church. It is covered with a motif of grapes and vines and has fourteen openings. This famous screen appears to have been the inspiration behind the renowned group of West Somerset screens, and there was a tradition that the Church of St. George that houses this treasure was built by Henry VII in gratitude for the bravery of Dunster men at the Battle of Bosworth, the royal benefactor lavishing wealth especially on the screen. Unfortunately, the story must be dismissed: most of the building is at least seventy years older than Bosworth Field.

The little town has a long history. It received a charter from Reginald de Mohun not long after the Conquest in return for a tun of wine value forty shillings, and up to Elizabeth's reign it was a busy port. It is referred to in Elizabethan documents as Dunster Haven, and many years before that Edward III commanded the bailiffs of Dunster not to permit "any religious persons to depart by the aforesaid sea-port without licence". The Castle was defended for Maud against Stephen; and in the Civil War, after being held for Parliament by the Luttrell of the day, it was handed over to the royal forces and commanded by Colonel Windham from 1643 to 1646. In the latter year Blake besieged it and, after a brave defence, Windham surrendered. Two years later, that redoubtable man Prynne was imprisoned there by Cromwell.

The wealth and fame of the town were built on its cloth-making, and 'Dunsters' were once known throughout the land. The octagonal wooden yarn-market in the centre of Dunster—often referred to as a 'butter-market'—was erected in 1609. Dunster market day was the big event for miles around then, and for many years after. An old man told Savage that when, in the 1820's, a more than usually large number of farmers came in to buy grass seed, it had 'a child-like resemblance' to what it was when he was a boy.

The yarn-market, the Castle, the Luttrell Arms, the Priory, the church, and the many other beautiful buildings are the visual reminders of a long, proud and prosperous past. They are, too, the source of wealth today, for in summer Dunster is crowded with visitors who come to see the many memorials of byegone days. A new industry has sprung up in Dunster, yet despite the influx of visitors, despite holiday camps and chalets, it manages—astonishingly enough—to preserve the almost medieval air that is its greatest charm.

Between Dunkery and the Exford-Whit Stones road lies a moorland region of great variety and delight. There are many possible routes to follow, but the best is from Rowbarrows to Nutscale, a steep and narrow valley the headwaters of which have been dammed to form a lake about a quarter of a mile in length, so providing a 36,000,000-gallon reservoir for Minehead. Above the reservoir the stream is exuberant, like all Exmoor waters, dashing impetuously over its boulders and singing its wild song of freedom. Past the intake wall, calmness and gravity reign: a placid sheet of water mirrors the burning disc of an August sun or the glory of an April sky. The narrow cleft of Nutscale is the home of wild things: the red deer harbour there; the fox and badger, the pony and otter may all be seen. There are small trees on the valley slopes—rowan, hazel, hawthorn, alder and beech—and every kind of Exmoor bird is found in the valley at its proper season. The mosses, lichens and wild flowers of the moor are here in abundance. It is a sheltered, prolific place.

South of the reservoir the character of the landscape changes. Chetsford Water, one of Exmoor's most beautiful streams, flows under its picturesque bridge out of the high moorland. Ember Combe, its tributary, passes a fine Bronze Age stone row. Lucott Cross is nearby, where a malicious ghost once haunted and—within the past twenty years—when the moorland mists came down the baying of the Yeth Hounds was said to be heard. A lonely, barren, lovely land.

The newcomer to Exmoor who wishes to experience the widest possible range of the moor's scenes and moods in one day could hardly make a better choice than the Rowbarrows-Nutscale-Chetsford Water walk.

Across the A 396, the Brendon Hills, in Berta Lawrence's words, stand as a bridge between Exmoor and the Quantocks.* They are the easternmost region of the National Park, dominated by the dome of Croydon Hill—heavily afforested—in the north, and by the long upland ridge from Heath Poult Cross to Raleigh's Cross in the south. This is farming country, pleasantly diversified with woodland walks and pretty hamlets.

In the mid-nineteenth century the iron mines brought prosperity and an influx of Welsh miners and quarrymen, for slate was a major industry too,

* See *The Exmoor Review*, No. 8, pp. 24–6.

especially near Treborough. Brendon top abounds with relics of the mining. A ruined cable-house reminds the visitor of the incline-railway down which the ore travelled to Watchet. The derelict shafts, not always very safely guarded, mark the site of the once-busy mines; grass-grown rubble is all that remains of the cottages where the miners lived. In the chapel called Beulah they left a more enduring memorial of themselves and of their faith—just as, at Leather Barrow and Cutcombe Barrow, Dun's Stone and Tripp Barrow, Bronze Age man made *his* bid for immortality before the darkness overtook him.

Though structured in a manner reminiscent of the Dunkery region, the Brendons are too enclosed and cultivated to offer the walker what Exmoor can give, but the plantations on Croydon and Kennisham can be explored by making use of Forestry Commission paths. The Haddeo Valley,* up past Bury and along Hartford Bottom, with tracks and lanes to Brompton Regis and out over Blagdon Hill, is pleasant country. There is a good open stretch of heath on Haddon Hill, and the long road over Brendon Top leads past sites that are of the greatest interest to both the prehistoric and the industrial archaeologist.

But if the essence of the Brendons can be distilled at one particular place it is at Raleigh's Cross, on the boundary of the Park. The inn was once a calling place for drovers and packhorse men, when Brendon was moorland, and goods were brought up from Bampton and flocks were driven down. The August Sheep Fair is still held nearby, and the plinth of the stone cross still stands in front of the inn. There are several traditional stories to explain the original purpose of the cross which gave the place its name. The strongest tradition connects it with Simon de Raleigh, Lord of the Manor of Nettlecombe, his body resting there while being taken home for burial after his campaign in France in 1387.

It seems fitting that history and legend should mingle in this way at this place, and that drovers and packmen, sheep fair and ponies, should all be linked with the inn and the road by which it stands, for Raleigh's Cross is in a very real sense the gateway to the Brendons, and discovery of this eastern outpost of Exmoor can profitably begin here.

* Now the site of a large reservoir

CHAPTER TWELVE

The Coast of Exmoor

THE coastline of the Exmoor National Park is justly famous. From North Hill in the east to Combe Martin in the west—a 'straight-line' distance of some twenty-four miles—the Vale of Porlock interposes the only considerable break in a picturesque range of hog's-back cliffs. Most of England's cliffs are flat-topped and, indeed, the Atlantic cliffs of the Hartland and Clovelly regions further west in Devon are of this type. But Exmoor's cliffs, belonging to the rarer hog's-back type, exhibit the striking scenic qualities characteristic of this structure. They begin their rapid fall to the sea a considerable distance inland, thus commencing a long, steep slope, only the lower portion of which is sea-eroded. The highest of the hog's-backs have fine escarpments below the belt of turf, gorse and bracken with which the upper slopes are covered, but on the lower cliffs vegetation creeps down almost to sea level. Another feature of the hog's-back type is the 'dead ground' between the cliff at its lowest 'walkable' point and the sea, caused by the extremely sharp final declivity. The consequent sensation of being suspended on thin air is even more alarming than the view from the top of a flat-topped cliff, where the waves break on jagged rocks two or three hundred feet below.

Again, the hog's-back cliffs are much more stable than the flat-topped cliffs, for the chief factor in cliff destruction is the frontal assault by the waves. Of course, the Severn Sea is not such a formidable antagonist as the Atlantic—the force of a wave on the Hartland coast has been estimated at 2,000 pounds a square foot in winter—but the comparatively small area open to attack protects the Exmoor cliffs. Nor are they as vulnerable to interior penetration. On a flat-topped cliff rain seeps down to the solid rock, channelling its way along the rock joints, washing out the bonding. In winter, the rain freezes and expands the joints until the cliff is honeycombed. The long, steep slope of the Exmoor coast causes the rain to run off seawards instead of sinking in to any great depth. Finally, the Devonian rock of the hog's-backs is harder than the Upper Carboniferous rocks of which the flat-tops further west are formed.

The eastern portion of the Exmoor coast is in Somerset. It rises abruptly to the summit of North Hill above Minehead, dominating the delightful little harbour. The whole of the Selworthy Hills, of which North Hill is part, is threaded by excellent tracks, and the heathy top provides some of the finest walking in the whole of the National Park. The gentle climb west to Selworthy Beacon (1,013) is the basic route, passing a good barrow cluster as it nears the high point, from which a fine panorama opens out: the woods of Grabbist, the fertile Vale of Porlock, Horner Woods and Dunkery, the bare uplands of the middle moor, the waters of the Channel —this is as good a spot as any from which to sample that variety of scene that is Exmoor's most remarkable feature. And 'in under' the Beacon, deep in the woods, is the lovely village of Selworthy, surely one of the finest in Somerset, its church a treasure house of history and beauty.

There are several routes from the Selworthy Hills to Porlock. A favourite is through the pleasant hamlet of Bossington and across the Vale. Shut in on three sides by moorland heights, Porlock looks north to the sea from which warm, moist air is funnelled by the configuration of the land, so ensuring that abundant crop and pasture growth for which the district is renowned. This is the one lush area in the whole of the Park and grows, so it is said, the finest barley in the world.

Porlock is still a fascinating place, even though so crowded in the summer. The old thatched cottages turn their backs and their chimneys— 'Porlock fashion'—to the street. Then there is the Ship Inn where Southey stayed and where he wrote some indifferent verses in praise of the town. His journal contains an interesting entry:

> This place [Porlock] is called in the neighbourhood 'The End of the World'.
> All beyond is inaccessible to carriage or even cart. A sort of sledge* is used
> by the country people, resting upon two poles like cart shafts.

Even today, when cars are more reliable than they used to be, the journey up Porlock Hill on the road to Lynmouth gives the traveller some inkling of the difficulties of Exmoor travel in the early days of motoring. Porlock Hill was first ascended by motor car for a bet in 1900, and for very many years after that the climb was regarded as an ordeal for vehicle and driver. The alternative route, up the Toll Road, irons out the worst gradients by making sweeping curves and contouring the precipitous cliff.

It would be pleasant to discover the abode of the 'person from Porlock' whose arrival at Coleridge's holiday farm—possibly Yearnor—according to the poet's own not altogether trusted account prevented the completion of *Kubla Khan*. It is tempting to hold this same busy-body responsible for two choice rhymes in the churchyard:

> Cease now, dear friend, and weep no more,
> I are not lost but gone before:
> Like as the bud ript off the tree,
> So death have parted you and me.

* Known locally in those days as 'a trackamuck'.

Long time in pain we did remain,
While o'er earth's plain we trod;
But now we're free, death eased we,
And glory be to God.

St. Dubricius's church has a peculiar truncated spire surmounting a low tower, both being clad in oak shingles. The story persists that the top of the tower was blown down in a great gale about 1700, but there seems to be no hard evidence to support the statement. The most noteworthy feature of the church is the magnificent Harington monument, considered to be one of the finest in England. This, however, is but the best of a quite outstanding collection of tombs and memorials. Some of the effigies afford ironical proof that the vandal is no modern phenomenon: 300 years ago amateur 'sculptors' were at work on them.

Porlock and its little 'port', Porlock Weir, amply repay discovery for both are rich in Exmoor history, having played a vital part in the life of the eastern moor during centuries when the sea route was the easiest way in and out.

From Porlock Weir the heavily wooded coastal stretch that extends west as far as Glenthorne can be explored. Perhaps the most rewarding area of all is Culbone Woods. This was once the site of an extensive charcoal-burning industry; the original burners were reputed to be a colony of lepers who lived and worked in the woods until they died. They were not allowed to cross over to the Porlock side of Culbone Water and it is said that there was a 'Lepers' Window' in Culbone church to enable them to join in worship there.* Certainly, the pits lie between Culbone and Glenthorne, placed close to the tiny streams that fall to the sea. Here and there, stone ruins mark the sites of charcoal-burners' huts, and a network of tracks connect the pits with each other and with the main route through Culbone Woods. The later burners were exempt from the prohibitions placed on the lepers and exchanged their charcoal at Porlock Weir for food and other necessities. Until about sixty years ago a large flock of feral goats lived in the coastal woods, so meat, milk and skins were plentifully available.

Another industry of the woods was oak-felling. Some of the saw-pits in which the trees were cut into planks can still be seen. Thousands of tons were sent out for shipbuilding, and it seems likely that the charcoal-burners used pieces left over from the oak-cutting. The registers of Culbone church (a building tiny enough to make credible its claim to be 'the smallest church in England') tell clearly enough the story of the decline of both these industries. The general depopulation of the countryside would have had its effect in any case, but the replacement of charcoal by

---

* See *The Exmoor Review*, No. 4, pp. 61 and 62.

coal in iron-smelting and of wood by iron in shipbuilding were special factors in the reduction of Culbone's population.

At County Gate—or 'Cosgate', to use the old name—Somerset meets Devon, 1,059 feet above sea level, and the coast road threads through the upland scenery on its way to Lynmouth and Lynton. It was along this road, though little better than a track then, that Coleridge came on his 'jaunt' from the Quantocks, young Hazlitt with him and silent, hero-worshipping John Chester limping along a little behind. They left Nether Stowey in the morning light and reached Lynton at midnight, knocking up an innkeeper who provided bacon and eggs the flavour of which Hazlitt remembered twenty years later. His description of the scenery through which they passed needs little change, though the smugglers are no longer an instantly identifiable race:

> We walked for miles and miles on dark brown heaths overlooking the Channel, with the Welsh hills beyond, and at times descended into little sheltered villages close by the sea-side, with a smuggler's face scowling by us, and then had to ascend conical hills with a path winding up through a coppice to a barren top, like a monk's shaven crown.

It was along this road, too, that the Minehead-Lynton coaches used to travel—*Lorna Doone*, *Katerfelto* and *Red Deer*. Not until 1920 were they replaced by motor coaches and their names transferred to those noisy smelly pioneers that "made connection with the London trains". The early buses had more trouble with the fierce hills at Countisbury and Porlock than the sturdy horse teams that did the journey in three hours and only once failed to get through. In summer the traffic was heavy, but in winter only one coach was run each week. Four-horse teams were used, an extra pair, ridden postillion, being hitched on for the Countisbury ascent out of Lynmouth where—and again at Porlock Hill—'the co-operation' of passengers was sought; in fact, most of them walked up the hill behind the coach, the heavy vehicle and luggage being all that the horses could manage.

The immediate vicinity of County Gate is an area of considerable historical interest. There are some good barrows south of the loop in the coast road, and just south of the barrows the steep slopes of the East Lyn and Oare Valleys begin—a pleasing route into Badgworthy and the Doone country. North of the road lies Old Barrow (fully described in Chapter One, pp. 16–18). The Glenthorne estate with its fine woods and coast track is private property and permission is needed to explore its features. The house has access to the main road by a drive that conquers the gradients with sweeping curves: a three-mile-long route over one mile of the hog's-back slope.

Coscombe, a little stream in a five hundred foot deep valley leading north from County Gate, is typical of the scenery here. The combe head comes right up to the road and is shallow enough at first, then deepens so rapidly that within a hundred yards or so the valley walls rise like mountains and the walker is shut off from the world. The combe is thickly wooded with oaks; bracken and hawthorn crowd the stream; in spring there is a profusion of primroses and the wild hyacinth. A hundred and fifty feet above the sea, the combe broadens out into a grassy clearing, and here the house was built. Whatever may be thought of the architecture, the situation is magnificent. Perched on its green pedestal, Glenthorne faces a sheer drop to the sea, and on all sides but the north great hills tower above it. Its builder, the Reverend W.S. Halliday, was of a humorous turn of mind, one of his favourite jokes being to baffle local antiquarians by burying Roman coins in likely places over Exmoor. It was the knowledge of this trick that made them deeply suspicious of any appearance of Roman remains and, consequently, delayed positive identification of Old Barrow until recent years (see Chapter One).

The determined walker can trace out the coastal track west of Glenthorne, passing through a succession of combes—Wingate, Desolate, and Coddow—and seeing one of the sights for which this coast is famed, if he has the map-reading ability to get him there. At the head of Wingate Combe a rough path leaves the main track and leads down the valley. At the seaward end the waters divide and the two streams plunge fifty feet to the sea, striking the rock projections with dramatic effect as they leap from ledge to ledge. By no means the best, Wingate is yet a good introduction to the remarkable series of coastal waterfalls between County Gate and the Cornish border at Marsland Mouth. Such falls are very unusual in the British Isles—indeed, except in Scandinavia, they are rare in Europe as a whole—and no stretch of coast in these islands can boast so fine a series as Devon.

At the entrance to Coddow Combe—a huge, gritty, grey ravine—the track improves. The stream has been diverted to feed the water tanks at the Foreland lighthouse, a building on a rock ledge high above the sea, which lashes it with spray in the winter storms. The stout, whitewashed enclosure walls, the trim yard, the immaculate paint-work, all combine to present that air of strength and efficiency characteristic of Trinity House establishments. In fog, an automatic mechanism sets off explosive charges every few minutes, and each night the great lantern flashes out the Foreland's own 'call-sign'. The fascination of the place is born of the conflict between the savage onslaught of the elements and the scientific ingenuity and human devotion pitted against them.

From the lighthouse it is a hard climb over the screes on the western slope of the Foreland, but the effort is worth making: at Great Red, a deep

Looking towards Hurlstone Point—the hog's-back cliffs of the Exmoor coast.

Great Red—where Foreland Grits and Lynton Slates join (see Chapter Twelve).

The track round Foreland Point.

The Vale of Porlock—the one lush area in the whole of the National Park.

The Rhenish Tower at Lynmouth.

Countisbury Church—not far from Arx Cynuit, where the Danes were overwhelmed.

Lynton and Lynmouth Harbour, taken from the Foreland.

gully north of Blackhead Point, the junction between Foreland Grits and Lynton Slates occurs; and once the 950 foot contour has been crossed a view of both sides of the promontory opens out, revealing the structure of the Foreland. It is then clearly seen as the remains of a range of hills running north and south, and deeply eroded to the east and the west by the sea. Erosion has cut much deeper on the Lynmouth side, capturing all the short streams that once flowed down the western slopes. The curve of Lynmouth Bay marks the present limit of marine encroachment. The summit of Countisbury Common provides a panoramic view of most of Exmoor's coast. Westwards, the bay sweeps round to the little harbour at Lynmouth and its famous Rhenish Tower. A gash in the almost sheer cliff behind the town marks the track of the cliff railway and leads the eye straight up to the sister town of Lynton hanging dizzily over the sea. Dark woods mass where the Lyn gorges cut back into the hills, falling steeply from the barren moorland where the rivers are born. On beyond Lynton the jagged outlines of the Valley of the Rocks can be seen; and westwards still, a bold coast, with Highveer dim and the great shoulders of the Hangman dimmer still behind. To the east, the coast can be traced back to Glenthorne and on to Hurlstone Point beyond Porlock.

The hamlet of Countisbury is reached by a track joining the road just by the little church of St. John the Evangelist. The low tower and scoured grey walls tell of a stern battle with the wind and the rain. Although there was a church at Countisbury before the Normans came, the present building is not ancient for, at a vestry meeting on 1 June 1796, the parishioners decided to pull down the old nave, which was very dilapidated. This they did, and built a new one for themselves, using local workmen and dispensing with the services of an architect. Richard Slocombe, William Lock, Richard Crocombe and John Fry may not have had the mysteries of Gothic Revival at their fingertips, but they planned a building that has endured. Encouraged by the success of this first venture, the parish got to work again in 1835 and took down the old tower before the winds did the work for them. The new one was up by the end of the following year at a cost of £150. The chancel was rebuilt and the north aisle added by the humorous Halliday of Glenthorne in 1846. The churchwardens' accounts are extant from 1678. Records of disbursements for ale consumed on proper occasions always loom large in such archives, but the entry for 1681, when a bellfounder received £5 for casting a bell and £3 for the metal he used, is worth quoting:

Paid for beer when the bell founder talk with the parishioners for casting the bell, and beer when the bell was cast, and beer when the bell was taken out of the peet . . .

And then, of course, there was beer when the parish fox-catcher (wages fifteen shillings a year, and responsible for wild cats and hedge-hogs, too) had a good day; and beer to drink "ye king's helth on the Crownation day"; and beer for the Fifth of November.

The church and a few cottages and the Blue Ball—that is all there is of Countisbury and, except for one great scene in the very distant past, not a lot is known of its history. But its name provides a clue to the importance it once had. There is now general agreement that 'countisbury' means 'the camp on the headland', and the fortress from which this name is derived is about half a mile west of the inn.* Approached from the Porlock side its massive strength is apparent, even though its great rampart has been subjected to 2000 years of weathering and erosion. Countisbury Castle is an Iron Age promontory fortress cunningly sited so that attackers had to rush uphill for over a hundred yards before they could reach the defences. In places its rampart still towers thirty feet above the bottom of the ditch: crowned as it undoubtedly was with a palisade, it must have been a formidable barrier to invaders. Wind Hill, the promontory that it guards, is a triangular-shaped eminence, unassailable on its two other sides, so steep are their slopes. Attack from the east was countered by this tremendous ditch and rampart.

The evidence that Countisbury Castle once played a major role in history may be found in Asser's *Life of King Alfred* and *The Anglo-Saxon Chronicle*. The story they tell may be summarised thus: in 878, during the reign of King Alfred, Hubba the Dane sailed with twenty-three ships from South Wales and landed somewhere on the Exmoor coast. He attacked the defending forces, led by Ealdorman Odda, at a place called Arx Cynuit. There was no water supply in the stronghold, so Hubba was confident of quick success, but the defenders rushed down the slope, killed Hubba and 800 of his men and captured their Raven banner—a unique achievement.

Various places have been suggested as the site of Arx Cynuit, but scholars are now in agreement that Countisbury Castle fits Asser's description best, a clinching argument being his statement that the fortress could be assailed only from the east. And Countisbury fits into the strategic picture: Hubba landed somewhere along the Exmoor coast—most probably at Porlock, a rich prize—and had a large enough force to contemplate extensive and sustained raiding as far east as Taunton or as far south as Exeter. Odda, however, was keeping watch from Countisbury and Hubba dared not move inland until he had dealt with the powerful force that threatened his lines of communication with his ships. He *had* to attack Odda, even though the Devon army was secure behind the fortress wall of Arx Cynuit. The rout of the Danes proved the quality of Odda's

* For a full account, see "Countisbury Castle" by Charles Whybrow: *The Exmoor Review*, No. 3, pp. 40–2.

generalship in choosing as his camp a stronghold that was already more than a thousand years old when he led his army there to thwart the Danes. The Iron Age men had built it strongly and sited it well, intending it as their protection against the Bronze Age people who made Exmoor's barrows and who, from their moorland home, were offering resistance to the invaders from Western Europe with their strange ways and their iron weapons.

Lynmouth and Lynton were little known to the rest of the world until the second half of the eighteenth century. After 1750, improved roads and the cult of the picturesque drew travellers to the wilder parts of England. Increasing leisure and wealth were accompanied by an aesthetic enjoyment of the desolate and unproductive uplands. Early in the century the practical Defoe struggled along the southern fringes of Exmoor, took one look at the rolling moorland, and expressed his opinion in a pithy and contemptuous sentence: "Camden calls it a filthy, barren waste, and so it is." By the end of the century such an attitude was impossible for any man of sensibility. A romantic delight in the lonely places was by then the mode.

Even so, poor communications still deterred the tourists. Really determined seekers of the picturesque, like Coleridge or Southey, got there on foot, but the number of visitors able or willing to do this was very small. For centuries Lynton and Lynmouth had been cut off from the outside world, and it was not until the nineteenth century that road and railway building opened them up as holiday resorts.

Early man left more permanent memorials of his existence in this district than did his medieval successors. The moors above Lynton abound in prehistoric remains (see Chapter One) and recent archaeological surveys have confirmed at least some of the nineteenth-century beliefs—usually associated with improbable 'Druid' legends—about Bronze Age relics in the Valley of the Rocks.

It seems that the Saxon settlement of Lynton and Lynmouth was slow and the result of infiltration rather than violence. This coastal area was gradually taken over; the lingering of the Celtic people is revealed by the survival of some of their place-names—*Lyn*: 'a torrent', for example. Nevertheless, there is ample evidence of the progress of Saxon settlement and cultivation in the *worthies* and *cotes* of the district.

According to Domesday the population of Lynton was then approximately 400. In 1801 it was 481. These figures tell clearly enough the quiet, uneventful story of the place for 800 years. Such history as Lynmouth and Lynton had in those days was of their own or nature's making: the annals of a few leading families; the deeds of the moorland sheep-stealers; the long struggle with the sea; the devastating power of the Lyn rivers in flood. Until the tourist traffic began, the grazing of the large moorland commons, the raising of store-cattle, and the production of oats and rye for home consumption occupied the men of Lynton. Lynmouth, of course, was busy with herring fishing and curing. The golden age of that industry coincided with the years in which the Wichehalse family flourished. The red-herring houses were built on both sides of the little harbour and were frequently swept away by storms or Lyn floods. In 1607, for example, the river changed its course and destroyed the curing houses on the Countisbury side. In their heyday the Wichehalses did their best to strengthen the sea and river defences, but from the Restoration until 1713—when the estates finally passed from their hands—their fortunes were declining, and their successors found the property expensive to maintain. Lynmouth decayed, and by 1750 the harbour dues were inadequate to sustain the port.

Even in the earlier and more prosperous period, there were fluctuations of fortune unconnected with flood or tempest. From time to time the herring shoals deserted Lynmouth, and the traditional reasons were advanced to explain the calamity: the parson had been unreasonable in his demands for tithe and the herrings left to punish him for his greed; or the use of herrings as manure in times of plenty had insulted the fish. In 1750, the lord of the manor sold the curing houses and they were turned into cottages. There was a revival of the industry from 1787 to 1797 but permanent recovery was impossible. Oysters were exported until the early years of the nineteenth century but this was a side-line compared with the once-flourishing herring trade. Bark and oats were also exported on a small scale, and coal and limestone came in, but the steep hills behind the little harbour prevented the development of the port.

It was only between 1628 and 1686 that the twin villages had a resident squire, and after the latter date they had neither squire, rector, nor hardly a visitor in the next 100 years of their remote life.

It appears that in 1790 the only inn was kept by a John Litson, 'At the Sign of the Crown'. In 1807 William Litson, a relative of John's, opened a hotel near the Valley of the Rocks and did very well out of it. Cottages and bungalows, and another hotel—The Castle—sprang up in the next few years. The Napoleonic Wars were doing Lynton and Lynmouth a good turn, for this first influx of visitors consisted chiefly of wealthy tourists whose Continental haunts were now closed to them: they found 'The English Switzerland' an exciting substitute. Among the pioneer visitors were the Marchioness of Bute, and Coutts the banker—influential examples that were bound to be followed. The roads from Barnstaple and Minehead were improved, and the inhabitants of Lynton and Lynmouth, having seen their opportunity, were assiduous in promoting the new industry. From 1850 development was rapid: new hotels, new houses, a pure water supply, the establishment of the Urban District Council in 1894—all of these were successive stages in the evolution of Lynton and Lynmouth as tourist resorts.

During the nineties, Sir George Newnes, the publisher, was a great benefactor of the two villages. He presented Lynton with its Town Hall and was responsible for many other developments during his residence at Hollerday House, his great mansion—destroyed by fire in 1913—spectacularly sited on Holiday (Hollerday or Haliday) Hill. His most remarkable achievement was the construction of the cliff railway, for it was he who chiefly supported the invention and who promised the bulk of the financial backing.

For many years the steep gradients between Lynmouth and Lynton had been a deterrent to visitors, who either walked or hired donkey transport at sixpence a time. The cliff railway changed all this. In 1870 a local engineer, Bob Jones, patented his invention; but it was not until Newnes and Hewitt (later Sir Thomas Hewitt, K.C.) took the project up that anything was done. Blasting was begun in 1887 and the track was laid on a gradient of one in one and three-quarters. The railway was opened on Easter Monday, 1890, the total cost, including the special Act of Parliament, having been £8,000. In 1908–9, the track was relaid and various improvements were made.

The two cars run on an endless cable and are gravity-driven. The water tank underneath the top car is filled with 500 gallons of water as the tank of the bottom car is emptied. When the brakes are released, the two cars slide smoothly up and down the rails, completing their 900 foot journey in one and a half minutes. There has never been an accident in the history of this remarkable railway which must be the safest in the world. In the early days of motoring, Lynmouth Hill was too much for motor cars, and the local company—which still controls the railway—transported them up and down the cliff. As late as the early twenties this service was still available: 7s. 6d. for small cars and 10s. 6d. for large ones.

The year 1890 also saw the provision of electricity, for on the same day that the cliff railway opened, the power station on the East Lyn—claimed to be the second hydro-electric plant in Britain—began to supply current; a surprising achievement for a place characterised for so many centuries by isolation and remoteness. It was not until 1921 that water power was supplemented by oil engines.

The nineties were, in fact, a period of rapid change and development. Eight years after the opening of the cliff railway, the first train ran between Barnstaple and Lynton over the narrow gauge line, nineteen miles long, constructed with much difficulty and at great expense between 1895 and 1898. Passing as it did through some of the loveliest scenery in England, and characterised by the quaintness of its rolling-stock as well as by the marked individuality of its personnel, the little railway won many hearts in its short life. In 1935, the last train passed over the metals, carrying 300 'mourners' and proceeding in sad solemnity to the wreath-decked buffers at the terminus.

As early as the seventies, there was a local agitation to obtain a railway for Lynton, but neither the London and South Western nor the Great Western could be persuaded that the venture was worth the risk. They were right, as it turned out. A local company was then formed, with Sir George Newnes as chairman. Its object was to link Barnstaple and Lynton with a narrow gauge, single-track railway. Such a line was considered more suitable to the hilly district than standard gauge and, since expense would be reduced by using sweeping curves rather than tunnels on the gradients, the narrow gauge (slightly under two feet) would be far more practical, and would mar the scenery less. The original estimate was £2,500 a mile for two foot gauge, compared with £8,000 a mile for standard gauge. On 27 June 1895 a Bill providing for the construction of the railway and for a capital of £70,000 passed through its final stage.

Work began in September 1895 but it was soon clear that many difficulties had been overlooked, in particular the tremendous amount of blasting that was necessary. Landowners demanded a higher price for land than had been estimated; and the bankruptcy of the contractors just before completion added to the company's problems. Instead of costing £2,500 a mile, the line cost double that figure. Yet the project was carried through, and on 11 May 1898 the first train ran from Barnstaple to Lynton.

From Barnstaple the line followed the Yeo valley, crossing a graceful viaduct seventy feet high before it reached Chelfham Station, four and a half miles out of Barnstaple. From Chelfham to Bratton Fleming the gradients stiffened, and just after leaving Bratton the line took one of those horse-shoe curves for which the 'toy railway' was noted. It was no rare thing for passengers to see hounds in full cry as the engine puffed along this section of the line at its statutory fifteen miles an hour. A huge 'S' bend by Westlandpound then led to Blackmore Gate, where the wildest section of the route began: the Great and Little Hangman gaunt against the sky and the coast of Wales dim beyond the Severn Sea. Then on, over the windy moor to Parracombe, passing Holwell Castle and the grey tower of St. Petrock's. At Woody Bay, a mile or so further on, the line crossed the 1,000 foot contour and so reached its highest point; and in the next three miles the travellers got their first views of Lynton—the wooded gorges of the Lyn rivers on the right, Countisbury ahead. Then, swinging round the spurs of the hills, the train finally came to rest at the Lynton terminus, a mile from the village and 800 feet above the sea.

There were four engines: *Lyn*, *Taw*, *Exe* and *Yeo*, and sixteen coaches. *Lyn* gave a lot of trouble. Owing to a strike in Britain, it was built in America and never seemed suited to its work. It was, however, a great favourite with its long-suffering attendants, who christened it 'Yankee' and bore with its unpredictable ways.*

---

* See *North Devon Story*: E.R. Delderfield (The Raleigh Press, 1952) for a full account of the railway.

Neither the beauty of the route nor the pronounced personality of stock and staff were proof against hard economic facts. Not until 1913 did the company pay a dividend—½ per cent!—and though Government subsidy enabled it to make a profit during the first world war, road transport was a deadly competitor afterwards. In 1923 the London and South Western bought it up, but they lost £60,000 in the next twelve years. The last train ran on Sunday, 29 September 1935.

The popularity of Lynton and Lynmouth is due entirely to their situation. There are few of the less pleasant features of typical twentieth-century 'seaside places' at either, but equally there is little of outstanding architectural interest. St. Mary's at Lynton dates partly from 1741, but was extensively altered in 1868 and 1893–1905. The Town Hall has a good deal of fanciful decoration, but might be worse. Most of the hotels vary from what Professor Pevsner calls "the grimness of some of Ilfracombe and Westward Ho! to the heavy-handed gaiety of fancy tile-hanging and turrets and gables with woodwork painted white". There are, however, a few examples of an earlier and better style: long low buildings of the early 1800's. A deservedly popular attraction is the Lyn and Exmoor Museum in Market Street. Established in 1962 by Lynton members of the Exmoor Society, it houses a remarkable collection of Exmoor exhibits ranging from ancient tools to modern pictures. The skill and enthusiasm of its voluntary curators have given pleasure and instruction to thousands and have preserved much that would otherwise have been lost. Down below in Lynmouth, the best feature is west of the quay: the cottages on Mars Hill, clinging to the precipitous sides of the cliff. The Rhenish Tower—reconstructed exactly as it was before the 1952 flood—was built in the late 1850's by General Rawdon, who used it to store salt water to supply his house with sea-baths. Originally a low, squat structure it was improved by Rawdon in 1860, when the upper courses, loopholes and machicolations were added. The name 'Rhenish Tower' is something of a mystery. Rawdon based the design on a painting that he saw in a friend's house, but there is no evidence whatever that this depicted a Rhineland tower. Whatever the geographical source of the inspiration, however, 'Rhenish' the tower is, and a deservedly well-loved feature of the Lynmouth scene.

The topography, structure and soil of the central moorland plateau have already been described (see Chapter Five). The water table, at its deepest, is only a few inches below the surface and the iron pan prevents effective drainage. It was over this desolate land that there fell on the night of 15/16 August 1952 one of the most violent rainstorms ever recorded in these temperate islands. At Longstone Barrow, a little over a mile away from the headwaters of the West Lyn and less than half a mile from the source of its principal tributary, the rain gauge recorded nine inches of rain between

11.30 a.m. on 15 August and 9 a.m. on 16 August. Only twice before in the period that records have been kept has this figure been equalled: in June 1917, at Bruton in the Mendips; and in August 1924, at Cannington in the Quantocks. It would seem that, for reasons not yet fully understood, this southern flank of the Severn Estuary is liable to sudden and unpredictable downpours of extreme violence.

The greater part of the Exmoor storm was concentrated in the hours between 7 p.m. and midnight on 15 August. So ferocious was the rainfall in these dreadful hours that sheet-flood over a foot deep was driven across the open moor, scouring away the thin soil as it descended the northern slopes of the plateau. At Simonsbath, four miles south-east of Longstone Barrow, the rain was even more violent, eleven inches falling between darkness on the 15th and dawn on the 16th. The whole of the catchment area of the East and West Lyn rivers and of their tributaries was subjected to a downpour of tremendous violence during that August night, but it was over the Chains—the area of the moor least able to absorb the vast precipitation—that the deluge was heaviest. It has been calculated that 3,200 million gallons of water fell on the Chains, and most of it in the concentrated venom of five disastrous hours.

What the layman called a cloudburst, the meteorologist described as "a cyclonic warm front thunderstorm, prolonged and widespread, with the thunder and lightning developing at points of concentration within the larger area of thundery rain".* Three days before the Lynmouth disaster a depression formed in mid-Atlantic and by noon on 15 August had reached the western English Channel, having sucked in warm air as it approached Brittany. Rain began in the Scilly Isles and at the Lizard early in the morning and by midday had spread to the whole of Cornwall, Devon and Somerset. Throughout that afternoon and night, north-east to north winds were blowing along the Exmoor coast, pushing the moist and unstable air up the steep northern slopes of Exmoor. The air currents within the depression, saturated with moisture from their Atlantic journey, were thus impeded in their eastward movement and an already slow-moving depression was held for hours over the most vulnerable area in its path.

Rain began at Lynmouth soon after midday and was fierce on the Chains by early afternoon. A chill wind blew in from the sea and heavy low-lying cloud hid the mountainous thunder clouds that were massing above the lower cloud rack.

During the fortnight preceding 15 August, rainfall on the moor had been heavy—at least three and a half inches. The catastrophic downfall of the 15th/16th thus came as the climax of a wet period and at a time when the

* See *Weather*, Nov., 1952, and the *Meteorological Magazine*, Vol. 82, for full technical accounts.

impermeable Chains had long since exhausted what very limited capacity they have to absorb water.

Such was the setting in which Nature prepared the devastating blow that overwhelmed Lynmouth. The vast deluge that descended on the Chains was refused by that waterlogged wilderness. Every ton of water that fell in those terrible hours found its way into the valleys and out to the sea; but in some of those valleys men had made their homes.

Down every one of the steep-sided combes in which the rivers rise, down every gully and depression in the northern slopes of the moorland heights that hang over Lynmouth the water descended. Farley and Hoaroak Waters united their tempestuous floods at the foot of Cheriton Ridge and hastened on to join the already-swollen East Lyn. The half-dozen streams that converge to form the headwaters of the West Lyn brought the torrents from the western Chains. At Barbrook Mill, another influx from Wool-hanger Common swept into the West Lyn, tearing down bridge and houses before starting the last deadly descent to Lynmouth.

The West Lyn falls 1,500 feet in four miles. The East Lyn, though less precipitous in its course, is also a very rapid river. Even in times of normal rainfall the rush of water down the steep gorges is an impressive sight. In a dry summer there may be no more than a trickle over the rocky beds, but rain over the Chains transforms this trickle into a torrent: a torrent made dangerous by the velocity of its fall and by the boulders strewn about the gorges.

Such, then, were the fatal factors: the enormous rainfall of 15 August, the impermeable pan under the Chains, and the steep courses of the Lyn rivers, produced a flood that no barrier could resist.

Down on the coast, where the two rivers meet, Lynmouth lay helpless in the path of the waters. The narrow valley constricted the flood and in so doing redoubled its fearful power. Not until it had rushed through the little town could the flood fan out into the harbour, staining the sea with a muddy dye that lasted for days. Boulders weighing ten tons and more, living trees uprooted from the wooded gorges, battered down the homes and hotels and the Rhenish Tower. The culvert through which the West Lyn was piped under part of the town and into the East Lyn was blocked with debris, and the angry river, impatient of the least restraint, swung back into its old course, mowing down the buildings that had been erected on the 'delta'. The boats in the harbour were swept out to sea, and cars— twisted into fantastic shapes—were hurled far into the bay. Bombardment from the sea and air could not have wrought worse devastation. Only those who endured the horrors of that dark night will ever know the full story of its tragedy and heroism as the waters rose and man-made things vanished in their path.

The heavy loss of life and the vast material damage brought a nation-wide response. The disaster fund was generously supported and the immediate needs of the stricken town were met by national and local organisations—public and voluntary—quickly and efficiently mobilised. The longer-term problem was to rebuild Lynmouth in such a way as to preserve its picturesqueness and its capacity to accommodate hundreds of visitors while ensuring that such a disaster could not happen again. For though it seemed unlikely that rainfall of the phenomenal magnitude of 15 August 1952 would occur on the Chains again for a very long time, it had to be accepted that Lynmouth was vulnerable to periodic flooding, and the menace of the moorland heights had to be faced.

There is general agreement that the long-term work was well done. The river was widened and the original bed was filled in, diverting this section eastwards. A new harbour arm and jetty provide safe anchorage, and a car park occupies the 'danger zone' where houses, shops and hotels once clustered. The rivers are now under control; and though silting of the harbour has followed the river-widening, and there has been some loss of shop and hotel property, the main object of the work has been achieved— Lynmouth is safe. In 1960, for example, after very heavy rain indeed, the river rose to its highest level since the disaster, but apart from some undermining of the new stone-walling along its banks no damage was done. The rebuilding has not diminished Lynmouth's attractions, but it has removed the periodic scourging that reached its frightful climax in 1952.

The Valley of Rocks can be reached either by the Valley road from Lynton or by the North Walk from Lynmouth, the latter being a most spectacular route into a very remarkable valley. North Walk is a mile-long terrace cut in 1817 by a Mr. Sanford, whose memory should be cherished by all who use the path. Poised half way down the cliff face of Hollerday Hill it commands superb views of the Severn Sea and of the Welsh coast, and leads into a valley which fascinates the visitor by its scenic splendours and the geologist by its enigmatic origins. The weird castellated turrets—Castle Rock (800 feet high), the Devil's Cheesewring, and Ragged Jack are the most famous—form a strange, distorted landscape: a visual strangeness accompanied by geological rarities. The Valley of Rocks is a dry valley and, instead of running seawards, it runs parallel to the coast, with a narrow ridge between valley and cliffs. The 'orthodox' explanation of these two unusual features is that, some ten thousand years ago, the Lyn rivers' outlet at Lynmouth was blocked by the Polar ice, the southern limit of which lay along the Exmoor coast. Ponded back, the rivers filled their valleys until they overflowed at the seaward end and sought an outlet by creeping along the ice margin in a westerly direction, deepening the valley now known as the Valley of Rocks. When the ice retreated, the original outlet at Lynmouth was cleared and the Lyn rivers returned to their former course, leaving the Valley of Rocks as a dry valley.

This is a neat and in many ways probable explanation, but as D.N. Mottershead pointed out:*

> ... the strange landforms of the Valley of Rocks are the result of a variety of geological processes operating in times past. These include the action of the sea in eroding the coastline, the weathering of rocks at depth, and the action of frost in a climate far colder than that of the present day ...

The factors he mentions must certainly have played a major part in the sculpturing of the grotesque pinnacles that attract the sight-seer and round which so many legends have been woven.

Lee Abbey, which stands upon the site of the old farmhouse of Lee or Ley, where the Wichehalse family lived for many years, never was an Abbey and was not built until 1850. It is a pleasant-looking place, however; a successful example of Victorian Gothic, despite Professor Pevsner's strictures and Murray's contemptuous "it is only a melodramatic abbey" (Handbook, 1872). Both the Abbey and the Folly near Duty Point owe most of their charm to their surroundings, but it was no unskilled hand that designed them, and nature has played a kindly part in weathering them harmoniously and covering them with an ivy mantle.

Crock Point is interesting as the only break in the long bastion of hog's-backed cliffs, and because of the landslip that once occurred there. Towards the end of the eighteenth century the ground was worked for clay by Dutchmen, who shipped the product back to Holland. When the digging ceased a farmer named Bromham took the land and for some years did well with it. One Sunday morning as he was sitting in Martinhoe Church a message was brought to him that his land was falling into the sea. For weeks afterwards clay was piled high on the beach 'in lumps as big as ships', and brightly-coloured—red, yellow, brown and white.

West of Crock Pits, the cliffs return to the hog's-back structure. The Woody Bay Cliffs are among the most spectacular on this coast, 900 feet high in places and heavily wooded, with so steep a slope that it is impossible to walk along them. The roads out of Woody Bay are remarkable examples of engineering skill; their hairpin bends would do credit to a Swiss mountain road. Inkerman Bridge carries one of the lanes over Hanging Water, a rapid little river that typifies the hog's-back streams. Rising on a moorish upland, it falls 900 feet in less than half a mile and cascades down the Woody Bay slopes to reach the sea in a thirty foot fall. Towards the end of the nineteenth century a syndicate was formed to develop Woody Bay, the aim being to rival Lynmouth; but before very much development had been accomplished a great deal of money had been spent and the scheme was abandoned. This lovely place is now National Trust property, an acquisition in which the Exmoor Society played a leading part.

* *The Exmoor Review*, No. 8.

The winding road from the bay climbs laboriously to the moorland hamlet of Martinhoe, passing a fine cluster of round barrows on its way. The church is worth a visit: both it and the farms nearby have that grey, battered look so disappointing to those who like prettiness more than the slates and rough stone walls that must keep out the western gales and rain. But those with a sense of history will delight in this tiny settlement where, for centuries, men have fought a stubborn battle with the elements and wrung a spare living from the obstinate earth. The hamlet figures in Domesday as *Matingeho* and it was not until the seventeenth century that *Martin* appeared—and then probably by analogy with nearby Combe Martin. The earlier name was derived from *hogh* ('a ridge') and the patronymic *Maetta*. Both the name and the wild setting bring Westcote's words to mind:

> Here the land is so uneven that you shall have these words of hoe and combe often repeated, which signify hills and valleys.

From Woody Bay to Heddon's Mouth is one of the finest cliff walks along this coast and, though Heddon's Mouth is much visited, the cliffs are left to their wild solitude because of the very difficult walking involved. Most people take the 'new' road out of Woody Bay and so miss what E.A.N. Arber* called the best of the hog's-back stretch—and nobody has ever known the Exmoor coast as he did. The finest sight of all is the Hollow Brook cascade. The stream rises near Martinhoe and falls to sea level in just over half a mile, its average gradient being about one in four. Between the road and the cliff there is a series of falls, the finest tumbling into a deep chine. Then, below the track, the Hollow Brook disappears over the cliff and leaps 200 feet to the beach, there entering a narrow boulder-piled gulley through which it passes to the sea. The first part of this lower and most spectacular fall—which can be seen only from a boat—consists of two cascades which unite half way down.

Highveer Point, the eastern rampart of Heddon's Mouth, is a bold promontory of bare rock through the northern tip of which the cliff track runs high above the waves. It is the largest and most spectacular headland west of the Foreland until Morte Point is reached. Wringapeak, the western arm of Woody Bay, and the aptly-named Cow and Calf near Hollow Combe, are striking, but they lack the stark isolation of Highveer. It gains, too, from its position as the bastion of the great cleave of the Heddon. The name 'Heddon' is derived from the Celtic *etin* (giant) and the valley through which the river flows to the sea seems well fitted to be the abode of legendary monsters. The walls are so steep—700 feet high, with a gradient of seven in ten—that, particularly on the western side, little grows, despite

* *The Coast Scenery of North Devon*, 1911.

the sheltered position which makes the Heddon cleave the warmest valley in North Devon. The impression from the summit of Highveer, however, is not of shelter and warmth, but of a starkly magnificent desolation: a wild antiquity made the wilder by the ruins of the limekiln on the western bank, so dignified by decay that they look like the remains of some stronghold. There is of course more colour on the eastern bank where gorse, bracken and heather are more plentifully interspersed with the grey of the screes. The great depth of the valley and the steepness of the sides indicate the erosive power of the river as, through the ages, it cut down towards the base-level that it reaches at its mouth. And even now, mature as it is, sobered by long life and the successful realisation of its fluvial dreams, it shows an occasional trick of the old rage and boils through the cleave, sweeping the shingle bar away and staining the sea with a muddy dye.

High above the Heddon gorge lies the hamlet of Trentishoe ('the fort on the ridge'). The tree-filled hollow on the hill, where the church and a few grey cottages nestle, may be reached by crossing the Heddon at its mouth and climbing up the west wall. A track at the top skirts the lip of the chasm and leads to the church: a fine upland way and well worth the fatigue of the climb. Both Trentishoe and Martinhoe were the scene of the early ministry of Bishop Hannington, who was killed in his African diocese in 1885. His was an energetic and lovable personality and during his curacy he was equally assiduous in visiting his scattered flock and in exploring the cliffs and caves of the coast. He dressed in a manner that gave offence to thoughtless people who were not compelled to make the journeys that fell to his lot. He wore, he wrote in his memoirs, "a pair of Bedford cord knee-breeches of a yellow colour, continued below with yellow Sussex gaiters with brass buttons. Below these a stout pair of nail boots wearing fully four pounds. My upper garment was an all-round jerkin of black cloth, underneath which an ecclesiastical waistcoat buttoning up at the side." Temple, the blunt-spoken Bishop of Exeter, fully appreciated the point of Hannington's unconventional dress: "You've got a fine pair of legs, I see. Mind that you run about your parish." And run about his parish he did, leaving behind him to this day the memory of a devoted, genial and courageous priest.

Holdstone and Trentishoe Downs, once bare in their moorland grandeur, are both barrow-crowned. A lonely road winds through the shallow depression that separates their twin summits, and west of Holdstone a track leads to Sherrycombe—scene of Exmoor's last coastal fall. It is a very swift stream, coursing foam-capped to the wild leap with which it ends. Few visitors to the National Park will ever see the Sherrycombe falls, the way down the ravine is too strenuous for all but the most determined. But for those who can make the effort the descent into Sherrycombe and the laborious climb up the eastern wall of the Great Hangman will provide an unforgettable experience, epitomising the wild beauty and healing solitude of Exmoor's incomparable coast.

Beyond the Great Hangman, at the foot of its gradual, well-tracked western slope, lies Combe Martin, where the Exmoor National Park ends.

CHAPTER THIRTEEN

Exmoor as a National Park

THE history of Exmoor as a National Park has not been happy. Since the designation of the Park in 1954 the conflict between amenity and agriculture has sharpened, and because of a fatal flaw in the National Parks and Access to the Countryside Act of 1949—under the provisions of which Exmoor, like all the other National Parks, was administered*—the Park Authorities have been powerless to prevent an annual loss of open moorland to agriculture and forestry, a loss which has accumulated over the years until it has reached alarming proportions. This is a problem that confronts all the National Parks of Britain, but for various reasons it is more acute on Exmoor: Exmoor is one of the smallest of the Parks; improved land and moorland were already closely interlocked when the Park was designated; and, finally, much of Exmoor's remaining moorland can, with modern techniques, be converted into better-quality pasture.

Exmoor, in fact, has become something of a test case for all the other National Parks in that its condition is much nearer crisis point than theirs. Faced with a deteriorating situation the Exmoor National Park Authorities and the Exmoor Society have undertaken detailed research into the problem and have explored possible solutions. The knowledge thus gained, and the prolonged debate and negotiations with other interested—and often privileged—parties, have resulted in a unique experience that may yet prove to be of incalculable service, for Exmoor's crisis will in time be repeated elsewhere, and the outcome on Exmoor is already seen to be vital to the fate of all Britain's National Parks.

It is the purpose of this chapter to examine the causes, the development, and the possible solutions of this complex problem, in the hope that the lessons of Exmoor may be learnt in time. The apparently irreconcilable interests of amenity and agriculture must be brought to a working compromise if the National Parks are to survive; and the Exmoor situation, because it is so acute, has produced a great deal of constructive thinking towards this end.

The National Parks Act of 1949 provided that certain areas of Britain should be recognised as being of particular importance to the nation as a whole. They were areas of wild natural beauty, each characterised by structural, topographical, vegetational and scenic features that gave them

* See the *Postscript* to this Chapter.

individual identity. In an industrialised age, when the population of an urbanised island was growing rapidly, they were seen as essential to the physical, social and mental welfare of the community. If the parks of London are its lungs, the National Parks were to be the lungs of the whole country. Access to the National Parks and the preservation of the individual identity of each were important factors in long-term social planning.

The National Parks Commission* was set up to advise the Minister of Housing and Local Government on the designation of suitable areas as Parks, to coordinate the work of the various National Park Committees and to assist them in dealing with Government Departments, but the detailed work of administering each Park was left to the local Park Committees. In the case of Exmoor the situation was complicated by the fact that part of the Park lay in Somerset and part in Devon. The result of this two-county division was a tripartite Committee structure. There is a Devon National Park Committee for Exmoor, a Somerset National Park Committee for Exmoor, and a Joint Advisory Committee. Both the Devon and the Somerset Committees are major committees of their respective County Councils, approximately two-thirds of their members being County Councillors and one-third being Minister of Housing and Local Government nominees whose names are put forward by the National Parks Commission. The County Councils delegate to their Park Committees their Planning powers and duties (within the boundaries of the Park) under the National Parks and the Town and Country Planning Acts, the Park Committees reporting back quarterly to the full Councils and requiring Council sanction for their proposed expenditure.

The Joint Advisory Committee has no executive power: it coordinates the activities of the Devon Committee and the Somerset Committee and considers matters which the two County Councils see as requiring a common policy. Both Councils are directly represented, and one-third of its members are nominees of the Minister, jointly appointed by the two Councils.

Despite the apparent strength of this administrative framework, the Exmoor National Park Authorities have been fatally weakened all along by two facts: first—and there is widespread ignorance of this—the land inside the National Park boundary was not nationalised, but remained in private ownership after designation; second, the Park Authorities have no Planning powers over agriculture or forestry. Although these two facts apply equally to all the other National Parks, the conditions already mentioned as peculiar to Exmoor made the situation worse there than anywhere else.

As was shown in Chapter Two, Exmoor farming changed very little from the time when Frederic Knight's experiments established the successful sheep-ranching methods until just after the second world war. By the

* Re-named the Countryside Commission under the provisions of the Countryside Act 1968.

St. Dubricius's Church, Porlock.

At County Gate—the problem of the fencing (see Chapter Thirteen).

A depressing scene—but the Countryside Act will help (see Chapter Thirteen).

Looking towards the Selworthy Hills—the taming of Porlock Common is clearly seen (see Chapter Thirteen).

A view of the moor from Lillycombe—the Countryside Act will save the heartland (see Chapter Thirteen).

The Anchor at Exebridge—just out of the National Park, but a wonderful resting place after a day's walk.

Wambarrow on Winsford Hill—supposedly haunted; certainly rifled.

Winsford Hill—a view to the west where moorland and fields mingle.

fifties, however, conditions had changed. Government support for farming, reinforced by modern reclamation techniques, made it profitable for the Exmoor farmer to take in moorland hitherto unimproved. Slowly at first, but at a quickening rate, fencing and ploughing began to eat into the heather and grass moorland. For some time the loss of moorland was apparent only to those who had an intimate and personal knowledge of Exmoor; inevitably, it was difficult for such observers to convince the Authorities that a serious problem was developing.

In 1965, however, the Exmoor Society—which had been founded by John Coleman-Cooke at a time when there was a plan to afforest the Chains and the Hoar Oak Herding—commissioned the compilation of a scientific record of land use over the whole of the National Park. The work was undertaken by Geoffrey Sinclair, Chief Field Officer of the Second Land Use Survey of Great Britain, and the Land Use Map that resulted was at once recognised as the first objective treatment of the Exmoor problem. The National Parks Commission, the Planning staffs of the Devon and Somerset County Councils, and the two National Park Committees were immediately aware that, for the first time, hard evidence was available about what was happening on Exmoor.

In the following year the Society, pursuing its policy of presenting facts and arguing only from these, published a pamphlet called *Can Exmoor Survive?* This proved to be a turning point in the Exmoor story, for its detailed and factual presentation of the problem lifted the discussion above the level of embittered and personal controversy and widened the debate from local to national dimensions. Very largely the work of two men— Sinclair and Victor Bonham-Carter (Editor of *The Exmoor Review*)*—the pamphlet was published in time to be the subject of great interest and debate at the National Park Commission's Conference held at Lynton in the autumn of 1966. Representatives of the other National Parks recognised in the Exmoor crisis a foretelling of the troubles that might in time afflict their own Parks on a comparable scale, and departed from the Conference realising that the fate of Exmoor was crucial, for action could not be confined to Exmoor alone. Only Parliament could amend the weaknesses of the 1949 Act, and amending legislation would apply to all the Parks. Equally, inaction in the face of Exmoor's problem would mean that the other Parks would, sooner or later, face the same crisis.

From this point onwards the Exmoor National Park Authorities conducted a reasoned, restrained, and yet determined campaign to persuade Parliament to give them the powers they needed to preserve a significant area of Exmoor as wild and open moorland.

In the spring of 1967 they published a map showing those areas of the

---

* Assisted by John Coleman-Cooke, Tom Spink (then Secretary of the Exmoor Society) and Charles Whybrow.

National Park which they considered it vital to preserve in their wild and open state, and followed this in August 1967 with their representations for amending legislation to the 1949 Act. In these representations they made two chief proposals: that the Park Authorities must be given power to control ploughing and fencing in the areas of 'critical amenity moorland'; and that there must be compensation for farmers who were in future prevented by amenity considerations from improving land in these areas. It should be stressed—for there was much misunderstanding and some misrepresentation of this point—that the Exmoor National Park Authorities did *not* ask for Planning powers over ploughing and fencing in the National Park as a whole, but only in the 'critical amenity' areas.

At the time that these representations were made the Countryside Bill was about to be presented to Parliament, and it seemed the most suitable measure to contain the clauses amending the faulty 1949 Act. The Minister of Housing and Local Government refused, however, to write the clauses into the Bill, and the Exmoor National Park Authorities then modified their proposals in an attempt to meet the strong objections to the imposition of Planning powers over agriculture even in a very restricted area of the National Park. In November 1967 they made further suggestions for amending legislation, this time seeking power to apply 'amenity conservation orders' to any area in those portions of the Park which they proposed to designate as 'Amenity Conservation Areas', coupling these proposals again with provisions for compensation and fair purchase.

The National Park Authorities made it quite clear that crisis point had indeed been reached on Exmoor by stressing that unless they received the powers for which they were asking they would seek the repeal of Section 5(1) of the National Parks and Access to the Countryside Act, 1949. This Section laid upon the Park Authorities (on Exmoor and in all the other Parks) the statutory duty to preserve and enhance the natural beauty of the National Park. They emphasised that the Countryside Bill as it stood was of no use at all to them when they were faced with that statutory duty. They reiterated that they were seeking additional powers only in a very small part of the Park, and they stated that if they did not get those powers then the character of Exmoor as a National Park would be irretrievably lost over the next decade.

At the Committee stage of the Countryside Bill an amendment embodying the Exmoor National Park Authorities' proposals was moved by a Labour M.P. (Peter Jackson, High Peak) and seconded by a Conservative M.P. (Marcus Kimball, Gainsborough); but despite widespread sympathy and the acceptance that the Exmoor situation was grave, the amendment was rejected because of the difficulties involved in compensation—a subject to which we shall return—and because of the Minister's fear that the proposals would prove so controversial that they might wreck the Countryside Bill as a whole.

It is inherent in the nature of such a book as this that the final events in the story cannot be told. At the time of writing (May 1968) there seems some hope that the forthcoming Town and Country Planning Bill may help National Park Authorities, who are at present faced with an impossible task. What can be recorded is that the pioneering work of the Exmoor Society and the devoted efforts of the Exmoor National Park Authorities have made the Exmoor facts available to all and have proved beyond doubt that the whole concept of National Parks has been endangered by the flaws in the 1949 Act.

A consideration of the statistics makes the dangers plain. The total area of the Exmoor National Park is some 170,000 acres. Of this, 43,567 acres is defined by the Park Authorities as 'Critical Amenity Moorland'—that is, open heather and grass moor, encroachment upon which will irretrievably damage the character and identity of the National Park by destroying those very qualities for which Exmoor was made a National Park. Of the Critical Amenity Moorland 9,934 acres are in the possession of the National Trust and Local Authorities and are, therefore, safe; but 33,633 acres are in private hands and are, therefore, at risk. The National Park Authorities considered that some 10,000 acres of the open moor could still be ploughed and fenced without doing harm to the character of the Park, but they believed that the 33,633 acres specified above must be preserved. In other words, the Park Authorities asked Parliament to give them adequate powers in just twenty per cent of the total area of the Exmoor National Park.

Seen in the light of these statistics the Authorities' case was, of course, eminently reasonable. If Parliament meant business when it passed the 1949 Act then there could be no valid objection to amending legislation that would make that Act work in just one-fifth of the total area of one of the National Parks that the Act itself was passed to create. Without amending legislation the existence of Exmoor as a National Park was threatened. Nor does a consideration of the pace at which moorland 'take' has been occurring on Exmoor do anything to weaken the belief that a way has to be found of stopping further erosion and enclosure of open moorland. Yet, seen in isolation, these figures encourage a dangerous over-simplification. There are other facts and other considerations. The farmers and landowners are not villains, eager to despoil a National Park. They are men whose property, lives, and livelihood are set within the Park boundaries. Their actions have hit the National Park hard—and may hit it harder yet—but they have, for the most part, greatly improved the agricultural value of the open moor that they have ploughed and fenced; and they are the legal owners of the land.

Since Exmoor became a National Park the average loss of heather and grass moorland to agriculture and forestry has been just over 1,000 acres a year. Seven hundred and ten acres of this was genuine agricultural improvement; 188 acres fell within the category of 'interference' (ploughing, not supported by sound follow-up measures and, therefore, reverting to scrub and rush); and 112 acres went to forestry.* These figures, derived from the Exmoor Society's Land Use Map, have been generally accepted as authoritative. The Ministry of Agriculture's own records for subsidy-aided schemes showed an annual loss of 600 acres. (This figure, of course, took no account of forestry, or of reclamation schemes carried through without grant, and was based on a definition of 'moorland' that did not quite coincide with that adopted by the Society.) Even if the Ministry's figure is taken as final, however, the situation was clearly deteriorating at an unacceptable rate. And the Ministry's figure drew attention to the grim paradox of the National Park: within its boundaries, one statutory body—the National Park Authority—was trying to fulfil its public duty of preserving and enhancing the natural beauty and individual character of the Park, while another statutory body—the Ministry of Agriculture—was fulfilling *its* public duty of aiding the farmer to restrict access by fencing and to alter character by ploughing. So contradictory were these two roles, both supported by public money, that the Ministry of Agriculture was unable to give the Park Authority advance notice of reclamation schemes. The first that the Authority knew of such plans was when fencing went up and ploughing began in critical amenity moorland areas.

The position of the farmers in the National Park must be understood. Exmoor farming has passed through hard times. Only skill and endurance have enabled the farmer to survive, for hill farming has been historically tough and barely rewarding. Post-war conditions and subsidies have given new life and hope, and the improvement schemes successfully carried out—involving the farmer in the expenditure of his own money, it must be remembered, since the subsidies do not cover the cost—have made many Exmoor farms economically viable to a degree never before approached Again, when Exmoor was designated as a National Park it had been for centuries the home of a farming community whose lives and work had contributed to its character. These people did not ask for their home to become a National Park: they asked to be allowed to get on with their job, and unfortunately this was not always compatible with the National Park concept and functions.

It is for these reasons that both the Exmoor Society and the Exmoor National Park Authorities have always insisted that measures to safeguard

* Forestry is now less of a problem than it was, thanks to a 'gentleman's agreement' (vulnerable because it lacks statutory backing) between The Forestry Commission and the Park Authorities, and to brilliant and original work by Roger Miles, Forestry Officer for Somerset. Private forestry interests sporadically pose their problems, however.

amenity must be accompanied by just compensation for farmers whose interests may thereby be damaged. There is no reason whatever why the Exmoor farmer should be expected to foot the bill for the preservation of amenities available to all comers.

Nobody who tries to draw the appropriate lessons from Exmoor's history as a National Park will succeed if he adopts an emotional attitude to what has happened. The blunt fact is that the Exmoor farmers have been doing their job very successfully and making sensible use of the Government agencies and subsidies available to them. It is pointless and unjust to 'blame' them for the unfortunate results. The cause of the trouble lay in the 1949 Act which did not anticipate the strength of the clash between agriculture and amenity and, consequently, made no provision to resolve the difficulties. The only fault that an unbiassed observer can lay at the farmers' door—and the individual farmer is exempt from this charge—is that the National Farmers' Union and The Country Land-owners' Association in their booklet *Reclamation in Exmoor National Park* (September 1967) showed an astonishing unawareness of the facts of the situation that they purported to describe. The inaccuracies and tendentious-ness of this publication did nothing to support the farmers' very real case.

Fortunately, the deadlock between agriculture and amenity is more apparent than real. To say that, however, is not to minimise the difficulties involved in trying to make the interested parties aware that they have a good deal in common. Patient and prolonged efforts to do this have as yet been little rewarded. Yet a recapitulation of the basic facts on which a satisfactory compromise can be based must at least be recognised as a constructive effort, and may be useful to those who will face similar problems in other Parks.

As has been shown, amenity must be given priority only in a very small part of the total Park—the 'critical amenity moorland' areas—and it is precisely here that *traditional* farming of high Exmoor, vigorously pursued and grant-aided, would give the National Park farmer a fair return and *at the same time* safeguard and enhance the natural beauty and individual character that constitute those very qualities for which the Park was created. For the wild, open, heather and grass moorland which provides the visitor with his chief aesthetic and recreational pleasures is not 'natural', if by that word is meant a product solely of nature.* The high moorland of Exmoor has been intensively grazed for centuries, the rough pastures being an essential part of the economy of farms on the borders of Exmoor in the days of the Wardens, and remaining essential to the farms that the Knights made within the Forest. Grazing and swaling (burning) of heather and grass moor have produced results that—together with the topography —constitute those qualities that rightly persuaded the Park Authorities to

* See Chapter Five.

pronounce these areas 'critical' and to declare that loss of those qualities would irretrievably damage the character of Exmoor. The vital areas of Exmoor—vital to its survival as a National Park—are a product of the labours of man operating on natural factors over a very long period in pursuit of a living. The problem—and the opportunity—is to make it worth the hill farmer's while to continue with traditional farming in traditional ways. If this can be done, then the tension between amenity and agricultural interests can be resolved.

It will be seen at once that such a solution would tackle simultaneously the twin problems of preserving open moorland and of compensating the farmer whose economic interests were thereby damaged. The present agricultural subsidies encourage the hill farmer to adopt a lowland system, but there is nothing unalterable or sacrosanct about these measures. A subsidy to hill farmers to continue with traditional methods would make agricultural and amenity sense, and need be no more expensive (probably less) to the taxpayer. In any case, if the nation wants its National Parks it has got to pay for them: and better to pay for them to be conserved, rather than—as now—pay for them to be destroyed.

In April 1968, Geoffrey Sinclair published an account* of new thinking about preservation and compensation which may yet prove to be capable of breaking the Exmoor deadlock. His words are an authoritative endorsement of the argument developed in the preceding paragraphs of this chapter:

The idea of compensation cannot be dropped, for it embodies elementary justice. Yet the idea, as pursued up to now, carries with it the stigma of 'charity' and—being merely a recompense for restriction—is *negative*. Again, since some 'critical amenity' moorland could never be successfully reclaimed and other areas could, it would be unfair to apply compensation at a uniform rate.

I have always argued that it is the efficient *traditional* management that has produced in our moorland a delicate balance between man and nature, pleasing to the eye and stimulating to the mind and body. Given proper hill care, it also produces a decent living: faced with subsidised competition, it is scarcely economic to maintain. In fact, hill farming proper is scarcely supported by the State at all, as aid for its cultivation merely introduces a lowland system. A prosperous traditional system satisfied the dual needs of both agriculture and amenity: cultivation effectively eliminates one and sometimes both.

Why do we allow our money to be used in this destructive manner? Why not convert present ploughing grants in 'critical amenity areas' into long-term maintenance grants, bolster moorland agriculture, and at the same time ensure its amenity attraction? More than anything else this seems to me to

* The Exmoor Society, *Newsletter No. 11*.

be a *positive* contribution acceptable to true hill farmers. There are many details yet to be settled, but a solution along these lines will encourage farmers to feel pride in farming in a National Park rather than consider it as an encroachment on their freedom . . .

No apology is needed for so long a quotation from Sinclair's article, for he and Victor Bonham-Carter have pioneered much of the constructive thinking, based on patient and detailed research, that even now offers some hope that the problems of Exmoor will be solved before irretrievable damage has been done and the heartland reduced to insignificant pockets of unimprovable moor. If present trends continue unchecked it is probable that the Chains will survive—though, as has been seen, they were once threatened by forestry—but there would not be enough wild and open moorland left to justify the continued existence of Exmoor as a National Park.

Parliament's failure to act, and governmental indifference to the problems—as almost cynically demonstrated in its treatment of the National Parks Commission and its bland promotion of a Countryside Bill that launches new countryside schemes while the National Parks decay —have been depressing features in this sorry tale. Against this may be set the careful constructive work of the Park Authorities, of the Exmoor Society, and the exciting new developments coming from the Dartington Amenity Research Trust. In the 1968 edition of *The Exmoor Review* Michael Dower (Director of the Trust) made the opportunities and the challenge abundantly clear:

> I am convinced that we can root our arguments for the protection of wild places . . . not only in visual (and now, perhaps, in economic) reasoning, but also in a strong base of social, functional and economic thought. Much exciting work has been done in America and is now being launched here to understand better how all the forces inter-act which make our landscape, and how we can use them for our wider benefit . . .

On Exmoor, because the problems have been so acute, hard thinking about these issues has reached a developed stage. The outline of a successful solution is clear: the details are being tackled and can be resolved.

As this book goes to press the great problem is how to persuade government to play its part. The apparent deadlock between amenity and agriculture can be broken by measures fair to both; but it would be a bold prophet who declared himself confident of a happy issue.

N.B. The Local Government Act of 1972 made sweeping changes in the administration of the Exmoor National Park. The new arrangements are outlined in Appendix I.

POSTSCRIPT

THE foreboding note on which Chapter Thirteen ended seemed entirely justified when those words were written, for the Countryside Bill, as it had been passed by the Commons, contained no provisions whatever to protect the National Parks from the kind of erosion that was destroying Exmoor. The best comfort that the Park Authorities could find lay in a vague hope that something might be done in the Town and Country Planning Bill. But since the Countryside Bill had seemed to all who were fighting for the 'critical areas' their one real chance, the Minister's refusal to accept their proposals was a heavy blow. It appeared then that a measure (the whole purpose of which was to increase provision of amenity and recreation), would pass into law leaving the National Parks—the creation of the very Act that the new Bill was designed to supplement and strengthen—as defenceless as before. The situation was the more bewildering and painful because the Ministry of Housing and Local Government had been informed in the plainest possible terms that the position was desperate. All expert testimony was in agreement and the Ministry itself had accepted the strength of the evidence. Those responsible for the National Parks and Access to the Countryside Act of 1949 could at least plead that its flaws were not apparent at that time: that they had not *intended* to leave the National Parks vulnerable. In 1968, on the other hand, the Minister was in possession of all the facts and, consequently, the position that he appeared to have adopted seemed indefensible. No wonder that those who cared about and were responsible for the National Parks regarded the Countryside Bill with feelings varying from weary indifference to outright cynicism.

Though the battle seemed lost, however, the Park Authorities did not give up and both they and the Exmoor Society continued to argue their case and to press for action. To everybody's surprise, the Government relented and an amendment to the Countryside Bill was introduced in the Lords, embodying provisions that went a long way to meet the views of the Park Authorities. This amendment passed into law as part of the Countryside Act in July 1968. Briefly, it provided that the National Park Authorities should submit to the Minister a plan covering the critical amenity areas requiring protection. If the Minister accepts the plan he will then issue an order making it an offence for anyone to plough or otherwise alter the character of land covered by the plan without first giving six months notice of his intention to the planning authority. This 'holding' period of six months is to be used to negotiate access agreements or to secure—compulsorily as a last resort—an access order. Alternatively, under other sections, covenants restricting ploughing and fencing can be made and compensation agreed.

This vital amendment applies, of course, to all the National Parks, but on Exmoor immediate steps have been taken to implement it. The Exmoor Park Authorities have already had a most fruitful meeting with other interested parties—the National Farmers' Union, the Country Landowners' Association, and the Timber Growers' Association—with the intention of producing an agreed plan for submission to the Minister by early 1969. There must be good hopes of success, for the critical amenity moorland map is already in existence, providing the essential basis for safeguarding the heart of the moor.

There is, of course, a moral in all this. In the darkest days the Exmoor Society never flagged in its efforts to arouse public opinion; and the Park Authorities, once in possession of the facts, pursued a steady and responsible policy undeterred by the many setbacks. That optimism about the future of Exmoor as a National Park is now possible is due entirely to the refusal of these two bodies—official and unofficial—to give up the struggle.

Note to the Second Edition. The forebodings of Chapter Thirteen were, in fact, more justified than the optimism of the above *Postscript*, which was written at a time when those of us who had been in the thick of the Exmoor conflict wanted to believe that a new day had dawned. Alas—not so! Since the Countryside Act was passed, moorland 'take' has continued. About five per cent of the critical amenity area was 'improved' in the four years between 1969 and 1973. The 'conservation' provisions of the amendment have not worked—and are not likely to. Section 14 of the Countryside Act (see Appendix I, pages 173 and 174) has proved to be a toothless wonder.

National Park Law and the Exmoor National Park

In Chapter Thirteen some account is given of the ways in which the National Parks and Access to the Countryside Act of 1949 proved inadequate. The deficiencies that were so apparent upon Exmoor were not, of course, peculiar to that particular Park, since all the National Parks of Britain were designated under, and administered in accordance with, the provisions of the 1949 Act. But for reasons made clear in that Chapter the flaws in the Act had greater consequence on Exmoor than elsewhere.

For ease of reference the provisions that proved to be mutually irreconcileable (and, therefore, hostile to the main purpose of the Act) are set out in this Appendix, together with statistical illustration of the rapid decline of the Exmoor National Park. These sections are followed by an outline of those provisions in the Countryside Act of 1968 that are designed to safeguard the critical amenity areas while paying due regard to the agricultural realities of the situation.

The National Parks and Access to the Countryside Act of 1949 imposed upon the National Park Authorities—which were constituted under the terms of the Act—the statutory duty "to preserve and enhance the natural beauty" of the Parks (*Section 5(1)*). It was also their responsibility to encourage visitors into the Parks "for open air recreation and the study of nature". At the same time (under *Section 84*) the Authorities were instructed to pay "due regard to the needs of agriculture and forestry". Agriculture within the Parks was expressly exempted from planning control, and though moorland was placed in a special category—in *Part V* of the Act—and provisions were made for access by agreement, those provisions proved ineffective. This was because, in the early days, such safeguards seemed unnecessary on Exmoor, the public having long enjoyed uninterrupted access to what had always been wild areas. In any case, landowners were understandably reluctant to conclude binding access agreements which offered them nothing in return. Later, when the pace of reclamation quickened, it seemed preferable to the owners of the land to continue to permit access to unreclaimed moorland and to deny it when agricultural improvements involved ploughing and fencing. Even if practicable, however, access agreements did nothing to ensure the preservation of the moorland character of the areas to which they applied.

Under *Sections 76* and *77* provision was made for acquisition for the purpose of access, but the procedures involved were elaborate, the funds available were limited, and the twin pressures of agricultural improvement and amenity value rapidly forced up the price of land. The Park Authorities, competing in the open market and requiring the sanction of the Finance Committees of their Local Authorities for such expenditure, were usually offering too little too late for such land as came up for sale within the National Park.

Finally, the 1949 Act made no provision for collaboration—or even discussion—between the representatives of the Ministry of Agriculture and the Park Authorities. The power to act and the means with which to act were vested in the agricultural authorities, while the statutory guardians of amenity were denied even the dubious benefits of an early warning system.

The helplessness of the Park Authorities under the 1949 Act is reflected in the table of Moorland Loss in the eight years from 1958 to 1965 inclusive, published in *Can Exmoor Survive?* (The Exmoor Society, 1966).

Region	Acreage Lost	Moorland Loss Rate	Acreage Improved	Acreage Interfered	Improvement Value
1	805	10·8%	795	10	98·7%
2	1,645	8·6%	1,360	285	82·7%
3	1,055	7·9%	605	450	57·4%
4	2,715	17·9%	1,955	760	70·0%
5	960	25·7%	960	—	100·0%
Totals:	7,180	12·4%	5,675	1,505	79·1%

Notes on Table

(a) The figures in Column 1 refer to the five Regions of the Moorland, viz: 1) Coastal Heaths; 2) Northern Heather Moorland; 3) Grass Moorland of the Centre; 4) Southern Heather Moorland; 5) Brendon Heaths. (See Chapter Five.)

(b) Moorland Loss Rate (Column 3) is a percentage of the heather and grass moor existing in 1958. Each individual percentage refers to the acreage lost in the individual region, e.g. Region 1 (the Coastal Heaths) had lost by 1965 10·8 per cent of the moorland that it possessed in 1958. The total in Column 3 is a percentage of the total acreage of heather and grass moor existing in the National Park in 1958.

(c) To the total under Column 2 should be added 900 acres afforested in Region 5, making a true total of 8,080 acres lost to agriculture *and forestry* in the eight years covered by the Table.

(d) "Interference" (see Column 5) is defined as "partial, unsuccessful or inconclusive improvement", resulting in a marginal condition typical neither of pasture nor of moorland.

(e) The *overall* Moorland Loss in those eight years was 13·75 per cent of the 1957/58 total, and the *average annual loss* over the period was 1,010 acres. For a reconciliation of that figure with the Ministry of Agriculture's figure see Chapter Thirteen.

In the Spring of 1967 the Exmoor National Park Authorities produced their 'Critical Amenity Land Map', from which the following statistics are derived:

Total area of the Exmoor National Park	169,900 acres
Total area of critical amenity moorland within the Park	43,567 acres
Area of critical amenity moorland owned by the National Trust or by Local Authorities, but excluding common land	9,934 acres
Balance of critical amenity moorland in private ownership and therefore at risk	33,633 acres

In August 1967 the Authorities published their *Representations for Amending Legislation to the National Parks and Access to the Countryside Act of 1949*. In this document they stated:

(a) that under the 1949 Act they were unable to perform their statutory duty of preserving the natural beauty of the Park and promoting public enjoyment of it;

(b) that in their opinion—under the conditions then obtaining—there would be no reduction in the annual rate of moorland loss;

(c) that if the 'critical amenity areas' shown on their map were not protected from ploughing and fencing then the Park would be irretrievably damaged.

They asked for amendments to the 1949 Act (a) to give them power to control ploughing and fencing in the critical amenity areas (*not* in the whole area of the National Park) and (b) to provide suitable compensation for farmers who were affected by these powers.

N.B. Reference to the Critical Amenity Land Map statistics quoted above will show that the Park Authorities were asking to be given control over ploughing and fencing in just twenty per cent of the Exmoor National Park (i.e. the 33,633 acres of critical amenity moorland that were at that time in private ownership and therefore at risk).

In November 1967 the Park Authorities, submitting modified proposals in an attempt to secure their inclusion in the Countryside Bill, stated that if they were not to be given powers "to perform a duty imposed upon them by Parliament then Parliament should remove the duty by repealing Section 5 of the 1949 Act".

The Countryside Act of 1968 contains the following vital Section:

14.(1) The Minister may, if satisfied that it is expedient, by order apply this section to any land in a National Park appearing to him to be predominantly moor or heath.

(2) The occupier of any land to which this section for the time being applies, and which is moor or heath which has not been agricultural land at any time within the preceding twenty years, shall not, by ploughing or otherwise, convert

any of the land into agricultural land unless he has given six months written notice of his intention to the local planning authority.

(6) In this section 'agricultural land' does not include land which affords rough grazing for livestock but is not otherwise used as agricultural land.

(7) In considering for the purposes of subsection (2) above, whether land has been agricultural land within the preceding twenty years, no account shall be taken of any conversion of the land into agricultural land which was unlawful under the provisions of this section.

N.B. See the *Postscript* to Chapter Thirteen for further details of the Countryside Act.

Note to the Second Edition. Under the provisions of the Local Government Act of 1972 the Exmoor National Park is now administered by a single Committee consisting of 21 members. Seven are ministerial nominees, selected to represent amenity interests. Eight are Somerset County Councillors. Four are Devon County Councillors. One member represents the West Somerset District Authority and one represents the North Devon District Authority. County Council control is still entrenched; and though the appointment by the National Park Committee of a National Park Officer is a step in the right direction, he is still dependent upon the County Councils concerned for his salary and his supporting staff. Moreover, he must still work within the defective provisions of the Countryside Act. Section 14 provided neither the stick nor the carrot (both are needed) and, with the vital issue of compensation unresolved, moorland 'erosion' is bound to continue. National resources are needed to conserve the critical amenity areas.

The greatest problem of all—and growing every year—is the massive invasion by car-borne visitors. How can the summer hordes be prevented from destroying the very qualities of beauty, peace and quiet that they have come to seek? Both open moorland and village communities are threatened by 'the season'; and the traffic control plans that have so far been formulated are pious gestures rather than positive policies. Nothing less effective than 'Goyt-Valley-Type' schemes can save Exmoor from its lovers.

APPENDIX II

Some of the Plants Commonly Found on Exmoor

Arranged According to Habitat

Drawn and Described
by

Audrey Bonham-Carter

Some Plants found on drier moors

1. Bell Heather—*Erica Cinerea*. Evergreen widespread undershrub, with small linear dark green leaves, and egg-shaped crimson-purple flowers.

2. Crowberry—*Empetrum Nigrum*. Evergreen prostrate trailing undershrub, with flat shiny leaves spirally up the stem, and tiny pale pinkish flowers at base of leaves. The berry turns from green through pink-purple to black.

3. Cross-leaved Heath—*Erica Tetralix*. Evergreen grey-green downy undershrub, with leaves in whorls of four up the stems, and rose-pink drooping flowers in groups at ends of stems. Also found in wetter moorland.

4. Heath Bedstraw—*Galium Saxatile*. Low, often prostrate, hairless perennial, with tiny white flowers in sprays, which have a sickly scent. Whorls of four/six little leaves up the stalk.

5. Ling—*Calluna Vulgaris*. Common evergreen undershrub, with small linear dark green leaves in two opposite rows, and purple flowers in numerous spikes, occasionally white. Sweet smell.

6. Heath Milkwort—*Polygala Serpyllifolia*. Small, often prostrate, perennial, with oval opposite leaves crowded together especially near the base. The flowers are small and attractive, usually dark blue or dark pink, sometimes in lighter blue or white.

7. Lousewort—*Pedicularis Sylvatica*. Low spreading semi-parasitic perennial, with toothed pinnate leaves, and bright pink flowers (each flower is two-lipped with upper lip longer).

8. Whortleberry (Bilberry)—*Vaccinium Myrtillus*. Erect deciduous hairless undershrub, up to 18 ins. high, with bright green shiny pointed oval leaves, and waxy pink drooping flowers. The berries are small, black, and good to eat.

9. Tormentil—*Potentilla Erecta*. Slender, often prostrate, perennial, thread-like stems, yellow flowers, leaves usually three-toothed. Hybridises often with creeping and trailing Cinquefoil *P. Reptans*, *P. Anglica*, thus hard to identify.

Plants found chiefly on peaty plateaux

10. Heath Rush—*Juncus Squarrosus*. Tough rigid rush, 6–18 ins. high, with wiry grooved leaves, and stiff leafless stems bearing terminal clusters of pale silvery-brown flowers. The egg-shaped fruits are larger than in most rushes.

11. Common Sedge—*Carex Nigra*. Variable sedge, with three-angled stems, narrow greyish leaves, and short unstalked flower spikes (one or two male, above two or three short sausage-shaped female flowers).

12. Stagshorn Club Moss—*Lycopodium Clavatum*. Becoming scarce on Exmoor. The main stem is creeping or rooting and longer than other Club Mosses, some-times extending for several yards, with closely set toothed green leaves. The cones are solitary or in pairs on long stalks, the cone scales yellow and toothed.

13. Purple Moor Grass (Flying Bent)—*Molinia Caerulea*. Variable coarse slightly hairy grass, forming dense tussocks, with a purplish look about the long branched flower head. The flat grey-green leaves turn to pale ochre in autumn, giving a tawny golden appearance over the ground. In winter, these tough leaves blow about and form large balls, hence 'flying bent'.

14. Bog Asphodel—*Narthecium Ossifragum*. Small creeping perennial, with tufts of flat iris-shaped leaves, green to orange in colour. The bright yellow star-shaped flowers, with orange anthers and fruit, grow in dense patches, lighting up boggy places with brilliant orange splashes.

15. Mat Grass— *Nardus Stricta*. Fine wiry hairless grass, forming dense mats, with very fine small flowers, the heads being on one side of the stalk.

16. Harestail—*Eriophorum Vaginatum*. Similar to Cotton Grass (see below) forming tussocks. It has a single erect head, pale yellow in flower, white and fluffy in fruit.

17. Heath Spotted Orchid—*Dactylorchis Maculata*. Small variable orchid, 6–12 ins. high, with leaves keeled and folded up the stem, spotted with black. The flowers, in short broad cylindrical spike, are pale pink, pale mauve or white, the petals spotted in dark crimson.

18. Deer Sedge—*Scirpus Cespitosus*. Densely tufted rush-like plant, with narrow wiry stems, flowering on the tips. It makes large areas of bright russet in autumn.

19. Cotton Grass—*Eriophorum Augustifolium*. It has several nodding heads on single round stems and long cottony threads when in fruit. It makes conspicuous white patches in boggy places.

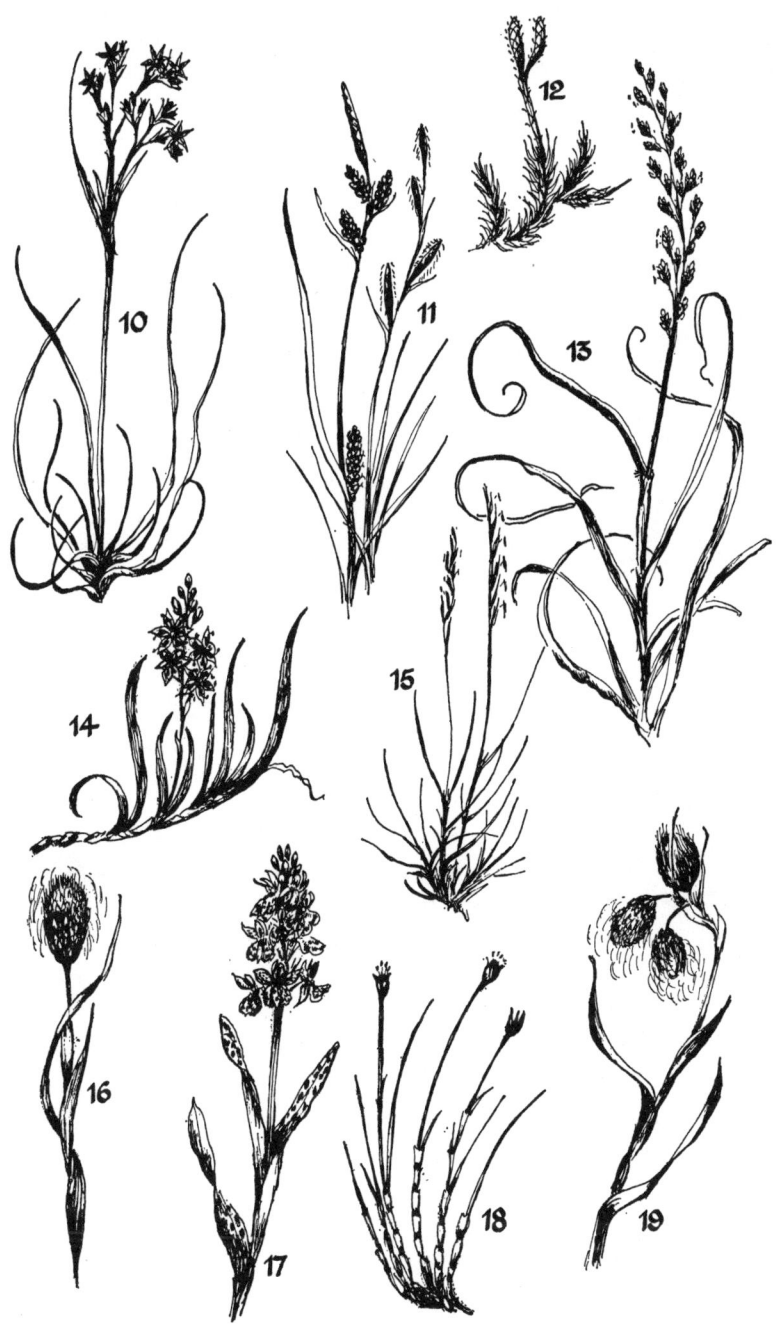

Plants found along rocky river valleys

20. Great Woodrush—*Luzula Sylvatica*. Grows in big tufts up to two feet high; has bright green, glossy, hairy leaves and chestnut-brown flowers in groups of three in loose clusters.

21. Hard Fern—*Blechnum Spicant*. An attractive little fern, 4–15 ins. long, with tough dark green leaves, once-pinnate. It is easy to distinguish as some of the inner upright leaves are thinner and wirier than the others.

22. Cow Wheat—*Melampyrum Pratense*. A weak semi-parasitic plant that grows in and near rocky places. Its yellow two-lipped flowers are found in pairs up one side of the stem, flowering often as late as September.

23. Wall Pennywort—*Umbilicus Rupestris*. Fleshy perennial, with thick round dimpled leaves and spikes of greenish-yellow flowers. The plant grows in walls and rocks.

24. Common Spleenwort—*Asplenium Trichomanes*. Small tufted fern, with dark green oval leaflets, opposite up a dark wiry mid-rib. The plant also grows in walls and rocks.

25. Black Spleenwort—*Asplenium Adiantum-Nigrum*. Small tufted graceful fern, with two or three shiny green triangular pinnate leaves or leaflets, toothed and pointed. The stalk is blackish.

26. Hartstongue—*Phyllitis Scolopendrium*. Distinctive fern, with undivided leaves, in tufts, long and strap-shaped. The plant varies considerably in size. The spore cases are in rows on the underside of the leaves.

Some plants found in acid boggy places

27. Bog Pimpernel—*Anagallis Tenella*. Slender hairless mat-forming perennial, with oval leaves, opposite up prostrate stems. The delicate shell-pink flowers open in the sun and form pools of pink among sphagnum moss bogs.

28. Marsh Violet—*Viola Palustris*. Small hairless violet, with shiny bright green leaves, almost kidney-shaped, and delicate pinky-mauve flowers veined with dark purple.

29. Marsh Pennywort—*Hydrocotyle Vulgaris*. The minute flowers of this prostrate creeping plant are found in whorls at the base of round disc-like leaves, which stand erect on a central stalk.

30. Lesser Spearwort—*Ranunculus Flammula*. Small-flowered buttercup found in wet places, with flesh-pinkish stalks and narrow lanceolate hairless leaves.

31. Bog Pondweed—*Potamogeton Polygonifolius*. The plant has broad oval bright green leaves and narrower floating leaves not joined to the stalk, also long stout flower stalks.

32. Bog Stitchwort—*Stellaria Alsine*. Weak hairless plant, with leaves more akin to chickweed than to other stitchworts, and white star-like flowers having petals shorter than the sepals.

33. Ivy-leafed Water Crowfoot—*Ranunculus Lenormandii*. This plant has shiny fleshy ivy-shaped floating leaves, and white flowers larger than those of the commoner *Ranunculus Hederaceus*.

34. Ivy-leafed Bellflower—*Wahlenbergia Hederacea*. Delicate hairless pale green perennial, with small blue campanula-like flowers on hair-thin stalks. The ivy-shaped leaves are also stalked.

35. Sundew—*Drosera Rotundifolia*. Strange small insect-trapping plant, with a rosette of stalked thick round reddish-green leaves, covered with red sticky hairs. These curve inwards to trap insects. The little white flowers are found in small heads on leafless stems springing from the centre of the rosette. At a casual glance, these plants appear as reddish patches of sphagnum moss.

36. Marsh St. John's Wort—*Hypericum Elodes*. This plant is unlike other St. John's Worts, having downy greyish leaves and yellow resin-scented flowers. It forms greyish mats in boggy places.

BIBLIOGRAPHY

As the footnotes in this book make clear, the indispensable source of information for the student of Exmoor is *The Exmoor Review*, published for The Exmoor Society by The Exmoor Press at Dulverton, Somerset. The Society also publishes a very full Exmoor Bibliography, which should be consulted to supplement the reading list given below.

AGRICULTURE
Baker, V., *Exmoor—An Economic Survey*, University of Bristol, 1949.
Orwin, C.S., *The Reclamation of Exmoor Forest*, O.U.P., 1929.

ARCHAEOLOGY
Chanter, Rev. J.F., *The Rude Stone Monuments of Exmoor, Transactions,* Devonshire Association, 1907.
Fox, Lady Aileen, *South-West England,* Thames and Hudson, 1964.
Grinsell, L.V., *The Ancient Burial Mounds of England,* Methuen, 1953.
Page, J.Ll.W., *Caratacus Stone on Winsford Hill, Proceedings,* Somerset Archaeological and Natural History Society, 1890.
Vowles, A. *Exmoor—the History of the Caratacus Stone,* Cox, Sons and Co., Minehead, 1959.

DESCRIPTIVE
Bourne, H.L., *Living on Exmoor,* Galley Press, 1963.
Delderfield, E.R., *North Devon Story,* Raleigh Press, 1952.
Delderfield, E.R. *Exmoor Wanderings,* Raleigh Press, 1956.
Hendy, E.W., *Wild Exmoor Through the Year,* Cape, 1930.
Page, J.Ll.W., *An Exploration of Exmoor and the Hill Country of West Somerset,* Seeley, 1890.
Peel, J.H.B., *Portrait of Exmoor,* Robert Hale, 1970.
Risdon, T., *Survey of the County of Devon,* E. Curll, 1714.
Snell, F.J., *A Book of Exmoor,* Methuen, 1903.
Vowles, A., *Dunkery,* Western Gazette, 1946.

THE DOONES
Brown, Ida M., *A Short History of the Original Doones of Exmoor,* Cox, Sons and Co., Minehead, 1901.
Rawle, E.J., *The Doones of Exmoor,* Barnicott and Pearce, Taunton, 1903.
Thornycroft, L.B., *Story of the Doones in Fact, Fiction and Photo,* Barnicott and Pearce, Taunton, 1948.

Vowles, A., *The Doone Valley and the Water-Slide of Lorna Doone*, Cox, Sons and Co., Minehead, 1937.

Ward, H. Snowden, *The Land of Lorna Doone*, Marston Low, 1904.

HISTORY

Brown, C.A., *The Lynton & Barnstaple Railway*, David and Charles, 1964.

Chadwyck Healey, C.E.H., *The History of Part of West Somerset*, Sotheran, 1901.

Chanter, Rev.J.F., *A History of the Parishes of Lynton and Countisbury*, J.G. Commin, 1907.

Green, E. *Notes on the History of Dulverton, Proceedings*, Som. Arch. and Nat. Hist. Soc., 1883.

Hoskins, W.G., *Devon*, Collins, 1954.

MacDermot, E.T., *The History of the Forest of Exmoor*, David and Charles, 1973.

Orwin, C.S., *The Reclamation of Exmoor Forest*, David and Charles, 1972.

Rawle, E.J., *Annals of the Ancient Forest of Exmoor*, Barnicott and Pearce, 1893.

Savage, J., *History of the Hundred of Carhampton in the County of Somerset*, W. Strong, 1830.

Sellick, R., *The West Somerset Mineral Railway*, David and Charles, 1962.

Tugwell, Rev.G., *North Devon Handbook*, Stewart, 1856.

THE WILD RED DEER

Collyns, C.P., *Notes on the Chase of the Wild Red Deer in the Counties of Devon and Somerset*, Lawrence and Bullen, 1862.

Edwards, L. and Wallace, H.H., *Hunting and Stalking the Deer*, Longmans, 1927.

Evered, P., *Staghunting on Exmoor*, Chatto and Windus, 1902.

Goss, F., *Memories of a Stag Harbourer*, Witherby, 1931.

Government Publication: Report to the Home Office of Committee on Cruelty to Wild Animals including Exmoor Deer, H.M.S.O., 1951.

Hamilton, A., *The Red Deer of Exmoor*, with Notes on those who hunted them from 1070 to 1906, Horace Cox, 1907.

Hewett, H.P., *The Fairest Hunting*, J.A. Allen, 1963.

Kerr, Eleanor, *Hunting Parson*, Herbert Jenkins, 1963.

Martin, E.W., *The Case Against Hunting*, Dobson, 1959.

Williamson, H., *The Wild Red Deer of Exmoor*, Faber, 1931.

Fortescue, J.W., *The Story of a Red Deer*, Macmillan, 1897.

JOURNALS AND PERIODICALS

The Exmoor Review (first published 1959—see p. 185)
Somerset and Dorset Notes and Records
Devon and Cornwall Notes and Queries
Transactions of the Devonshire Association
Proceedings of the Somerset Archaeological and Natural History Society
Proceedings of the Devon Archaeological Society

Index

(There are no entries in this index for authors whose works are listed in the Select Bibliography)